THE IRISH TIMES
BOOK
of the
YEAR
1999-2000

EDITED BY
PETER MURTAGH

Gill & Macmillan

Gill & Macmillan Ltd
Hume Avenue
Park West
Dublin 12
with associated companies throughout the world
www.gillmacmillan.ie

© 2000 *The Irish Times*
0 7171 3147 5
Index compiled by John Loftus
Design by Identikit Design Consultants, Dublin
Print origination by Carole Lynch
Printed by Butler & Tanner Ltd, Frome, Somerset

A catalogue record is available for this book
from the British Library.

1 3 5 4 2

Contents

Introduction

The *Irish Times* occupies a unique place in Ireland: no other national daily newspaper produced primarily for the people of this island is owned by a trust — a trust that sets down in writing the aims of the paper and the obligations of those who work for it. No other newspaper places such emphasis on fair, accurate reporting; no other newspaper instructs its journalists to give special consideration to the reasonable representation of minority interests and divergent views.

This mission statement, as it might be known in today's terminology, was fashioned in 1974 when the then shareholders bought themselves out and placed ownership of the paper into The Irish Times Trust Ltd. The change occurred to secure the future of *The Irish Times* as an independent newspaper concerned primarily with 'serious issues for the benefit of the community throughout the whole of Ireland, free from any form of personal or party political, commercial, religious or other sectional control'.

To this end, the Editor and staff must adhere to an editorial policy with certain objectives, outlined in a Memorandum of the Trust. These include supporting constitutional democracy, the discouragement of discrimination of all kinds, and the promotion of a friendly society that is enriched by education, the arts, culture and recreational facilities and where the quality of spirit 'is instinct with Christian values'. They also include the promotion of peace and tolerance and opposition to all forms of violence and hatred; and the promotion of understanding of other nations.

Anyone familiar with the issues and events that have shaped life in Ireland, north and south, for the past 30 years will recognise how principles such as these can be — and are — applied in the day-to-day working life of an *Irish Times* journalist. The values espoused in the Memorandum underpin our work, the aim of which is described thus: 'to enable the readers of *The Irish Times* to reach informed and independent judgments and to contribute more effectively to the life of the community…'

To this end, around 280 full-time and contract journalists are employed by *The Irish Times* across a variety of departments: home, foreign and business news, sports, features, arts, comment and analysis, and also at Ireland.com, the *Irish Times* website. Within Ireland, the paper maintains staff correspondents in Belfast, Waterford, Cork, Limerick, Athlone, Galway and Sligo, as well as a large team of reporters and specialists in Dublin. We have a full-time office in London with two correspondents, plus a correspondent in Edinburgh. Our spread of reporters within these islands stands unmatched by any other Irish newspaper.

Further afield, the paper maintains the largest stable of foreign correspondents of any Irish media outlet. These include correspondents in the United States, Mexico and Brazil; France, Belgium, Germany, Italy, Spain, Russia and Israel; Kenya, South Africa, India, China, and Australia.

Why do we do this? The simple answer — which happens also to be the right answer — is that our readers expect no less. How, for instance, could an *Irish Times* reader be informed adequately on a matter of such importance as the euro if their primary source of information was second hand, recycled material produced by a media organisation in the UK determinedly hostile to the currency? Readers of *The Irish Times* demand to be informed about world events through the eyes of journalists who know and understand Irish interests. If something major occurs in, for example, China or the United States, readers of *The Irish Times* expect to read about it through the reporting of familiar names like Conor O'Clery or Joe Carroll — correspondents who are in constant touch with Dublin and who understand the concerns and interests of Irish people.

Backing up our reporting staff in Ireland and abroad is a team of commentators with views as diverse as those expressed by Dick Walsh, Vincent Browne, John Waters, Breda O'Brien, Fintan O'Toole and Kevin Myers.

Apart from the accuracy of its reporting and the depth of its comment and analysis, *The Irish Times* also has a reputation for quality writing: articles that capture the essence of a moment, reflect an unspoken emotion or simply make us laugh. There isn't a newspaper in the English-speaking world that wouldn't be proud to count among its writers the likes of Maeve Binchy, Kathy Sheridan, Tom Humphries, Roisin Ingle, Frank McNally and Kathryn Holmquist.

This book is an anthology of some of the best writing to appear in the paper between September 1999 and September 2000. It is by no means a definitive selection — it is my selection and consequently suffers from all the flaws and biases that one person's choice reflects. Six days a week, almost every week of the year, *The Irish Times* publishes something over 100,000 words a day — about equal to a medium sized novel. Some of the best appears on the pages that follow; the rest appears every day, Monday to Saturday, at a newsagent near you…

I want to thank a number of colleagues who helped in the production of this book. Conor Brady and Gerry Smyth who asked me to compile and edit it; Fintan O'Toole, who agreed to write an essay on Ireland today, thus providing a link between this volume and his own, much acclaimed, *The Irish Times Book of the Century*. I must also thank Kusi Okamura for her cheerful assistance in tracking down material, Picture Editor Dermot O'Shea, his colleague Peter Thursfield, and their picture desk staff (Rosie Thursfield, Terry Thorpe, Mick Crowley, Derek Grant and Paul Hayden); and also the numerous colleagues and friends who drew my attention to pieces they felt should be included. Thanks also to Fergal Tobin and Deirdre Greenan and all at Gill & Macmillan for bringing it all together. The final choice was my own — I only wish I had had more pages. In an ideal world, much that was left out would have got in.

Peter Murtagh
The Irish Times
September 2000

Ireland 2000

SOME images of Ireland in what was regarded by journalists as a slow news week at the end of August 2000:

The most compelling and intimate political drama in the Republic is coming to a head, not in the Dáil, at a tribunal of inquiry in Dublin Castle or even in Brussels, but in the most obscure of European Union countries, Luxembourg, and in the headquarters of an institution that few Irish people had even heard of at the start of the year, the European Investment Bank. The bank's directors quietly refuse to vote for the Irish government's chosen nominee for the position of vice-president, the disgraced former Supreme Court judge Hugh O'Flaherty. In the most dramatic example of a new kind of civic democracy, public anger at the nomination eventually leads to O'Flaherty's decision to withdraw his candidacy. Some new form of civic power has been stirred in Ireland, but the first to recognise it is not the supposedly responsive local political institutions but a faceless, faraway Eurocracy.

A popular young comic actor, Robbie Doolin, best known for his role in a bland and gorm-less TV soap called 'Upwardly Mobile', dies as a result of a late-night fracas on a Dublin street. As his coffin is carried into Saint Bernadette's church in Crumlin for his funeral Mass, it is draped with a tricolour and crowned with a black beret, apparently confirming widespread reports that he was associated with the terror gang responsible for the most hideous atrocity of the Northern troubles, the Omagh bomb of 1998. Upwardly mobile Ireland still has its dark secrets.

A group of British soldiers is held hostage by a gang called the West Side Boys in the bush in Sierra Leone. The voices on the radio that inform Irish listeners of the progress of negotiations for their release have the clipped, precise tones of the English officer class. But the soldiers, it turns out, are almost all Irish. Most are from Northern Ireland, two from the Republic. Irish lives, in the most unlikely places, still spill over the neat borders of nationality and statehood.

Two soccer players are kicked out of the Irish international squad preparing to play Holland after they are arrested on charges of drunken behaviour and causing criminal damage to a car. The airwaves and newsprint are full of outrage at the way these well-paid men have 'let down their country'. Most of the anger is directed at the elder of the two, Phil Babb. No one finds it odd to accuse Babb, a black Londoner, of disgracing his country, Ireland. He has become, quite naturally, a symbol of the nation. Yet on those same night-time city streets, a black Londoner is vastly more likely to be the victim, rather than the alleged perpetrator of a crime, and to be told in no un-certain terms to go back where he belongs.

An all-too-familiar violence returns to the working-class housing estates of Belfast and other towns in Northern Ireland. Men are singled out for assassination. A young girl is badly wounded when shots are fired through the window of her home. Families are intimidated out of their homes in a delib-erate campaign of 'ethnic cleansing'. But this time both the perpetrators and the victims are Protestant, as the UVF and the UFF fight out a vicious feud. The familiar violence has taken a bizarre turn.

And through all of this, by far the most famous Irish person in what are now known as 'these islands' is someone who was completely obscure a few weeks previously. Anna Nolan, a contestant in the British 'real life' voyeuristic game show 'Big Brother', touches on many of the clichés of Irish womanhood. She is an ex-nun, an exile and, with her warm personality, has become a surrogate mother to all the other contestants. But she is also an out-of-the-closet lesbian, astonishingly at ease in a media-saturated virtual reality. She has mastered the art of delivering intimate true confessions for the all-seeing eye of a vast TV and internet audience. She just might be the model for Irishness in the new millennium.

BETWEEN them, these more or less random images give some sense of what it was like to be Irish at the turn of the century. The strange had become familiar and the familiar strange. The big picture was made up of odd, incoherent details. Old stories were playing themselves out in unsettling new contexts. Flagrant exposure went hand-in-hand with continuing secrets. Contradictions abounded. It was all, in other words, not that different from what it was like to be Irish at the turn of the previous century.

From the perspective of the year 2000, indeed, it was possible to see that the really odd time in Ireland was the period between the 1920s and the 1980s, when it was possible to pretend that Irishness was a simple thing that fit into a single frame. In those years, albeit at the expense of a great deal of denial and repression, the fusion of nationality and Catholicism had created one powerful set of values and institutions that any citizen could either identify with or, at worst, reject. We came to believe that there was something natural and inevitable about this state of affairs. Only now, after it has all collapsed under the weight of violent conflict, political corruption, church scandal and a new kind of globalisation, can we see that it was neither.

If that collapse creates a rueful sense that 'Ireland' has gone to the dogs, it is well to remember that Ireland has always been going to the dogs. The distinctive values of the nation are perpetually being swamped by the forces of bland international modernity. The young have always been increasingly vulgar, feckless and hedonistic. The deep-seated values passed down from our immemorial ancestors are forever on the verge of extinction. Material progress always seems to heighten rather than to dispel an underlying sense of unease. So it was in Ireland at the start of the 20th century, when many of the country's leading artists and thinkers felt an urgent need to form or join associations dedicated to rescuing the nation from the terrible fate of becoming just another outpost of global modernity. So it was in the year 2000 when neither the joys of surviving the millennium nor a barrage of stunning economic statistics could dispel a pervasive mist of discontent.

If, in the latter half of 1999 and through most of 2000, the people running the country often seemed completely at sea, most notably in the farcical handling of the O'Flaherty affair, it was, in some ways, hard to blame them. The basic belief that animates the behaviour of governments is that success will be rewarded and that spectacular success will be rewarded spectacularly. Here, then, was a Government that had achieved, or at least presided over, two epic improvements in the quality of Irish life which, taken together, ought at least to have cut off some of the major sources of gloom.

However slowly, painfully and uncertainly, devolved democratic institutions had been re-established in Northern Ireland. The IRA had agreed to something that most sane and sensible commentators thought would never happen — independent inspection of its arms dumps. The notion — in the realms of science fiction until very recently — that Martin McGuinness would be a minister at Stormont in a government led by David Trimble had become an accepted, almost unremarked, fact. The biggest source of depression and despair in Ireland, the daily grind of horror and atrocity, had begun to dry up.

After the Northern Ireland conflict, the next worst reason not to be cheerful had been mass unemployment. While the problem had not been entirely solved and its long-term social consequences remained very evident in high and persistent levels of poverty and illiteracy, the improvement was startling. The notion that Ireland entered the new millennium with sober predictions that, by the end of 2001, unemployment would be below four per cent would have seemed, just a decade before, an impossible dream.

In 1987, the unemployment rate was 18 per cent and thoughtful commentators were telling us that there would never again be full employment. In the first half of the 1980s, the number of people at work in the Irish economy actually fell by six per cent. Since 1993, by contrast, it has grown by an astonishing 25 per cent. The biggest economic problem is getting enough people to fill the available jobs.

And it's not as if the surprisingly unhappy mood could be explained by the Irish suddenly becoming dour and thrifty. If there was still a nagging fatalism at the back of the mind, whispering that it was all too good to last, it manifested itself in a determination to spend it while we've got it. The most eloquent numbers in this regard were the 00s on the registration plates of the armada of automobiles on the new motorways. But the bigger numbers were even more striking. In 1998, private consumer spending in the Republic totalled £30.8 billion. In 1999, it reached £34.6 billion. In 2000, the Economic and Social Research Institute estimated that £39.5 billion would pass through the tills and credit card accounts. And in 2001, we will, apparently spend almost £44 billion. Here, conclusively, is evidence of the Irish contempt for the domination of money. We despise the stuff so much, we can't wait to get rid of it.

How could it be, then, that in the most important electoral test of the year in the Republic, a by-election in South Tipperary, the Fianna Fáil vote, at just 22 per cent, suffered a cataclysmic collapse? How could an important, but seemingly obscure issue like the appointment of Hugh O'Flaherty to the EIB ignite a fire-storm of public rage and render the Government virtually helpless? If 'it's the economy, stupid', how did the Irish people wise up?

Some of the discontent is rooted simply in the fact that a sense of being well-off is not shaped only by how much disposable income you have. The ability to afford one's own house is still, in Irish culture, a crucial mark of prosperity and, from being the cheapest in Europe in 1989, Irish houses had become among the most expensive 10 years later. A typical urban house that cost 11.3 times the average annual disposable income in 1989, now costs 18.2 times the average. Basic health services, meanwhile, plunged ever deeper into crisis with recent improvements (like, for example, the availability of epidural pain relief for women in labour) actually being undone in some parts of the country. And that sense of the quality of life becoming tangibly worse was reflected most obviously in the sheer difficulty of getting from A to B. The chaos in public and private transport, bringing greatly increased journey times, meant that a small island had become, in a sense, far bigger. A hefty slice of the global economy had been plonked down on the rickety infrastructure of an underdeveloped country, and the strain was all too obvious.

Yet the rage that gripped the public was not mere road rage. It was clearly provoked by much more than the daily stresses and irritations of a society that had outgrown its own public structures. For behind it was a clear feeling that, whatever it actually was in the 21st century, Ireland still mattered to its citizens. Unfamiliar as the place had become in so many ways, it still existed as an idea. And that idea still contained many of the things that people at the start of the 20th century, about to embark on the painful process of inventing a modern nation, had wanted for it: a sense of justice, a feeling of belonging, a capacity to be proud of ourselves, a notion, however vague, that there was an 'ourselves' to be proud of. The precise content of that notion was hard to pin down, but it was made concrete and tangible by its obvious absence. For what became ever more apparent as the year went on and the revelations from the tribunals continued to unfold was that the Ireland that contained these desires hadn't just slipped away in a process of economic and social change or been stolen from us by perfidious Albion. It had been deliberately and cynically betrayed from within. Some people at the very top of the heap had owed more loyalty to the Cayman Islands than to Ireland. Some citizens blessed with resources had turned themselves into 'bogus non-residents', here but not here, part of Ireland when the goodies were being given out but mysteriously vanishing into a virtual exile when the obligations of citizenship were to be met. And while everyone was equal before the law some people had turned out to be more equal than others. Unfortunately for him and the Government, Hugh O'Flaherty happened to give a name and a face to a previously incoherent sense of injustice and impunity.

In an odd way, all of the revelations, by pointing up the absence of a public community of which Irish people could be proud, served to remind them that they still wanted one. The joys of shopping, however enthusiastically embraced, didn't quite fill the hole where a society called 'Ireland' should be. Retail therapy didn't quite assuage the anguish of finding ourselves at the start of a new century, right back where we had started the old one, in an unsettled, fluid place that needed to be re-invented as a republic.

Fintan O'Toole
The Irish Times
September 2000

Journalists and Photographers

Dick Ahlstrom is Science Editor of *The Irish Times*. He writes on science matters on a day-to-day basis and edits a weekly page, Science Today, published on Mondays.

John Banville is a novelist and Associate Literary Editor and Chief Literary Critic of *The Irish Times*.

Alan Betson is an *Irish Times* photographer who joined the paper in 1993 after working with the INPHO sports photo agency. He is a regular winner in various categories of the PPAI awards and was Photographer of the Year in 1997.

Maeve Binchy is a novelist. She has written a variety of columns in *The Irish Times* for many years and in April 2000 announced in the Weekend supplement published on Saturdays that she was retiring.

Rosita Boland is a feature writer with *The Irish Times*.

John Bowman is an historian and broadcaster.

Conor Brady is Editor of *The Irish Times*.

Mark Brennock is Political Correspondent of *The Irish Times*. A former Northern Editor and Foreign Affairs Correspondent, he has written extensively on the Troubles and on Irish foreign policy.

Vincent Browne is an *Irish Times* columnist and RTÉ broadcaster.

Colin Byrne is a professional caddie who carries the bag of European tour professional Greg Turner. He has been writing a column for *The Irish Times* for the past two years.

Cyril Byrne is a staff photographer with *The Irish Times*. He has won numerous awards for his work and mounted several exhibitions.

Mary Canniffe is Investment Editor at *The Irish Times*.

Joe Carroll has been Washington Correspondent for *The Irish Times* throughout President Clinton's second term in office. He is due to retire at the end of 2000.

Tony Cleyton-Lea is a freelance music journalist and critic.

Denis Coghlan is Chief Political Correspondent of *The Irish Times*.

Sarah Cottle is a Sligo-based freelance reporter.

Kevin Courtney is a freelance music journalist and critic.

Siobhan Creaton is Finance Correspondent of *The Irish Times*.

Paul Cullen is Development Correspondent of *The Irish Times*. He has written extensively about the problems of sub-Saharan Africa, as well as about Irish, international and local aid and development programmes. Recently, however, he has been covering the Flood Tribunal and is a regular broadcaster on the subject.

Jim Cusack is Security Editor of *The Irish Times*. He has written extensively on crime, the Garda Síochána and the Troubles. A former Northern Editor, he is co-author (with Henry McDonald) of *UVF*, a study of the loyalist paramilitary group.

Deaglán de Bréadún is Foreign Affairs Correspondent of *The Irish Times*. He was formerly Northern Editor.

Penelope Dening is a UK-based freelance author and journalist. She writes regularly in Weekend. Her most recent book was a biography of the model Twiggy.

Miriam Donohoe is a Political Reporter with *The Irish Times*.

Katie Donovan is a feature writer with *The Irish Times*.

Mary Dowey writes on wine in Weekend.

Keith Duggan is an *Irish Times* sports journalist, specialising in Gaelic games.

Jim Dunne is a reporter with *The Irish Times* and a former Senior Finance Editor with the paper.

Louise East writes a column, Winging It, in Weekend.

Jack Fagan is Property Editor of *The Irish Times*.

Elizabeth Field is a food writer.

Peter Hanan is a freelance caricaturist. His work appears regularly in Weekend and he also illustrates the Saturday Profile each week.

Mary Hannigan is an *Irish Times* sports journalist who writes an off-beat column in Monday's sports supplement looking at the Irish and British football scene.

Nuala Haughey is a staff reporter.

Justin Hynes is *The Irish Times* Formula 1 racing correspondent.

Kitty Holland is a staff reporter.

Mary Holland is a columnist with *The Irish Times*. She is a regular broadcaster and also writes for *The Observer* newspaper.

Eddie Holt is *The Irish Times* TV critic and a lecturer in journalism at Dublin City University.

Kathryn Holmquist is a feature writer specialising in parenting and health-related issues. She also writes a weekly synopsis of the provincial press, Paper Round, which is published on Mondays.

Joe Humphreys is a staff reporter.

Tom Humphries is a sports writer and columnist with *The Irish Times*. He writes Locker Room, a column that appears in Monday's sports supplement and spent much of 1999/2000 on secondment in the United States before covering the Olympic Games in Sydney.

Roisin Ingle is a staff reporter and is currently based in Northern Ireland.

George Jackson is a Northern-Ireland based freelance reporter.

Matt Kavanagh is an *Irish Times* photographer. He has won the PPAI Photographer of the Year award on two occasions. He is currently working on a book of photographs of international jazz musicians.

Cathy Kelly is a novelist.

John Kelly is a broadcaster and writer. He hosts The Mystery Train, a personal selection of music broadcast on RTÉ radio 1 and writes a weekly column on music in Weekend.

Geraldine Kennedy is political editor of *The Irish Times*.

Frank Kilfeather is a staff reporter.

Elaine Lafferty is a Los Angeles-based correspondent for *The Irish Times*. She has also reported from Kosovo and from Central America.

Pat Langan has been a staff photographer with *The Irish Times* since 1970. He covered Northern Ireland until the early 1980s. He has made several studies of bad housing, social deprivation and the Travelling community. He has also contributed to several books.

Eric Luke is an *Irish Times* photographer who joined the paper in 1990 after 17 years with the *Irish Press*. He won second prize in the news category in the World Press Photo Awards in 1997.

Lara Marlowe is Paris Correspondent of *The Irish Times*. She has also reported extensively from north Africa, the middle east and former Yugoslavia.

Seamus Martin is International Editor of *The Irish Times*. He is a former South Africa and Moscow Correspondent.

Dara MacDonaill is an award-winning photographer who began his career in 1979 as a messenger boy with Lensmen press and PR agency. He worked with Sportsfile, a sports photo agency for three years, and later for Independent newspapers before joining *The Irish Times* in 1998.

Frank McDonald is Environment Editor of *The Irish Times*. His latest book, *The Construction of Dublin*, is published by Gandon Editions.

Frank McNally is a staff reporter. He also writes a humorous column in Weekend.

Emer McNamara is a freelance journalist. She moved to Manorhamilton in Co. Leitrim in the autumn of 1999 seeking a new life, which she described in a weekly column, Living on Main Street. In June 2000, she found financial pressures forced her to return to Dublin.

Eoin McVey is a Managing Editor at *The Irish Times*.

Brendan McWilliams is a meteorologist. For the past two years he has lived in Darmstadt in Germany, from where he dispatches his daily Weather Eye column, while also working for EUMETSAT, the European meteorological satellite organisation.

Frank Millar is London Editor of *The Irish Times*. Born in Northern Ireland, he has an unrivalled understanding of Northern Ireland and Anglo-Irish politics.

Frank Miller has been a staff photographer with *The Irish Times* for 10 years. Prior to that, he worked for the *Irish Press*. He has worked abroad extensively for *The Irish Times* including in Indonesia, Turkey and Rwanda, and has twice won the overall award in the Eircell/PPAI press photographer awards.

Sean Moran is *The Irish Times* GAA Correspondent.

Gerry Moriarty is Northern Editor of *The Irish Times* and has reported from Belfast during the period of negotiation and implementation of the Belfast Agreement.

Orna Mulcahy is Deputy Editor of Property Times and also writes a column on restaurants in Weekend.

Kevin Myers writes Irishman's Diary. He reported from Northern Ireland in the 1970s. Apart from his column, he is also a regular broadcaster on RTÉ and Today FM, and writes a column in the *Sunday Telegraph*.

Breda O'Brien is a columnist with *The Irish Times*.

Bryan O'Brien is an *Irish Times* photographer. Twice overall winner of the Eircell Press Photographer of the Year, he is also a consistent category winner. He went to Sierra Leone with Concern and in 1999 held an exhibition of his work in Arnott's exhibition hall.

Tim O'Brien is Regional Development Correspondent of *The Irish Times*.

Conor O'Clery is Asia Editor of *The Irish Times*. A veteran foreign correspondent, he has been Northern Editor, London Editor, Moscow Correspondent and Washington Correspondent. His latest book, published by the O'Brien Press, *Ireland in Quotes*, is a history of the 20th Century.

Padraig O Morain is Health and Children Correspondent of *The Irish Times*.

Kevin O'Sullivan is Environment and Food Science Correspondent of *The Irish Times*, and is also a deputy news editor.

Fintan O'Toole is a columnist with *The Irish Times* and author. He writes extensively on politics, current affairs, the arts and cultural matters, and is theatre critic for the *New York Daily Post*.

Kathy Sheridan is a staff writer with *The Irish Times*.

Lorna Siggins is Western Correspondent of *The Irish Times*, based in Galway. She is also the paper's Marine Correspondent.

David Sleator joined *The Irish Times* as a staff photographer in 1998. In 1993, 1995 and 1996 he received the Freelance Photographer of the Year award; and in 1999, he won the Eircell/PPAI Political Photographer of the Year award.

Joe St Leger has been an *Irish Times* photographer for 10 years. He has won several Irish and international awards for his news and feature work.

Peter Thursfield has won the PPAI Photographer of the Year award three times. In recent years, he has combined taking pictures with photo editing at *The Irish Times*.

Terry Thorpe works on *The Irish Times* picture desk and is an accomplished rock concert photographer.

Martyn Turner has been drawing political cartoons for *The Irish Times* since about 1976. In the intervening 24 years, he has produced numerous books of his work and contributed to many others.

Gerry Thornley is *The Irish Times* Rugby Correspondent.

Nicole Veash is a freelance correspondent based in Latin America.

Michael Viney writes Another Life, a weekly column in Weekend dealing with nature and environmental matters. He lives at Tallamh Bán, near Louisbourg in Co. Mayo, overlooking the Atlantic Ocean and Inis Turk island.

Declan Walsh is a Dublin-born freelance journalist who has based himself in Nairobi in Kenya from where he covers east and central Africa for *The Irish Times*.

Michael Walker is *The Irish Times* British football correspondent.

Dick Walsh writes a column on Saturdays. He is a former Political Editor of *The Irish Times* and has written extensively about Fianna Fáil.

John Waters is a columnist with *The Irish Times*.

Johnny Watterson is a sports writer with *The Irish Times*.

In Time's Eye, which appears daily on the Editorial page, is written by Y, a distinguished retired *Irish Times* journalist. For some years in the 1980s it was also written on alternate days by H, another former *Irish Times* journalist.

It is in the nature of newspapers that journalists change positions and locations fairly regularly. The biographical notes above are accurate at the time of going to press.

Being Ill Has Never Been So Much Fun

Maeve Binchy

I know it does sound a bit like a vegetarian writing a press release for the meat board. But it's not quite as it seems. It's not so much a health book as a cheer-up book and since I am a manically optimistic person then my credentials should be fairly reasonable for that.

It all began two years ago this month when the artist Wendy Shea came home from one hospital with a new hip and I came home from another hospital with another new hip. At that time we each brought a great number of get-well cards with us. Just like old Christmas cards, it's a problem knowing what to do with them.

I looked at all mine again and saw the funny messages on some and the pressed flowers on others and the expensive art cards and I thought it's insane to keep all these in a suitcase so that I can take them out when I'm really old and prove to myself that I was loved in 1997. And lovely as they were they're not the kind of thing you can recycle, crossing out 'Dear Maeve' from whoever and putting in your own message. This way insanity lies.

So with great regret I let them go but I kept thinking that there must be some way of harnessing such generosity for a good cause. I noted with darkening brow that the greetings card industry, which has plenty of money already, gets more and more as soon as anyone goes to hospital.

So why couldn't there be a little book not much dearer than a card, I thought? Something you could send to people in hospital and they could send on to someone else when they had read it, or keep it on their shelf in case they forgot to cheer up one day and needed to be forcibly cheered. And the royalties could go to a charity.

A brilliant idea, and since there wasn't such a book, Wendy Shea and I have produced one in aid of the Arthritis Foundation. It's not just about arthritis; it's about everything.

It's a funny thing writing a book in aid of charity. You can be quite shameless in telling everyone how great it is and dragging them into bookshops to buy it because they know the money isn't going to buy you a yacht or a diamond brooch.

Nothing is quite as easy as it sounds. Why don't I ask someone to embroider that for me on a sampler and I could put it on the wall of my study.

Charlotte Norwood hanging an exhibition of prints from the Neptune Gallery watched by her seven-month-old daughter Phoebe, prior to the opening of the 34th Irish Antique Dealers' Fair in the RDS. Photograph: Matt Kavanagh.

I think everything is basically very easy and that I'll have it finished in a couple of weeks, so it always comes as a huge shock when there are problems, as of course there always are. It was easy to know what any cheer-up book that I might write would not be.

It would not be a preparation for the next world. Nor would it be bedpan humour. And not alternative cures and remedies. And certainly nothing in the area of 'Pull Yourself Together and Stop Bellyaching'.

This little manual had to be suitable for all sorts of people — some who were seriously ill and did not want their position trivialised, some who were going to be perfectly fine, and for some who didn't really know which category they were in. We wanted to let people know that it was appropriate for any kind of ailment and they wouldn't have made a terrible error of taste and given some horrific offence by having sent it to a friend who was poorly.

And of course once I began to write the book the real problem became clear. It was not what to put in, it was what to leave out. The list of contents alone was about eight pages long.

This book was going to be the size of the Yellow Pages; it was going to defeat totally its purpose of cutting a swathe through the get-well card industry. It would fit in no envelope for convenient posting. Any patient who would be strong enough to have it on the bed would be strong enough to leave hospital.

And then, with a blinding flash, I remembered that when you're in hospital or at home in bed with 'flu you don't actually want to read long detailed things; you want to read short things and then fall asleep and wake and read another short thing. And you want funny drawings to make you laugh.

So I left out most of it. We lost things like the story of a great nurse known as Dracula who could always find a vein.

And we lost the great argument about whether it is reassuring or over-familiar to be addressed by your first name in hospital. But there's lots of good advice left, like: how to alienate all your visitors and ensure you remain entirely unvisited; how to annoy the person in the next bed; how not to be ashamed of your wobbly bits and keep covering them up.

There are imaginative tasteful gifts to give people — it's full of heroic, inspiring tales of weak-willed people who managed when it was utterly necessary to give up food, drink and smokes. These weak-willed people are all me actually, but that just makes it more personal and honest.

The book was edited for us by Mary Maher of this newspaper and we used to have sessions where we would fall about laughing at Wendy's drawings, though why I should adore pictures of myself

Raonid Murray, a teenage girl killed in a horrifying midnight knife attack just 200 yards from her home. She was found lying in the lane about an hour later by her sister and a group of friends, who happened to be passing by.

looking enormous and insane I have no idea. Innate good humour verging on the illness of elation, I imagine.

And that's what kept us all going. That and the great news that this book — though written for an Irish publisher, Poolbeg — has also been taken up by publishers in England, America, Canada, Australia, Sweden, Germany and Holland. And the royalties will go to the relevant arthritis charity in each of those countries as well.

This was not intended to be the definitive book on every ache and pain ever endured; it was certainly not a leadership manual from two women who considered themselves model patients.

But I really do think that there might be something in it which would entertain or inform, and certainly pictures that will delight. I'd love to think it might be on people's hospital bedside cabinets next week, and with it I send my personal, best wishes, my thanks for the contribution to the charity and one of my few certainties in life — a reassurance that nothing on earth is as bad as it might seem at 4 a.m.

Aches & Pains by Maeve Binchy and Wendy Shea (Poolbeg, £4.99)

TUESDAY, 7 SEPTEMBER 1999

Victim's Stunned Friends Pay Tribute at Her Removal

Jim Cusack

Hundreds of teenagers, some in school uniform, gathered in stunned silence yesterday evening for the removal service of Raonaid Murray, the teenage girl stabbed to death in south Co. Dublin at the weekend.

St Joseph's Church in Glasthule, packed to capacity for the arrival of her coffin, stayed open until midnight to allow her friends and relatives to hold a vigil. The suburban village came to a halt as

Police sketch of a man wanted to help in the investigation into the murder of Raonid Murray.

the mourners spilled out from the church grounds to the roadway opposite Presentation College where her father, Mr Jim Murray, is headmaster.

Father Eamonn McCarthy, a friend of the Murray family since he served in Ballybrack parish in the 1980s, said prayers over the coffin. He told a hushed church that there were not enough words to express the desolation and pain being experienced by the community and whole nation over Raonaid's death.

He said it was hard to reconcile what had happened with a loving God. He asked for prayers for the family who were devastated. He also referred to the fact that another family might soon experience the tragedy of finding out that one of its members was responsible for Ms Murray's death.

Before the 5.30 p.m. service, Ms Murray's friends gathered outside the church, girls in the blue uniform of St Joseph of Cluny school which she attended up to two years ago on one side. On the other were more recent friends from the Institute of Education and from Dun Laoghaire.

Their parents and the neighbours and friends of the Murray family filed into the church past the shocked teenagers. The church is only 50 yards from the spot where Ms Murray and her friends used to gather in the evenings outside Sandycove DART station up to a few months ago. Members of the same little group, standing in ones and twos outside the church, were among the most bewildered and lost of the mourners.

The funeral service takes place today at 10 a.m.

FRIDAY, 10 SEPTEMBER 1999

Patten Leads Full Circle to Belfast Agreement

Frank Millar

Logically and inevitably — and for Mr David Trimble and many Ulster Unionists, doubtless painfully — the Patten commission yesterday led us full circle back to the Belfast Agreement.

From the outset it should always have been clear that Chris Patten would locate his commission's report in the context of the Good Friday accord which gave him his terms of reference — in the assumptions its signatories (presumably) made at that time, and on the presumption of the agreement's survival and successful implementation.

And the last governor of Hong Kong showed himself more than ready to engage with those parties — well, one party actually — which now appeared surprised that he should have discharged his side of the deal.

For there was no mistaking he had the Ulster Unionist leader in his sights when he reminded yesterday's press conference how his commission had come about.

'It is impossible to find a political solution to the problem of policing in Northern Ireland,' he declared. 'That is why the politicians agreed last year to pass the issue to this independent commission. Since they could not agree on the answers, we were asked to suggest a way forward. We believe that it is possible to find a policing solution to the policing problem, but only if you take the politics out of policing.'

Certainly he didn't have Ian Paisley or Bob McCartney in mind when he issued the challenge to the assembled press. Ask them, he exhorted: 'What on earth did they think they were signing up to? What on earth did they think we were likely to recommend when we were asked to look at issues like ethos, composition, training and structure?'

Mo Mowlam might have wished Mr Patten hadn't spelt it out quite so bluntly. However, Mr Trimble can expect to hear the implicit charge oft repeated in the days and weeks to come. As Mr McCartney predicted in this newspaper on Wednesday, another political explosion is set to rip through the heart of unionism. And many thousands of angry unionists may well answer the rallying call to 'Save the RUC'. But is it likely they will turn out to damn Mr Patten without turning their fire also on the man who (in the minds of many of them at least) handed the policing issue over to him?

If Mr Trimble is at all sensitive about this matter, he showed no sign of it yesterday. In first angry flush, he dismissed the Patten report as 'a shoddy piece of work'. Clearly he had never anticipated that the Royal title would be scrapped. Clearly it was Mr Patten, moreover, who had failed to grasp the logic of the Belfast Agreement.

In strictly Ulster Unionist terms, the logic seemed perfectly clear. Sinn Féin has accepted that Northern Ireland is part of the United Kingdom and its members would sit in a Northern Ireland Executive — in effect becoming ministers of the crown. Fair enough to assume, then, that title and badge as symbols of allegiance to the state should no longer be thought contentious.

In the world beyond Glengall Street, of course, such logic would be readily dismissed as wholly disingenuous. For all that, there can be no doubt the Patten proposals on title and symbols present Mr Trimble with another mighty problem. There need be no doubting, either, his personal sense of the

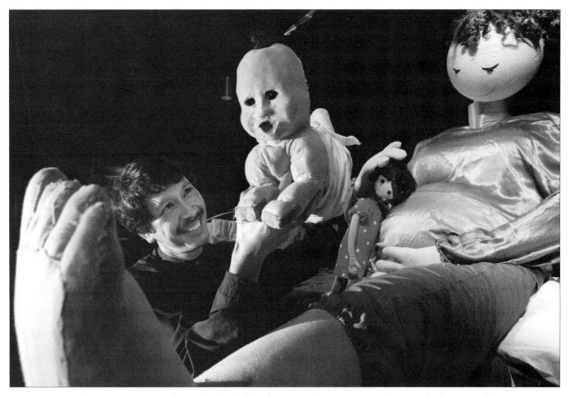

Puppeteer Stephen Stoetzer, from the Netherlands based Poppentheater Hans Schoen, with the main characters from 'Cuddle at Sea', which started the International Puppet Festival 1999 at the Lambert Puppet Theatre. Photograph: Alan Betson.

'pain' acknowledged by Chris Patten yesterday. Nor should anyone make light of the danger, painted by the UUP leader yesterday, that in their anger over these symbolic changes, unionists might well reject whatever else they consider good in the report.

One of the most telling pieces of commentary preceding yesterday's publication of the report was a television interview with the mothers of the two RUC officers murdered in Lurgan just weeks before the second IRA ceasefire. As the camera panned to the gravestone, it lingered on the engraved RUC harp and crown as one mother explained it was for this her son had died.

There, in raw and simple terms, is the truth of it: the real, intimate, enduring sense of loss and pain for those whose loved ones have served and fallen over the last 30 bloody years.

Chris Patten tried to reach out directly to this community of RUC victims. Insisting he intended no 'slight' to the sacrifice and service of thousands of RUC officers, he affirmed: 'We are transforming the RUC, not disbanding it.' But the greatest memorial to them, he offered, was 'the vision' of 'a peaceful Northern Ireland with agreed institutions including an agreed police service'.

Members of the commission, and British ministers, would have been concerned to hear Sir Ronnie Flanagan venture that the 'pain' might be worth the preferred 'gain', provided greater acceptance of the police service was indeed the result. If he is to present himself credibly as the man to carry the reform process through, they will expect Sir Ronnie to accept that making the service more acceptable to both communities should be done because it is right, and without calculation of the result.

However they will have been immensely relieved to hear Sir Ronnie echo Mr Patten's assurance: 'Certainly not, this is not disbandment.' His force, he said, stood ready for radical change in the context of a stable peace and a political settlement. And there was no doubt about the Chief Constable's determination to remain at the helm.

Sir Ronnie's role will be pivotal during the crucial consultation period ahead both in terms of restraining any premature rush to judgment by Dr Mowlam and ensuring that reforms proceed in a way consistent with the security assessment and for the impact of his leadership of the force in relation to the mood and disposition of the unionist political class, and the wider public beyond.

Ultimately, of course, that political class has the big choices to make — and they extend beyond the immediate policing issues raised by Patten.

Mr Patten knows to expect no quarter from Dr Paisley and Mr McCartney. Yesterday merely confirmed their darkest fears about the nature, purpose and direction of the peace process itself. They will be unremitting in their opposition to it and to Mr Trimble.

But whither Mr Trimble? Some commentators drew comfort from his relatively restrained performance yesterday, while some close to him think he has no choice but to continue to try to ride a number of horses. However nationalists, and many others, openly wonder how long he can sustain the dual role of constructive engagement and outraged opposition.

Ironically, from Mr Trimble's viewpoint, the most benign interpretation on offer yesterday came from a very shrewd nationalist observer. The biggest pain, he ventured, was still for Sinn Féin: a party which had supported the long war, now preparing to sit in a partitionist government and share responsibility for a police force drawing its very title from the polity so long denied. 'It seeks to make of a failed political entity a successful one,'

he remarked on the process begun by the Belfast Agreement now brought full circle by Patten.

Wasn't that part of the logic which drove the Ulster Unionists, against all expectations, to buy into the Belfast Agreement, 'inclusivity' principle and all? Can they really consider Sinn Féin an acceptable partner for government while resisting its inclusion on the new policing board? And if they fear (and many of them genuinely do) the 'corruption' of the police service, can they long resist the challenge to see police powers devolved to the Assembly?

That was the big 'prize' offered yesterday by Patten. Beyond the debate about policing, Mr Trimble must decide if he still considers the prize worth having.

MONDAY, 13 SEPTEMBER 1999

A Triumph of Will Pushes Cork to Ultimate Triumph

Sean Moran

Cork 0–13: Kilkenny 0-12

The rain came down and in the crowd of 62,989 neutral thoughts might have dwelt on the pathetic fallacy. Might the heavens have been weeping for the re-emergence of the traditional powers in yesterday's Guinness All-Ireland hurling final? Or for the dire quality of the match, particularly in the first half?

As the afternoon drizzled along, something of the storied history between Cork and Kilkenny must have echoed down the generations, because for the final quarter the match opened up.

With nowhere left to hide, no strategems worth keeping up their sleeves, the realisation dawned that nothing that had happened already this season mattered anymore. The record of four months' hurling would now be written over 17 minutes.

There was an epic intensity as Cork's young outsiders chased down the Leinster champions, and although Kilkenny resisted the winning surge until the last six minutes, the scoreline drifted beyond their reach and stayed there, bobbing around at a point during the frantic closing minutes before Pat O'Connor blew up the last All-Ireland final of the millennium.

It had all started so scrappily. Rain and wind combined to make the surface slippy and the ball unreliable. Twenty-three wides (13 to Kilkenny) disfigured the first half.

Between the puck-outs the hurling wasn't bad, but at 0-5 to 0-4 to Kilkenny at half-time, it wasn't easy to find anyone who could remember a poorer 35 minutes in a final.

Given Kilkenny's exploits this season a low-scoring match suited Cork. And there was more to please Jimmy Barry-Murphy and his selectors. Kilkenny's half backs, awesome in the second half against Clare, never got a grip on the game. Fergal McCormack moved around intelligently and varied the target for Donal Cusack's puck-outs.

The Cork defence laid the foundations of this victory by restricting a team which had averaged 29 points per match to 12.

But it was the forwards who did it in the end. Timmy McCarthy, in his first championship match exactly three months ago, had had at times the air of the headless chicken. But through the summer his vision on the ball has sharpened and yesterday his was as big a contribution as anyone's.

Three points from play and a number of incisive runs were topped by his move to centre field in the last quarter which was heralded by the Cork management as one of the main reasons they turned the match.

The second half had been a long pursuit up to then. Although Alan Browne celebrated his half-time introduction with a point within 20 seconds of the

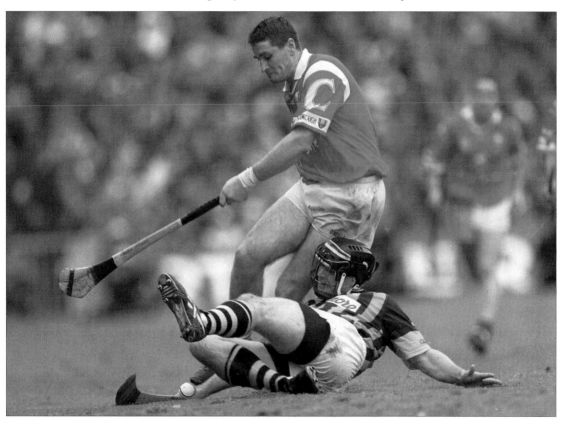

Fergal McCormack, Cork, in action against Pat O'Neill, Kilkenny. Photograph: Ray McManus/Sportsfile.

restart, Kilkenny reeled off four unanswered points. Joe Deane missed a free, Mickey O'Connell a 65.

With their challenge creaking, Cork got a break. DJ Carey missed a straightforward chance to push Kilkenny five points ahead, 0-10 to 0-5. A minute later, Kevin Murray — sent on, amidst some confusion as to who was going off, because the Cork bench felt they needed a goal — swung over a point.

From there to the end, the match soared out of its sticky mediocrity as points were traded with sufficient disproportion to bring Cork back into the hunt.

Seánie McGrath ended 70 minutes as the star which his extrovert talents have always suggested. From an early stage he was skinning Willie O'Connor but the ball didn't run for him. Two wides were followed by one dropped short as he tried to ensure accuracy.

Yet he never lost the faith, and between the 55th and 62nd minute he took centre-stage for a crucial soliloquy. One point from a clever Joe Deane pass and another set up by McCarthy prefaced his third — a sprinkling of stardust in the right corner under the Hill.

Jimmy Barry-Murphy said he knew his team would win when that one cleared the bar to tie up the scores at 0-11 each.

There was so much which defied general expectation in the match, and yet so much that had been foreshadowed. Kilkenny were never raging favourites for the match, but they were widely expected to win. Yet despite the draining experience of losing last year's final, yesterday was more unexplored territory for them than it was for Cork.

With their attack moving smoothly and menacingly all summer, Kilkenny had never been put to the pin of their collective collar to win a match. As goals hurtled in during their short Leinster campaign, neither Laois nor reigning All-Ireland champions Offaly could live with them.

Ultimately decisive was Cork's experience of going into big matches — more often than not as outsiders — which went down to the wire and proved time and again their exceptional capacity to combine classy hurling, irrepressible self-confidence and icy composure.

In the wind and the rain, there was an easy case to be made for the conditions suiting the physically solid and experienced practitioners whom Kilkenny had dotted around the field. Pat O'Neill emerged through the rain of the counties' last final meeting in 1992 to claim the man-of-the-match award.

Seven years ago he made his name by repudiating a wobbly reputation that season and the consequent bombardment which Cork were encouraged to unleash on top of him. Yesterday,

Designer John Rocha and his wife Odette in the Morrison Hotel for his September fashion show. Photograph: Bryan O'Brien.

the plan was to keep the ball as far away from him as possible; it largely worked.

John Power had earned many plaudits on his comeback to the Kilkenny team this season. Forceful and crafty up until yesterday, he had epitomised the improvement of the team's attack. Willie O'Connor has ruled the left flank of Kilkenny's defence all decade.

Nonetheless, when the day was done there was a feeling that we had seen the passing of a generation of hurlers and the arrival of another. Finals make their own heroes, and whereas few could be surprised that Brian Corcoran responded so hungrily to his first visit to the top table since that final seven years ago, the anticipated summitry of his meeting with Power never materialised.

Corcoran won the day and was able to move around his defence and play the role of general which the season has demanded of him.

With Power subdued, the spin-off effects for the rest of the attack never surfaced. DJ Carey had a very quiet conclusion to his hitherto sparkling year and drew his first All-Ireland final blank in five outings. Looking fractionally caught for pace on the heavy ground, he was also marked by two imposing athletes in Seán hAilpín and Diarmuid O'Sullivan.

At one point in the first half, Carey made his move, but O'Sullivan, whose beefy presence under the high ball had been looking a little shaky, kept his concentration and matched his man stride for stride, harassing him like a bulldog all the way. Late in the second half, Carey sliced through onto a chance but, squeezed for space, his kicked shot went wide.

Amidst the gloom of their highly-rated half-forward line shutting down, Kilkenny's one ray of hope was Henry Shefflin. The young full forward had generally made his best contributions to the cause when matches had loosened up a bit as contests, but yesterday he was very good and the one Kilkenny forward to raise his game for the final.

At centre field, Cork's captain Mark Landers gave a fine display in the first half and contested the

sector well with Andy Comerford, before the injury which had threatened his participation in the weeks before the match forced his withdrawal in the 51st minute.

Mickey O'Connell never really got going and found no opportunity to open his shoulders and go for points. His long-range frees and 65s weren't on line either, but he refused to be demoralised and threw himself around, scrapping for every squirming ball in the hectic finale.

It summed up the win. The sight of one of their cocky stylists, an under-achieving final behind him, frantically diving into the mud demonstrated the triumph of will. And one triumph led exuberantly to another.

TUESDAY, 14 SEPTEMBER 1999

Music in the Key of Love

Penelope Dening

Single? In want of company, if not a bit more? The quicksand of the office romance being no go — even assuming you've an office with other people in it at all — what does the discerning singleton do who WLTM a potential LTR with GSOH?

As those initials suggest, there's always the lonely hearts' columns, although phoning and listening to the messages can be a dispiriting and, at 50p a minute, expensive business. When the man whose ad proclaims 'Wide musical tastes' informs you on the audio message that what he meant was 'the Levellers, Led Zeppelin and Frank Zappa' and the one who wrote 'I write opera, woo women with sensuous trombone' sounds like Julian Clary and is looking for a buxom blonde who likes leather and ironing, it's time to think again. All introduction agencies include a profile of cultural interests in assessing clients. However, these can be pretty vague. An interest in the theatre could mean 'The Mousetrap' or 'Waiting For Godot'; film might mean Bertolucci or 'The Spy Who Shagged Me'.

The embarrassment factor in the search for romance, is high — at least for me. Work provides a carapace of bravery and as a journalist I can beard the fiercest of lions in the darkest of dens. But one-to-one with a potential LTR, with nothing to talk about except the litany of past failures (admit to being a writer and you're finished) and I'm a quivering wreck.

However, one introduction agency offers a civilised way through the getting-to-know-you obstacle course. The idea for Classical Partners came to Michael Lamb and Diane Walters at an outdoor concert in France three years ago. 'It was a lovely evening,' Michael explains, 'and there were all these people on their own, not talking to each other, and it just seemed such a waste.'

My own experience is that I just don't go to concerts on my own. Where's the pleasure if there's no one to share it with? Then there's the misery of the interval with everyone else chatting and laughing and you're re-reading the programme for the nth time, along with all the other sad no-hopers.

So it was that I found myself last Sunday at the Queen Elizabeth Hall in London for a forte piano recital by Andreas Staier. It wasn't hard to spot the Classical Partners contingent. While everyone else in the foyer was dressed for a baking afternoon, this lot wouldn't have been out of place at a wedding and all the women had newly washed hair. Being similarly outfitted (black dress, nothing too outre) I was soon spotted by Diane and immediately introduced to 'old hand' Noel.

Noel looked 50 but later admitted to 64. That's why the events, as the concerts are called, are so important: age, he said with practiced charm, is rarely chronological. 'Now, admit it, Penelope, if you had been sent my profile through the post, you'd have thought "64 and past it" and not given me a second look.' Noel — a sometime professional violinist — admits to 'several moderate successes' over the two years he's been a member. What did he mean exactly? 'You will just have to speculate on my precise meaning,' he said, with the discretion of the gentleman he undoubtedly is.

Classical Partners currently has 1100 people on their books, ranging from those like me (keen but musically illiterate) to professional musicians. The age range — if Sunday is anything to go by — is equally wide. Membership costs £345 a year.

At present Classical Partners is solely UK-based, with offices in London and Manchester. 'Our strength is that I know all the members,' Diane explains, 'both through personal interviews and through the events.' Similar musical tastes are important, however, and are elicited from the questionnaire members complete when they join providing a detailed breakdown of preferred composers and periods. (They even have jazz events.) 'We wouldn't match a Mahler-lover with someone with a passion for Gilbert and Sullivan,' she says.

Those in their 30s can expect to get a match every two weeks, but if you're a women in your late 40s or 50s it can be more difficult, so Classical Partners offer a deal where for the price of a half-yearly membership you are guaranteed six matches, however long these take to come through. Meanwhile there are always the events — about three a month — which are signed up for separately. These include 'soirées', usually featuring young, up-and-coming musicians, held in private houses. According to Noel, this is the best place for meeting people, much better, he says than the one-to-ones. Next weekend there's a gala evening with the Royal Opera in Windsor Castle. In October there's a weekend in Paris.

A meal — either before or after — is always part of the evening's festivities. Last Sunday there were about 40 of us, and by the time we sat down to eat we were already a cohesive, if rather noisy, group. Everyone I met was interesting, from the 27-year old Russian piano teacher to the pathologist from Oxford with whom I exchanged telephone numbers. Before anyone gets too excited I should point out, that she's a she. But, hey, you can't have everything.

Emer McNamara, standing in Upper Main Street, Manorhamilton, Co. Leitrim. Photograph: Alan Betson.

THURSDAY, 16 SEPTEMBER 1999

Living on Main Street: Manorhamilton Transfer

Emer McNamara

'Wherever you go — that's where you are', are words that resonate for me every time I walk up Main Street in Manorhamilton, where I now live. I should be more specific: I actually live on Lower Main Street, a postal address which baffles most of my Dublin friends, not to mention the credit card companies. 'Don't you have a house number?' they ask, before I explain you could mark the envelope with just my name and 'Manorhamilton' and it would get to me.

It's part of the economic reality of Dublin these days that I would choose to live full-time in a place which I would not describe as my natural habitat. I'm bringing all the complications of modern, urban life with me to this tranquil town. Transplant EastEnder's Bianca to rural Ireland, and you'll get where I'm coming from — without the bad fashion choices of course.

I moved here because it finally dawned on me that I would never be able to buy a house in Dublin and I was sick of spending my time worrying about how freelance work would pay the rent on my apartment.

'And, you know, I own a lovely house,' I'd sob to friends in The Front Lounge. 'Yeah, in Leitrim — duh,' being the usual response.

It's a sign of how critical things became for everyone that, a year and a half later, these friends started buying in what I'll kindly refer to as 'the suburbs', while simultaneously telling me how lucky I was to own a house anywhere — even in Leitrim.

How I bought the house in the first place is all part of the mini-soap playing out, right here, in down-town Manorhamilton. Having moved house nine times in eight years, my ex-partner (and father of my child) and I finally landed here in May, 1997.

With the benefit of hindsight, that many house moves might have indicated that all was not well on the domestic front. In fact, things were in such terminal decline that I bought the house without ever seeing it. This bizarre gesture was meant to indicate that I no longer cared where I lived, as long as the relationship was right.

The gesture turned out to be in vain. And so it was that I found myself, after six months and a lot of DIY, with a house in Leitrim, a small child, and my ex-partner living 10 doors up the street.

The prospect of entertaining everybody with the comings and goings between a house in Lower Main Street and a house on Upper Main Street did not appeal to me in my then fragile state. But it's amazing how economic realities change your perceptions, aided, of course, by the support of someone who loves you.

The return here after my one-and-a-half years in Dublin was clinched by my new partner, Tony, when he embraced the move with enthusiasm. He grew up in Ballyfermot and, as he has spent the past five years in Manhattan, to say it's been a culture shock for him is something of an understatement.

Work takes him to Dublin two to three days a week, but he swears he enjoys the drive and the pace of life here, though adjustment to reality continues. He still doesn't get that salad means coleslaw here, not Caesar, and I've a sneaking suspicion he draws his understanding of small town life from Straw Dogs. Then again, maybe that's because he's an actor.

I bought the house for £47,000. It has four bedrooms, a converted attic for my office, a living-room/ kitchen and a basement with three rooms I haven't even tackled yet. The garden is 130 feet long, and it comes with a small mews attached, referred to in these parts as 'd'outhouse'.

I'm going to renovate it as an apartment, to supplement my income and take advantage of the recently introduced tax incentives. I don't let the fact that I know zero about gardening or tourism put me off and, anyway, the move here is not so much a choice as a necessity.

Let's put it this way, I don't expect to be decked out in Birkenstocks and track-suits anytime soon. Nor do I take any notice of the 'organic lifestyle' gang, who keep going on about keeping the old fruit trees in the garden, because, you know, I might want to make damson jam. I've secretly been stocking up on weed-killer, which I use with abandon anytime they're not looking over my shoulder.

The thing which makes it all worthwhile is my son Leo's happiness. He, of course, is oblivious to the difficulties and challenges which surround our choice.

My first weekend back in Manorhamilton, the owners of the Mace supermarket, Noel and Rose, said their 'hellos' to me, while Leo looked at them and said, 'That my mum you know'.

It was like he was proving that I really existed, since people here have only seen him with his father every second weekend since my unexplained exit a year and a half ago.

Thankfully, he no longer needs 'play-dates', since kids here move up and down between each other's houses with an ease and freedom that makes me think, 'Now that's how it should be.' He also gets to spend more time with his father, something about which he is delirious. Nobody has asked directly, but I know there is curiosity about who exactly the new Dublin fella in my life is. Since Tony is divorced, his nine-year-old daughter Hannah lives in Dublin with her mother and step-father, but we're looking forward to her visits here in the near future.

What people will make of the new addition to my family, I don't know. I presume it will just add

Benedictine Sisters from Kylemore Abbey Connemara at the launch of the Irish Cancer Society's Terry Fox Runs. From left: Sr Anna Sweeney, Mother Clare Morley (Abbess), Sr Karol O'Connell, Sr Dorothy Ryan and Sr Marie Bernarde Crosson. Photograph: Bryan O'Brien.

to the speculation. But we have given up worrying about this, just like we've given up worrying whether or not we will bump into my ex-partner in the pub. Anyway, we've heard from our sources that he doesn't drink in the one we like, and that there's an 'X' on the door anytime we're in residence.

My main preoccupation late at night is fantasising about the chicken wings in Elephant and Castle and the memory of Chinese take-away from the North Ocean in Clontarf. They've recently installed an ATM machine on Main Street, so maybe a Chinese take-away could be the next big news.

I'm here for eight weeks now, and have finally sent my 'We've moved house' cards to all the friends I was afraid would think I was mad. But maybe that's what it takes to escape the jaws of the Tiger — madness and the willingness to take risks.

Hannah recently asked Tony why he was living in 'Manorhatten', confusing his old US address with our new abode. It captured the surreal quality of the move more eloquently than I could, proving that wherever you go, that's where you are.

SATURDAY, 18 SEPTEMBER 1999

A Chase Against Time

Louise East

I bumped into a friend in a nightclub on Saturday and we sat down for a good chat. The rationale of having a good chat beside a heaving dance-floor, a six-piece swing band and speakers the size of American fridges escapes me now, but I'm sure there was one. We screamed at each other about our respective love-lives for a while before she started to stare at a man shaking his stuff on the dance floor.

Somewhere in his mid-30s, he was slightly tubby with hair that had gone on a retreat and decided that the busy world of hair growth was just not worth the hassle. He was simultaneously dancing and staring longingly at the lead singer on stage; understandably, as she was the lead singer and

possessing of a marvellous voice, long dark hair and teeth that almost did that audible sparkle thing as in the toothpaste ads.

'Now how old would you say she is?' asked my friend, with a moody look in her eye. I guessed at mid-30s. She agreed and then said 'What about him?' I decided he was also just west of 30 and did my best to look receptive, in case she felt like enlightening me as to what she was on about. Without any further guessing games, she came to the point. Which was that there was a lot of lies passing themselves off as truths to the effect that men just get better-looking as they get older, while women peak at the age of 25.

Think of all the articles bemoaning the advent of wrinkles and grey hair and cellulite, that usually gripe at how unfair it is that men just go grey at the temples and look distinguished. This is simply not true, or at least it's only half of the story.

Picture the people you know who are starting to show the first signs of ageing. My friend and I listed off baldness, ear hair, nasal hair, beer bellies and jowls as unfortunate male symptoms and decided they were just not equalled by female thirtyness symptoms — a few lines, and spreading hips. Colleagues are muttering rather indignantly that I have no need to be worrying about ageing yet, and that may well be true for the moment. But ageing is beginning to feel like an event more hyped and more maligned than the millennium. This is in no small part because the old chestnut about men ageing better than women is usually coupled with the one about thirty-something men wriggling out of relationships and dating younger women.

Books such as The Rules abound, which take as a given that after a certain age, women will have to get their man with traps as ridiculous as those of Wily Coyote. Most men nod sagely and agree that on the whole the males of the species are terrible divils for not wanting to settle down.

In last Sunday's *Observer*, William Leith wrote an entire article entitled 'Can't Commit, Won't Commit' in which he dredged up psychologists, psychotherapists and sitcoms such as Ally McBeal to explain why men are desperate to wriggle off the hook. 'A lot of men won't commit, and are not planning to. They simply are Not Ready. So they sit at home and in bars, waiting, flicking through girlie magazines and looking at exposed flesh on the Internet. And sleeping around.'

To be honest, I have always believed this to be true and to a certain extent, it is. There definitely comes a time when men who have not got hitched start to shadowbox with anything that resembles commitment. Unfortunately, this can be the very time when women decide that they're finally ready to settle down or maybe decide they want to have kids before it's too late.

I'll never forget the chill that went up my spine on hearing that one male acquaintance gave a slight shudder as a 30-something single woman bounced up to him with a kiss and a fine welcome. 'Lordy, women like that terrify me,' he reportedly muttered. 'Just dying to get married.' It seems curious to me now that I immediately accepted that although this was deplorable behaviour on his part, it was also representative of how all women and men in their 30s felt. I felt the first grip of panic at the thought of being in my 30s, single and seen as a man-hunter by society in particular and men in general.

The thing is, as my wise but indignant friend pointed out, it was not a state of affairs reflected in real life. In the last year or so, a huge number of my female friends have split up with medium to long-term partners. Almost without exception this was because they felt there was no point continuing if there was no long-term future to the relationship. Not one of these break-ups was because the woman wanted to settle down and the man was doing a 100-metre sprint in the other direction.

In fact, one American friend has put an end to two relationships in the past year with men whom she describes as 'scarily ready and willing for marriage and families'. Then there's the tale of a male friend who has been engaged three times and is finally getting married next year — sure he's in love with his fiancée but he's even more in love with the idea of marriage.

There is a curious dichotomy between what is perceived to be true — that women are desperate for marriage and men are running scared — and what is actually happening. As usual there is a huge complexity, a huge variety of greys in the real life version — women and men who would do anything to get married; women and men who don't want anyone cluttering up their lives, and women and men who only want the right someone cluttering up their lives.

But what is constantly appearing in black and white is the idea that woman are sitting ducks, waiting to mate and willing but unable to find anyone to oblige. It's the most sexist, ageist lot of nonsense and it fosters a huge paranoia among women in their 30s and women in their 20s who are heading that way. None of us is quite paranoid enough to believe the theory was cooked up by fat, bald, hairy thirty-something men contemplating a lonely middle age, but it's only a question of time.

FRIDAY, 24 SEPTEMBER 1999

Most Militia Leave Dili to Count its Many Dead

Conor O'Clery

The young man pulled his T-shirt up to his nose, peered over the little round concrete wall, drew back, blessed himself and hurried away through the old tyres and junk in the back yard. The rest of the kids in line — some as young as 10 — did the same.

The well at the back of Manuel Carrascalao's house in Dili was yesterday a centre of pilgrimage and a macabre attraction. The youths were arriving back in the capital from the mountains where they ran to escape the militia terror two weeks ago.

Just below the rim of the well was the putrifying body of an independence supporter. 'There are 20 more down there,' said the young man. It

Collette O'Reilly, the first lady wheelchair competitor home in the 98FM Dublin City Marathon. Photograph: Frank Miller.

was impossible to tell if this was true, as one could not see deeper into the well.

Now that the United Nations peacekeepers have arrived in Dili and most of the pro-Jakarta militia have gone, the counting of the dead has begun. It is proving very difficult, with eye-witnesses still hiding or shipped out to West Timor, and with evidence possibly covered up by the militias and Indonesian soldiers. In addition, most of the territory is still inaccessible.

Everyone knew there had been killings in the last two weeks at the house of Manuel Carascalao, a prominent member of the East Timor Resistance Committee (CNRT). This had been the scene of an earlier massacre on 17 April, when the Aitarak militia had murdered more than 20 refugees hiding there. But things were not so simple at other alleged massacre sites.

It was widely reported last week, for example, that the Dili Diocesan Centre nearby had also been the scene of the murder of 20 or so people. The fine old Portuguese building is now a gutted skeleton where yesterday a strong wind caused the twisted, dangling remains of the corrugated iron roof to creak and groan like banshees.

A line of three bullet holes in one wall, with several more much higher up, indicated some shooting, but of blood or bodies among the ankle-deep debris there was no sign. A police station near the airport was another alleged massacre site, with bodies said to have been piled high in a cell, but the rooms showed no signs of slaughter.

It was the same at Bishop Carlos Belo's house on the seafront, where witnesses reported two dozen people killed, mainly by gunfire in the days after the 4 September announcement that East Timor had voted to break with Indonesia. But the priests and nuns there say only one person was shot dead.

Except for the Carrascalao house, people were killed in Dili mostly in separate incidents, 'one here, one there, maybe 100 altogether', said Father Francisco as he supervised the preparation of lunch in the garden beside the burnt-out residence.

UN peacekeepers have also yet to turn up evidence of large-scale killing sites. 'If there were massacres, where are all the mass graves?' asked Brig David Richards of the British Contingent of the International Force for East Timor (Interfet). 'In Sierra Leone there were bodies all over the place. I haven't seen that here.'

'There is some evidence that there have been some awful acts,' said Maj-Gen Peter Cosgrove, the Australian commander of Interfet. 'I'd like to see a professional investigation coming in rapidly.'

A senior Red Cross official, Mr Symeon Antoulas, said in Dili yesterday that because of very limited information, 'we cannot confirm reports of mass killings'.

He also disclosed that the International Committee of the Red Cross estimated the number of displaced persons in East Timor at 150,000, and not 600,000, as a Jakarta newspaper said last week.

'It maybe was enough to kill here and there to cause terror and achieve their ends of making the population flee, especially with their record of massacres earlier this year,' said another senior aid official, speaking anonymously.

A similar strategy of inducing fear — and also testing the resolve of the UN peacekeepers — seemed to be in operation yesterday in the unpredictable streets of Dili, where the militia and some elements of the Indonesian military caused several incidents.

Three truckloads of Indonesian soldiers of East Timorese origin, who are withdrawing from the capital of the former Portuguese colony, careered through the town yesterday morning, firing in the air at three locations and being pursued first by Gurkhas of the British army and then by Australian soldiers before driving off.

British marines later chased a militia man through an Indonesian army (TNI) barracks after shots were again fired in the air, almost causing an angry confrontation with the Indonesian soldiers. The militiaman got away but later the British soldiers rescued him from a crowd which a British officer said was 'kicking him to death' because they recognised him as a member of the Aitarak militia.

The withdrawing TNI also burned another barracks in the capital yesterday as it proceeded with a reduction from 11 to six battalions, causing further stress in the relationship between Interfet and the multinational army. Gen Cosgrove criticised their action as 'destroying the chance to build the city rapidly'.

With 3,000 UN troops now in East Timor, Interfet has tightened its control of Dili since it arrived and has now surrounded the airport with deep defence bunkers and machine-gun posts.

The most serious challenge facing Interfet in the coming days is likely to be not in Dili but west of the city near Liquica, where militia members were reportedly gathering for a confrontation. The reports of this build-up were being investigated, said Gen Cosgrove, who would not detail what he planned to do to prevent a *de facto* partition of East Timor.

MONDAY, 27 SEPTEMBER 1999

Paddy the Pigeon Knocked Down Without a Flap

Frank McNally

It was no way to treat a war hero. It took Paddy the Pigeon nearly five hours to fly back to England with news of the D Day landings in 1944, as all around him birds with the same messages were getting shot down, lost or distracted by French female pigeons.

But his Dickin medal for gallantry was disposed of in less than a minute in Whyte's auction rooms in Dublin at the weekend, and for less than the catalogue's estimate.

The sole consolation for Paddy, who was from Co. Antrim, is that the medal — known as 'the animal's Victoria Cross' and one of only 53 awarded — will stay in Ireland.

A £5,500 opening postal bid from the US was quickly overhauled by one in the room for £6,000, and that was that. Immediately after the hammer fell, the auctioneer's phone rang with a press query, provoking inevitable jokes about Charlie Bird. But apart from that, there was general anti-climax that the medal had gone so quickly.

The buyer turned out to be a businessman, Mr Kevin Spring, from Templeogue, one of Dublin's best-known pigeon-fanciers and, as a commandant in the FCA, a military man.

With his double interest in the medal, he had nursed an intention to buy it for several weeks. 'I told nobody, hoping it wouldn't attract much attention,' he said. 'So when the papers got hold of it, I was afraid there'd be a lot of bidders.'

He was ready to pay 'substantially' more for it, but declined to say how much. At 6,000, though, he is convinced he got the bargain of the year, even

The World War II Dinkin Medal, awarded to Paddy the Pigeon. Photograph: Joe St Leger.

if the auctioneer's commission pushed the price to nearer £7,000. 'The *Irish Independent* had an article about good and bad investments recently, and this was in the second category. I predict time will prove them wrong,' he said.

Indeed, within minutes the investment was already paying off, with the presentation to him of a commemorative gold, pigeon-shaped tie-pin.

The other star item in the day-long sale, a group of medals relating to republicanism from the Fenians through 1916 and beyond, went to an American bidder for £5,000. A medal from Louth's 1957 All-Ireland victory, almost as rare as an award for pigeon bravery, was withdrawn; while a file of documents handled personally by Hitler failed to reach its reserve price of £1,000.

The sale, which featured everything from an 1879 medal for the 'technical execution on porcelain and original grouping of flowers' (£50) to one for 'best bull' at the 1894 Spring Show (£120), raised about £150,000.

FRIDAY, I OCTOBER 1999

Getting Onto the Directors' Merry-Go-Round of Irish Business

Mary Canniffe

The names that have so far emerged as being on an official list allegedly associated with Ansbacher (Cayman) Ltd, College Trustees, or companies linked to them, is like a who's who of Irish business in the 1970s, 1980s and 1990s.

They range from chairmen or directors of the State's largest banks to chairmen of State-owned commercial companies and State advisory bodies to the top echelons of public companies.

The series of directorships held by some of those whose names are already in the public domain is an indication of how limited the top circle of Irish business was in the 1970s and 1980s and into the 1990s. For example, Mr Jim Culliton was a director of CRH, a chairman of AIB and of the RTÉ Authority; Mr Michael Dargan was a chairman of CRH, of the Fitzwilton Group, a director of Bank of Ireland and a chief executive of Aer Lingus; Mr Tony Barry is chairman of CRH, a director of Bank of Ireland, Greencore and DCC.

An examination of the membership of the boards of the biggest public and State-owned companies today shows in most cases that the top business circle remains the preserve of a relatively limited number of people. That is not to suggest that all or even most of the members of the top business circle had anything to do with the Ansbacher accounts or that there is necessarily anything sinister in people holding a number of directorships.

But it suggests that governance of the State's top companies still remains in the hands of a relatively small group, often from similar backgrounds and with broadly similar education, who socialise together and, in general terms, seem to perpetuate their own presence at director-level by appointing each other to different boards. It is interesting to look at a sample of the cross-directorships in Irish business today.

A number of the Jefferson Smurfit Group directors hold other directorships: a former EU commissioner Mr Ray McSharry, who came to business from politics, is also chairman of Eircom, a director of the Bank of Ireland, Ryanair and Green Property and chairman of London City Airport, the airport controlled by companies associated with Mr Dermot Desmond. Mr Howard Kilroy, who retired as Smurfit president and chief operations officer in 1995, is governor of the Bank of Ireland, and a director of CRH. Smurfit president and chief operations officer Mr Paddy Wright is a director of Aer Lingus. Ms Mary Redmond is a director of the Bank of Ireland, the Campbell Bewley Group and a member of the board of the Labour Relations Commission.

The Taoiseach, Mr Bertie Ahern TD, assisted by cartographer Ms Lorraine Nerney, studies the infra-red mapping system at his launch of the Ordnance Survey Ireland 175th Anniversary Exhibition in the Old Jameson Distillery, Bow Street. Photograph: Cyril Byrne.

Mr Martin Rafferty is chairman of Ulster Bank Capital Markets, United Drug and Readymix and a director of Ulster Bank and Greencore.

Aer Lingus board chairman Mr Bernie Cahill is chairman of Greencore and Irish Food Processors and a director of Murphy Brewery Ireland Ltd, part of Heineken BV.

As previously mentioned, Bank of Ireland's chairman is Mr Howard Kilroy. Other directors include Mr MacSharry and CRH chairman Mr Barry. Another director Mr Paddy Galvin is also chairman of PV Doyle Holdings, a director of Greencore, Irish Shell and Gallaher (Dublin) Ltd and Mr Pat Molloy is a director of Eircom, CRH and Kingspan.

At AIB, director Mr Ray McLoughlin is managing director of James Crean and a former director of the Custom House Docks Development Authority and the National Board of Science and Technology. AIB director Mr Don Godson is chief executive of CRH. Chairman Mr Lochlann Quinn is deputy chairman of the Glen Dimplex Group.

At CRH, aside from Mr Barry and Mr Kilroy are Mr Molloy (also Bank of Ireland, Eircom, CRH and Kingspan) and former IDA Ireland chief executive Mr Kieran McGowan (also Elan, Enterprise Ireland, An Post National Lottery and Drury Communications).

Another CRH director Mr Tony O'Brien is group managing director of Cantrell and Cochrane, chairman of Anglo Irish Bancorp and a director of The Enterprise Trust. A former Aer Lingus chief executive Mr David Kennedy who joined the CRH board is also chairman of Drury Communications and a director of Jurys Doyle Group and Lifetime Assurance.

In a small state there is a relatively small pool to draw from in appointing directors to publicly-quoted companies and government boards, so it is probably not too surprising that many of the same well-known names pop up when appointments are being made to State boards and semi-State bodies.

It is certainly not surprising that many of the members of the boards of the main banks for example are well-known business people in their own right. The aim in appointing non-executive directors, as pointed out by the Cadbury Committee on Corporate Governance, is that the company can benefit from the business and other experience they can bring to the board.

But there are some interesting links between the top players in business. They range from the old school tie, to colleges, rugby or tennis clubs. Schools such as Blackrock College, Clongowes, Gonzaga and Belvedere and University College Dublin seem to have produced many of the elite of business, while many belong to clubs such as Fitzwilliam Lawn Tennis Club or rugby clubs such as Lansdowne.

There are two sides to the debate on how people rise to the top in Irish business. There is the argument that Ireland is a classless society where anyone can become a leading business person. Proponents of this argument would point to the rise to the top, from relatively modest beginnings, of Bernie Cahill, chairman of Aer Lingus and of Greencore and Dermot Desmond, founder of NCB Stockbrokers and former chairman of Aer Rianta.

The counter argument is that Irish business is dominated by a small number of people who share similar 'moneyed' backgrounds, attended the same schools and socialise together in the same clubs and help each other up the business ladder. Advocates of this line would argue that the directors of many of the publicly quoted or State-owned companies

come from this circle of people and would cite as an example Tony Barry, the CRH chairman and director of Bank of Ireland and Greencore and DCC.

While some of the same names still keep reappearing at the top echelons of Irish business, it is clear that not all of them come from similar privileged backgrounds. Though it is clearly easier to get to the top from such a background, the so called 'golden circle' appears to have widened. Nowadays, entry to the circle is easier for people who start or grow businesses or achieve political status.

This may be because as people make money in business, many tend to mix in the same circles where opportunities to do business together can arise. As people get to know each other, connections are made and appointments to boards can follow. Regardless of their route to the top, the end result is that the top level of Irish business is dominated by a small circle of people.

MONDAY, 4 OCTOBER 1999

Mayo Women End Decade of Misery

Keith Duggan

Mayo 0–12: Waterford 0–8

The storied corridors of the Hogan stand echoed their last yesterday and to the sounds of an emerging voice as Mayo, a county accustomed to heartbreak at this venue, took its first women's All-Ireland title from a team that had set the standard for the sport. The westerners simply out-ran and outgunned a Waterford team that lacked the dash and incision which had formed the bedrock of their pre-eminent position in the women's game for most of this decade.

It wasn't the exhibition of open play and skill that had been anticipated; in keeping with the

Diane O'Hora, Mayo football captain, holding up the cup after beating Waterford in the All-Ireland Final at Croke Park. Photograph: Alan Betson.

men's competition over the summer, this was a game of frequent fouling and low scoring.

Mayo, though, were true to their promise and rushed at Waterford with renewed intensity in the second half, having stolen the momentum in the dying seconds of the initial 30 minutes. For a 15-minute period after the break, they overwhelmed their fancied opponents, steaming into an 0–9 to 0–4 lead after 34 minutes and while character alone saw Waterford slash into that gap, eventually cutting it to just one, there was a poise to Mayo which belied their youth.

Central to their cohesiveness were Christina Heffernan, the 22-year-old midfielder who stretched the Waterford defence with long, perceptive balls and Diane O'Hora, the nippy captain who fired three points from play in the second half.

While the attack was, as usual, enterprising — Sinéad Costello linked brilliantly with O'Hora and Sabrina Bailey broke free for an invaluable point seconds before the interval — the victory was founded on solid defence.

Helena Lohan was a revelation at full back, rock solid under the dropping ball and generally imposing, while Nuala Ó Shé got to grips with the troublesome Geraldine O'Ryan, who did much to keep Waterford hopes pulsing.

The defending champions opted for a dramatic restructure at the throw in, with full back Annalisa Crotty operating at midfield and full forward Claire Ryan dropping back to the wing. The result seemed to throw both teams; eight minutes passed before a score was registered, this a Claire Ryan point.

Waterford's most productive period followed, with Geraldine O'Ryan a live wire in the corner and Crotty's athleticism telling down the middle. The first half was still young when Mayo goalkeeper Denise Horan executed a double save from Áine Wall and Julianne Torpey. Only after Heffernan tapped over their first score — a free after 13 minutes — did Mayo begin to play with the fearlessness which carried them to this stage.

And although Waterford were steady early on, at no stage did they illustrate the dynamism of old. They had problems at centrefield; Mayo's Clare Egan picked up where Heffernan left off at half-time, fetching at will and driving clever ball for Costello and Marie Staunton to race onto.

Six minutes into the second half, they were putting distance between themselves and Waterford on adrenalin alone, with corner back Imelda Mullarkey finishing off a sweet sequence which left the scores at 0–9 to 0–4.

That provoked a stately Waterford response, with Olivia Condon and Martina O'Ryan turning enough possession for Geraldine O'Ryan and

Niamh Barry to translate into scores. A fine, curling shot by Barry after 48 minutes left them trailing by just 0–9 to 0–8 and it seemed as if they had weathered the storm.

Mayo's subsequent response again underlined the value of youth; whereas older teams might have got spooked at such a swift erosion of their lead, they simply set about rebuilding it.

They succeeded with surprising ease; Heffernan again pitching a measured ball for Costello to switch to O'Hora who nonchalantly delivered. Same story five minutes later and Mayo had three chances to push themselves into the comfort zone before Costello brought them to the threshold of dreamland with two minutes remaining.

These Mayo women then, end a decade of misery for the county's GAA fans — nine All-Ireland finals in 10 years had been lost by Mayo sides at Croke Park prior to yesterday. None of that mattered when O'Hora became the last GAA player to file up the fabled stairs to address the crowd from the Hogan stand, which will be no more by this evening.

MAYO: D Horan; N Ó Shé, H Lohan, I Mullarkey (0–1); M Heffernan, Y Byrne, N Lally; C Egan, C Heffernan (0–4, frees); M Staunton; C Staunton, S Costello; D O'Hora (0–5, 2 frees), S Bailey (0–1), M O'Malley. Subs: O Casby for C Staunton (1 min, inj); S Gibbons for M O'Malley (54 mins). WATERFORD: S Hickey; T Whyte,

A replica of the Dunbrody, a three-masted barque originally built in Quebec for the Graves family of New Ross in 1845. The replica is under construction in New Ross. The original ship carried Irish emigrants to North America in Famine times.

A Crotty, N Walsh; M Troy, S O'Ryan, J Torpey (0–1); M O'Ryan, O Condon; F Crotty, M O'Donnell, N Barry (0–2); A Wall, C Ryan (0–2, 1 free), G O'Ryan (0–3). Subs: B Nagle for F Crotty (39 mins); P Walsh for M O'Ryan (53 mins).

THURSDAY, 7 OCTOBER 1999

Haughey and a Tale of Shopping for Shirts

Mark Brennock

It was 10 a.m. in Paris one day in late February 1980, and Mr Haughey had decided to go shopping for shirts.

The previous day the then Taoiseach had met the President of France, Mr Valry Giscard d'Estaing. The official business over, Mr Haughey retired to the Irish Embassy where he was staying. The Minister for Foreign Affairs and the officials travelling with him went to their nearby hotel.

The next morning was to be free of official engagements, so two of the officials in the hotel and Mr Lenihan were surprised to be summoned to the embassy for 10 a.m. 'What are we going to do now?' an official asked Mr Haughey when they arrived. 'We're going shopping,' said Mr Haughey.

Two limousines left the embassy that spring morning, the one in front carrying the Taoiseach and the Irish Ambassador to France, Mr Hugh McCann; the one behind carrying Mr Lenihan, the deputy secretary of the Department of the Taoiseach, Mr Pádraig Ó hAnnracháin, and the Government press secretary, Mr Frank Dunlop. 'Where are we going?' Mr Lenihan asked. 'Shopping,' replied the official who had asked Mr Haughey.

After five or 10 minutes, the car pulled into a *cul de sac*. As Mr Haughey alighted smartly from his vehicle, a small man emerged from a shop on to the pavement and bowed from the waist. 'Monsieur le Premier Ministre,' he began. He explained that he was very honoured by Mr Haughey's presence.

The five men went into the shop, sat down and were given coffee. The source does not recall the name of the shop. Three or four men emerged from a back room carrying boxes. They carried the boxes, a dozen or more, out to the limousines.

Mr Haughey saw one of his officials had an expression of bemusement on his face. 'Shirts,' said the Taoiseach. 'Shirts,' he repeated. 'You know they have a bust of me here.'

The shirts each had the initials 'CJH' embossed on the breast. This would have matched the dulled silver cufflinks that Mr Haughey regularly wore with the same initials engraved on them.

The small man who had bowed outside on the pavement gestured interrogatively at the four men accompanying Mr Haughey. 'My security,' said the Taoiseach by way of explanation, referring to the Minister for Foreign Affairs, the Irish Ambassador, the deputy secretary of his department and the government press secretary.

The small man said that in honour of the occasion his security men should each choose a silk tie, which they did.

The party left in the official cars, without any apparent sign of money changing hands. The shirts appeared to have been bought on account. The source, who does not wish to be identified, says he has told stories such as this for many years, but if he had written them before people would have thought he had made them up.

SATURDAY, 9 OCTOBER 1999

Five Goals that Led to Six Days of Hell

Mary Hannigan

MONDAY: 'Glory, glory, Man-u-NII-tid™,' sang the alarm clock (available in all good megastores), so loud it scattered the early morning birds chilling out while digesting their worms on the clothes-line outside the window.

Leapt out of bed, throwing David Beckham duvet cover on to official Manchester United™ bedroom carpet. Turned on official Manchester United™ bedside lamp, stepped in to official Manchester United™ slippers and threw on official Manchester United™ dressing gown. Pulled back official Manchester United™ curtains and looked out window. Lovely morning. Cloudless sky. Sun shining. Smiled contentedly. Turned on TV3's 'Breakfast Time' show, doubling audience in one fell swoop. Tucked in to semi-chewed chicken kebab left over from night before. Tomato sauce had congealed a little, lettuce a little limp and black, but who cared? It was a beautiful morning. It felt good to be alive.

Then. Suddenly. Remembered. Stamford. Bridge. Nil–One. Nil–Two. Nil–Three. Nil–Four. And Nil–Five. Sick feeling in tummy. Quivering lower lip. Thought of smirk on face of Chelsea supporting pal. Will to live? Lost. Back to? Bed. Tried to reverse result in dream. Kidnapped Gustavo Poyet, shot Dennis Wise and reminded Chris Sutton he was brutal. Dropped Lettimino' Taibi, Phil Neville, Nicky Butt, Mickhael Silvestre, Henning Berg, David Beckham and Andy Cole and played with flat back nine (with Jaap Stam sweeping just behind). Didn't work. Still lost. Heavily.

Rang work. 'I won't make it in today — I think it's serious: stomach cramps, tension headaches, depression, dodgy goalkeeper.' 'Mmm, funny that — all 27 Manchester United-supporting members of our work force rang in to report the very same bug, but our 43 ABUs have arrived early, hale and hearty and grinning like they'd just won the National Lottery. No problem though, you'd be no use to me today anyway, so you needn't come in 'till tomorrow — and you can come in late if you like.' 'Really! That's damned decent of you — what time?' 'Ooooh, five past Taibi. Ho, ho, ho.' Back to bed. Tossed and turned. Kept seeing Italian goalkeeper (cost: £4.5 million) stranded in no-man's land, doing a mighty David James impression. Scary stuff.

Woke screaming. Many times. 'Schmeichel! Come back! We miss you! Keano! Even with a crutch you'd be more useful than Nicky! Ooh, Wisey has pinched me on the thigh so I'll knee him right in front of the ref, get myself sent off and reduce my already strugglin' team to 10 men, thereby guaranteeing that they'll be even more humiliated by these West London fancy boys than they'd have been if I'd stayed on the field in the first place' Butt. Got up. Checked answering machine. Thirty-three messages. 'Chuckle, chuckle, gloat, gloat, you're not singing anymore… five? Count 'em,' said all 33. Back to bed. Difficult to sleep. Tears on pillow created deafening squelching sound with every toss and turn.

TUESDAY: Stayed in bed all day. Lost job. Didn't care. More to life than work. Like competent goalkeepers.

WEDNESDAY: Chirpy Everton fan made contact. Important question for him. 'Your old goalie, 93-year-old Neville Southall, he's at Torquay now, isn't he?' 'Affirmative.' 'Well, d'you think he'd fancy a move to Old Trafford?' 'No chance — he wants to win things this season.'

THURSDAY: Taibi breaks his silence. Talks to press. 'I'm not affected by the criticism — I don't believe my form over my four matches has been that bad,' he says. (This means he thinks he can get worse.) 'I have only played four games, not 25, and it is too early to pass judgment,' he says. (No, it's not.) 'I am sorry we lost but, as far as I am concerned, I am satisfied,' he says. (Satisfied? Christ.) 'I am not affected by the controversy in the press. Morale is high, the players are behind me,' he says. (Well, naturally they're behind you when you spend much of your time trying to cut out crosses on the halfway line.) Wake up to discover Sir Alexander the Ferguson has got off on a motoring offence because he had diarrhoea. 'This One Will Run And Run,' says the *Guardian*'s headline on the story. 'Loo lucky lad Fergie,' says the *Star*. 'Reigning cramps,' says *The Daily Mirror*. 'Sure, Fergie was always full of…,' starts an Arsenal acquaintance before he's interrupted. Can the week get any worse?

YESTERDAY: Oh yes, it can. Martin Edwards has sold off a bunch of his shares for zillions and zillions of pounds and is all set to become chairman of the plc — this means Sir Alexander will have a maximum of £12.62 to spend on new players over the next three seasons and that Roy Keane will be offered a Snickers bar and two cans of Pepsi to stay at Manchester United. Which means he won't.

TODAY: Played the official 'Treble' video over and over for 16 consecutive hours as a gentle reminder of the happy days. Spoke to positive-thinking United fan and felt the better for it afterwards. His conclusions: normal service will be resumed so long as:

(a) Keane returns from injury yesterday;

(b) United find a goalkeeper who will stop their supporters from reminiscing fondly about Jim Leighton's performance in the drawn 1990 FA Cup final against Crystal Palace;

(c) Phil Neville retires to run a pub;

(d) Mickhael Silvestre realises attempting to nutmeg oncoming attackers is not a good idea;

(e) Nicky Butt joins Oldham;

(f) Paul Scholes stops trying to imitate Nicky Butt by kicking opponents;

(g) David Beckham stops attending London fashion shows on the eve of important games;

(h) Henning Berg stops scoring for the opposition;

(i) Jaap Stam is taught Italian so he can warn Massimo Taibi to keep his legs closed;

(j) Spurs stop laughing at United's derisory offers for Sol Campbell and agree to hand him over;

(k) Ryan Giggs is asked 'any chance of you playing a few games this season?'

If conditions a to k are met then United have a chance of finishing fourth behind Arsenal, Chelsea and Leeds this season, he concluded. Feeling better already.

Sadhbh O'Brien (4) from Knocklyon, Dublin at the Supertoys 'Toys on Test' event in Dublin where the top selling toys tipped for Christmas '99 were unveiled. Photograph: Joe St Leger.

TUESDAY, 12 OCTOBER 1999

Day of Six Billion Marks Watershed for Out-Of-Control World Population

Paul Cullen

Take hold of your wrist and feel your pulse. Wait for the familiar thump-thump. Then think: every time your heart makes a beat, the world's population grows by two people.

In the time it took to read the paragraph above, at least 25 more people have started living and breathing on this Earth. By the time you finish this article, the world's population will have grown by the size of a small Irish village.

Like your heart-beat, population growth is incessant, relentless. Every year we add about 78 million inhabitants to the planet, the equivalent of a new Germany. Numbers mushroom and multiply to the point of meaninglessness, and no one seems to be in control.

Today is the Day of Six Billion, a somewhat fictional birthday organised by the United Nations Population Fund (UNFPA) to mark the approximate arrival of Earth Citizen Six Billion.

Tuesday's child, wherever he or she is born, will arrive in a crowded, cluttered world, filled unevenly with the bounty of modern technology and 20th-century wealth, and the crass poverty endured by the majority of the planet's population.

It was as recent as 1960 that the Earth's population passed the three billion mark. In 20 years' time, we should be breaching the eight billion barrier, though no one really knows this for certain.

Population forecasting is an inexact science, and tiny changes in women's fertility rates (the average number of children a woman has during her child-bearing years) can make a huge difference in population size further down the road. But all the experts agree on one thing: the only way is up.

Population is the single most important yet overlooked issue determining the future of the world. But the West, with its own population growth under control, wrongly assumes it's an issue for developing countries. The latter plead that poverty must first be eradicated before women start having fewer children. In many states, large young populations serve as cheap labour or cannon fodder for national armies.

Population issues boil beneath the surface of

Ms Maria Meagher from St Mary's Secondary School, Killester, Dublin tries out a golf swing analysis device during the official opening of the new Biotechnology and Chemical Sciences Building at Dublin City University. The £16.5m science facility was opened by the Minister for Education and Science Mr Micheál Martin. Photograph: Frank Miller.

most of the world's conflicts. Serbs are quick to claim that they were in the majority in Kosovo until a few decades ago, after which they were out-bred by the ethnic Albanian community. The genocide in Rwanda and the brutal civil war in neighbouring Burundi are partly attributable to land pressures in two of the world's most densely inhabited countries.

You don't need to go to India or China to witness the effects of growing population. Just look at the effect of a relatively small increase in population in Ireland over the past few years. Suddenly, housing lists are soaring, and Dublin is in gridlock. Meanwhile, the countryside is being consumed by concrete, our rivers and lakes are polluted and CO_2 emissions are increasing.

Sure, life goes on, and society adapts, but what emerges in the new, more crowded Ireland is different from what went before — high rise in place of housing estate, urban anonymity instead of squinting windows, forest trails instead of wild bogland. This may or may not be a good thing, but we should at least be talking about it.

Globally, rising population is the main cause behind the destruction of rain forests, over-fishing, desertification, global warming and just about any environmental calamity currently threatening the Earth.

So why isn't there a greater outcry? One reason is that population growth has defied all interventions thus far. There's a mathematical inevitability to the growth curve. The rate of increase is slowing down and will eventually level off completely, but not before the world's population reaches at least 10 billion.

The second reason is that the doom-sayers of the past have been proved wrong. They were right about the rise in population, but wrong about the world's ability to provide food and water for the extra billions.

The 18th-century thinker, Malthus, was so wrong about Europe's ability to feed itself that his name has become a by-word for pessimism.

'The battle to feed all of humanity is over,' declared the leading Stanford University professor, Paul Ehrlich, in his 1968 million-seller *The Population Bomb.* 'In the 1970s, the world will undergo famines; hundreds of millions of people are going to starve to death in spite of any crash programmes embarked upon now.'

Dr Ehrlich's theories were nonsense — both the US and Europe are still paying their farmers not to produce food — but they were highly influential. Western family planning groups used them to justify coercing poor countries into invasive and untested methods of controlling women's fertility. Force was often used in the dash to reach quotas and targets. But none of this worked, except in China, and the world's population kept rising.

One reason the population debate has been so muted in Ireland is because of the controversial stance of the Catholic Church on birth control. Throughout the 1970s and 1980s the church led the opposition to the use of artificial contraception and abortion to stem population growth in the developing world. With some justice, it can now be seen, it argued that the world could cope with the growing numbers.

Scientists like Ehrlich made the mistake of modelling their predictions on behaviour in the animal kingdom. Biologists talk of the 'carrying capacity' of a herd of deer, demonstrating that numbers increase until no more food can be foraged and the population crashes. Then the cycle is repeated.

However, humans can anticipate the future and make changes to their environments to cope with expected changes. New technologies have driven the increases in food yields and now genetically modified organisms may produce further increases in output.

The reason the Earth's population is increasing is quite simple: death rates have declined but birth rates have not. Medicine has found ways to keep people from being born, but their application has encountered many political, cultural and religious objections. These are slowly being removed. Even though the birth rate is falling, the number of births is going up. More women are having fewer babies.

But growth is concentrated in the poorest countries. For a population to replenish itself, women must average about two children each in their lifetime. However, in developing countries outside China, women average four children. In Africa, the total fertility rate is six. Only AIDS is now serving to curb this growth.

Population growth brings with it rapid and massive urbanisation. Three-quarters of the populations of Europe and the Americas live in cities, but the corresponding figure in Africa and Asia is only one-third.

But as the countryside grows ever more crowded, millions of people in the developing world are heading for the cities. Rapid urban growth puts immense strain on the most basic resources, such as water, electricity and sewerage.

The results can be seen in the favelas clinging to the hillsides of Rio de Janeiro, the tombs used as homes in Cairo's City of the Dead and countless other shanty-towns in the poorer quarters of the planet's mega-cities.

Internatilich, the Netherlands, the most frequently-cited example of a rich and densely-populated country, 'can support 1,031 people per square mile only because the rest of the world does not'.

The main population problem, Ehrlich concludes, is in wealthy countries. 'There are, in fact, too many rich people.'

Recognising that coercion has failed, and wary of entering into fresh rows with religious groups, UNFPA now talks in generalised terms about educating girls and improving women's status as ways of slowing population growth. The goal of population control has now been replaced by respect for reproductive rights; helping people limit the size of their families, safeguarding their fertility and the births of their children as they choose.

But is this enough? For poor people everywhere, large families are still the best insurance policy for old age. In conditions of chronic unemployment, low wages and no social security systems, children are more than a blessing, they are a source of income.

According to UNFPA, 'unless the rich countries of the industrialised north address the root causes of poverty and all its attendant dangers, the task of reducing population growth will remain an unfair burden on the world's poor'.

Tell that to the 2,000 people who have been born since you started to read this article.

WEDNESDAY, 13 OCTOBER 1999

Mandelson Plunges Coolly in at the Deep End

Gerry Moriarty

A journalist wanted to ask this question of Peter Mandelson when he gave his high noon press conference at Castle Buildings, Stormont, yesterday: 'Mr Mandelson, you've now met the Ulster Unionist Party and Sinn Féin — any regrets on your appointment?'

The reporter, probably wisely, bottled out. Mr Mandelson didn't. The new Northern Secretary, a couple of hours into his Belfast brief had indeed held talks with David Trimble and Martin McGuinness, and later faced encounters with Séamus Mallon and the Rev Ian Paisley. He was treating it all very earnestly.

Mr Mandelson swapped his beaming smile of Monday when he was appointed by his buddy Tony Blair to a demeanour gravely in tune with the serious politics ahead. But there was no doubting that this was an energetic politician delighted to be in from the New Labour cold and itching to get on with the business.

It would take more than Mr Trimble and Mr McGuinness re-rehearsing their entrenched positions on government and guns to rattle him. It's too early to predict whether with the passage of

'But there was no doubting that this was an energetic politician delighted to be in from the New Labour cold and itching to get on with the business.' Peter Mandelson arrives in Northern Ireland. Photograph: Eric Luke.

time the 'Northern problem' will deflate his eagerness, as it has done for several of his predecessors.

With the Mitchell review entering its closing stages, Mr Mandelson will have a short honeymoon period. He left no one in any doubt yesterday of where he stands on the Belfast Agreement.

'There is no alternative to the Good Friday agreement. There is no plan B. It is that or nothing.'

There has been much levity, particularly from Dr Paisley, about Mr Mandelson with his previous high mortgage problems now having free bed and board at the grand Hillsborough Castle, just outside Belfast. But he has yet to lay his head there, because after a busy round of meetings and engagements yesterday, he flew back to London — with his red ministerial boxes filled to the brim with briefing notes that will keep him working deep into the night.

It was clear as Mr Mandelson and Dr Mo Mowlam stood together on the steps of Castle Buildings yesterday that Northern Ireland is going to be treated to a difference in style, if not in substance. Where Mo Mowlam was informal, Mr Mandelson, with a certain aloofness and plummy accent, is more in the urbane mould of Sir Patrick Mayhew.

On his stroll through Belfast city centre yesterday afternoon, he appeared a little uncomfortable. It was a far cry from the rousing walkabout Dr Mowlam did on her first day in the city over two years ago. But nonetheless, Mr Mandelson was accorded a civil and friendly reception, despite a few cries of 'Bring back Mo'.

Most people in Northern Ireland recognise that jobs don't come much more difficult than that of Northern Secretary. They were prepared to give him a fair wind.

The leader of the Conservative Party, Mr William Hague, was not so generous: he told the BBC in London that Mr Blair had shown 'tremendous arrogance' in returning Mr Mandelson to Cabinet. 'We will work with him, we will encourage other parties in Northern Ireland to work with him, but we are entitled to say this about him and his appointment: "If Roland Rat was appointed Northern Ireland Secretary I would say everyone should work with him, but I would still point out he was a rat."'

Mr Mandelson is said to be as sharp of mind and mouth as he is of face, but there were no heated words yesterday. He appeared careful in his dealings with Sinn Féin, the UUP, the DUP and the SDLP, sounding out what they had to say, working his way quickly into his new post.

He paid generous tribute to his predecessor, but implied with a touch of arrogance that he was there because Mr Blair realised he was the best man for the job.

Dr Mowlam appeared in better form yesterday than on Monday when she looked very downbeat on learning she was being shifted back to London, just as the Mitchell review reaches endgame. It was a case of ring out the old, ring in the new, as in the morning her papers were bundled into a big Range Rover for transport to London, while in the afternoon a removal van starting bringing her successor's files into Castle Buildings.

Officials at the Northern Ireland Office came out at noon yesterday to applaud Dr Mowlam and wish her well on her way. After the press conference, it was the most natural thing in the world that she should work her way along the ranks of journalists to shake their hands and exchange good wishes. She also paid an emotional farewell to the staff. It was a sad moment — Dr Mowlam made many friends here.

Now the North has a new act — a 'class act and a big hitter', according to those who know him well. All the politicians who met him yesterday — including Dr Paisley, who is bitterly opposed to the Belfast Agreement — showed respect for Mr Mandelson.

There will be hard verbal scraps ahead, but all the protagonists seemed energised by the arrival of the new man. As one official put it, 'At least he'll liven things up again.'

THURSDAY, 14 OCTOBER 1999

Andrews Admits Change of Mind on PfP

Dáil Report

The Minister for Foreign affairs admitted that the Government had changed its mind about its approach to membership of Partnership for Peace (PfP). Mr Andrews was opening a debate on a motion approving Ireland's participation in PfP. 'To those who claim that this Government changed its mind on PfP, I say yes we have, and we are not afraid to admit that we can change our minds in the light of new facts and changed circumstances,' he said.

He added that Fianna Fáil had openly and fully recast its views on PfP in crystal clear terms in its European election manifesto. 'In that manifesto, we restated our commitment to military neutrality. We emphasised our readiness to consider participation in Petersberg tasks under the Amsterdam Treaty. And we stated our intention to join PfP, subject to Dáil approval, as a logical extension of our existing policy, and not as a departure from it.'

Mr Andrews said it was not true that participation in PfP would oblige Ireland to engage in peace-enforcement operations. Irish involvement in any peacekeeping or peace enforcement operation was voluntary, subject to Dáil decisions and required a UN Security Council mandate. 'Participation in PfP does not alter this situation.' It was not true, the Minister said, that Ireland would be obliged to participate in exercises.

'Any participation in PfP exercises would be entirely voluntary and at our discretion. In any event, we have served alongside NATO countries in UN peacekeeping missions for over 40 years, and I see nothing inappropriate in training with such countries for peacekeeping purposes.' Rejecting claims that there had been insufficient debate on the issue, the Minister said the record of debates and statements in the House and elsewhere, including the media, should be looked at. 'Look at the explanatory guide on PfP, which was published under my direction in May of this year, and which is seen by other PfP nations as a model of its kind.'

The Minister said that for the past 40 years, Ireland had been actively engaged in UN peacekeeping, which was a defining element in Irish foreign policy and a matter of justified public pride.

The reality was that the UN was increasingly reliant on regional security organisations to support and carry out missions on its behalf. Ireland had already moved into the new UN approach to regional peacekeeping through its participation in the SFOR operation in Bosnia and the KFOR operation in Kosovo.

It was Government policy that Ireland should stay in the mainstream of peacekeeping. 'Our Defence Forces must have a full voice in preparations for peacekeeping missions and, understandably, Ireland should not be absent from PfP, a forum in which best practice is being discussed.'

Mr Andrews said: 'We neither need nor wish to join military alliances, but we do need to co-operate actively with the principal regional organisations involved to maintain peace and security in Europe. And we will do so in keeping with our distinctive peacekeeping traditions.'

Welcoming the motion, the Fine Gael spokesman on foreign affairs, Mr Gay Mitchell, said his only regret was that it had taken the Government so long to come to the realisation that this was the right thing to do.

'I regret, in particular, that Fianna Fáil has so seriously misled people for so long as to what membership of PfP involves and made promises about a referendum, which they are now breaking.'

Fianna Fáil, he said, began its road-to-Damascus conversion to PfP with an article by the Minister in *The Irish Times* on 28 November last year. Mr Ahern, according to Mr Mitchell, had said as opposition leader in 1996: 'PfP involves joint exercises with NATO on sea or land. Will they take place in Ireland? Will we be able to choose the NATO countries with whom we wish to have

Sleeping Beauty cast members Gerry Walsh, left, as Dame Lola Lampost and Richard Gibson as the bumbling King Underfoot pictured to announce the opening of their show at St Anthony's Theatre, Merchants Quay. Photograph: Cyril Byrne.

exercises? Will we have British troops back in the Curragh, the French in Bantry Bay, the Germans on Banna Strand, the Spanish in Kinsale and the Americans in Lough Foyle? Is that what we are talking about, or will we take part in exercises abroad under NATO command?'

Mr Mitchell said he knew that Fianna Fáil's weasel words that things had changed were nonsense other than if they meant: 'That was opposition and this is government.' But Fianna Fáil cynicism and U-turns should not blind people to the facts. 'PfP does not present any participant with any commitments other than voluntary participation in those PfP programmes. It is not a treaty in any sense and PfP membership certainly does not imply any mutual defence commitments or membership of NATO or any commitment to NATO membership.'

The Labour leader, Mr Ruairí Quinn, said that the Government had stumbled to where it found itself today. 'It has duped the Irish people along the way. No amount of obfuscation in this House, or reference to legal and constitutional principle, will hide that, and the public know it too.'

He said that what might go some way to restoring the Government's credibility would be some kind of explanation as to why it changed its mind.

Membership of PfP represented a significant departure in foreign policy, he said. 'There is a fear, and a genuine one, that the Taoiseach must address because it is clearly evident within his own party that PfP is a means to backdoor entry into NATO. It is a fear that I believe to be groundless.'

Mr Quinn said that the manner in which the Government had decided to join PfP deeply offended many people, not just within Fianna Fáil but right across the State. 'Instead of an open debate and decision involving the Irish people — which I believe would have endorsed this Government's decision to join PfP — we have mounting cynicism that the Government is pursuing some secret agenda in respect of our foreign policy.'

The debate on the motion continues today.

THURSDAY, 21 OCTOBER 1999

A Soft-Spoken Man, Never an Easy Touch

Dick Walsh

Liam Cosgrave spent much of his time challenging Jack Lynch, in government and opposition, but when Lynch retired, Cosgrave called him the most popular Irish leader since Daniel O'Connell.

Cosgrave is not given to exaggeration: Lynch was not only the most popular but the least divisive politician of our time.

His appeal was neither effusive nor patronising: he took people as he found them and, since they were usually friendly, so was he. But he never confused a homely welcome for the tribute of a grateful populace.

He remembered people in crowds, not as supporters or clients, but as if they were neighbours. And, travelling in his company, it was easy to believe that he had neighbours in every town and village in the land.

They were people of every class and creed and almost every political persuasion (he deeply mistrusted anyone who was in two minds about violence). They had names and families and lives outside partisan politics.

On a fair day in Dromore West, Co. Sligo, I saw a man reach through the steam rising from a cluster of damp overcoats to shake his hand. Lynch recognised him straight away, remembered a death in the family and wondered if the man's sons had got home from England for the funeral.

He didn't indulge in begrudgery and rarely provoked it. Pat Magnier of Labour, in a half-hearted attempt to do him down, once handed a photograph of Lynch in a dress suit to an elderly neighbour in Blackpool.

'There's Jack for you, now,' said Magnier, 'hob-nobbing with the crowd from the oil companies.' He looked around at a basin filling with water from

Dessie O'Malley, Charles Haughey and Kathleen Reynolds pictured at the Jack Lynch funeral in Cork. Photograph: Mark Kelleher.

a leaky roof. The old woman peered at the photograph and slowly smiled: 'Ah, Jesus, will you look at him. Didn't he come on grand.'

None of this should be taken to mean that, in politics, Lynch was a soft touch. In the early 1970s he was successful not just on one front but on three.

It was difficult enough to survive the arms crisis and the fierce internecine struggles it provoked; all but impossible to persuade Edward Heath of Dublin's right to a say in Northern affairs.

He managed both and then, with Paddy Hillery, negotiated Ireland's membership of the Common Market. Ironically, in the general election of 1973, Fianna Fáil lost office but increased its share of first preference votes. Cosgrave led the Fine Gael–Labour coalition and Lynch, in opposition, became known as the real Taoiseach.

Years later, outside a meeting of European heads of government in Bremen, Germany, a shrewd Danish journalist, Karl Tofte Jensen, of *Politiken*, said: 'A fellow might think that because he speaks quietly, your Mr Lynch is an easy mark. That would be the fellow's first mistake. And, maybe, his last.'

That was at the close of the 1970s when Lynch was back in office and negotiating, first with the formidable pair of Helmut Schmidt and Valery Giscard D'Estaing, on the establishment of a European Monetary System; then with Margaret Thatcher on the thorny question of Britain's EC contributions.

Representing his views on two films for Granada Television, I had an opportunity to watch at close quarters (for a journalist) as he worked on highly technical financial and diplomatic projects.

Ireland held the EC presidency for the first time, so both Community and national interests had to be borne in mind. His commitment to the

EC was strong, his grasp of detail impressive and his openness to change surprising.

Like most political leaders he was reluctant to admit — indeed, preferred not to discuss — decisions which friends as well as critics considered to have been mistakes.

Take Charles Haughey's restoration to the Fianna Fáil front bench in 1975. Lynch thought it an act of Christian justice: the minister, whom he'd sacked in 1970 had done his time.

Others felt it was bound to be a disaster for the party, for the country and for politics.

He blamed circumstances rather than some flawed theory about spending our way out of recession for the failure of the 1977 election manifesto. And he wouldn't hear of the argument

that the practice — implementing the promises — turned out to be worse than the theory.

But the judgment which springs to mind today is that of Justin Keating, one of the most perceptive members of the Fine Gael–Labour coalition of the 1970s, who said, when it looked as if Fianna Fáil was bound for defeat: 'History will be kind to Jack Lynch.'

Twice in the past 10 years Lynch and I happened to be in neighbouring rooms in St Vincent's hospital and we visited each other from time to time. Our conversations were not about politics but about hurling and his youth in Blackpool.

The first time I saw him he was taut as a coiled spring in a red jersey as he shot a point for Cork

Eleven-year-old Thomas Delaney from Galway at the annual week-long Ballinasloe Horse Fair. Photograph: Bryan O'Brien.

which set the crowd in Limerick's Gaelic Grounds reeling with admiration. The best of it was that, as he crouched by the sideline 40 yards out, he knew he could depend on wrist and eye; he wasn't going to miss.

'There you are,' said my father, 'and he's a TD and a barrister to boot.'

'Or not to boot,' said the cool Corkman beside us. 'Didn't he throw the boots away at half-time.'

You could tell the story about many another player-turned-politician — if they were good enough — but only in Lynch's case is it close to being the whole truth. His wife Máirín, his native Cork, politics and hurling were his life.

And a good life it was.

SATURDAY, 6 NOVEMBER 1999

Eye on Nature

Michael Viney

Recently I spent a few days in Killadoon, Co. Mayo and saw a greater variety and a greater number of birds in half-an-hour's walk along the boreens than I have seen in a couple of hours in the Bray/Greystones area. I counted 20 sparrows in a group when I would be lucky to see two or three here.

Derek H. Pullen, Bray, Co. Wicklow.

Sparrows are social birds. After the breeding season they roam in flocks seeking suitable food sources such as seeds and cereals.

My buddelia attracted quite a few butterflies this year despite a fall-off in numbers. Some were very interesting — one large, brown/gold one had deep-purple patches on its wings, almost identical to the colour of the flowers.

E. McDonagh, Batterstown, Co. Meath.

It was a peacock, one of most beautiful native butterflies.

WEDNESDAY, 10 NOVEMBER 1999

Herbal Crisis

Kathryn Holmquist

The health food industry is angry at the Department of Health's decision to place St John's wort — whose botanical name is hypericum — on the Irish Medical Board's prescription-only list from 1 January 2000. What many have yet to realise is that St John's wort, and other herbal medicines on the list, will not be legally available even with a prescription because they do not have product authorisation which is required to sell drugs on prescription.

Also on the list are blue cohosh, or squaw vine, used to support women during labour, and gingko, the most widely used herbal remedy in Europe and a scientifically proven remedy for memory loss related to normal ageing. Europe's largest manufacturer of gingko is in the Republic, yet ironically, from 1 January, people here will not be able to buy the herb.

The prohibition of St John's wort, gingko and other herbal medicines has come about as a result of EU legislation that 13 of 15 EU states are choosing to ignore in favour of their own legislation governing the sale of herbal medicines. Only the Republic, by placing herbal medicines on the prescription-only list, is following the letter of the EU law, which says that any substance with a pharmacological effect is a medicine, says Michael McIntyre, chairman of the European Herbal Practitioners' Association.

'It's a total farce,' says Dr Dílis Clare, a GP and university-trained medical herbalist, who arrived in Galway from London two weeks ago to open a new practice combining 'orthodox' and traditional medicine. Without St John's wort and gingko, two of the most important remedies in her herbal apothecary, Dr Clare says that she might as well close up shop and return to London, where these herbal remedies remain freely available.

Dr Dílis Clare, a general practitioner specialising in herbal medicine. Photograph: Joe O'Shaughnessy.

The hype about hypericum — St John's wort — has clouded the real issue, which is that consumers have a right to avail of herbal medicine, which has a 2,000-year-old tradition, and they also have a right to be protected. The EU and the Government need to develop a system whereby safe, quality-controlled herbal medicines are prescribed by informed experts under a system of regulation, asserts McIntyre. A university-trained medical herbalist (there are five university programmes for medical herbalists in Britain), he believes the Republic should introduce a system of training and regulation which would limit the use of herbal medicines to licensed practitioners. The Irish Herbal Practitioners' Association has been talking to the Department of Health about this possibility, so far without success.

Herbal medicines have scientifically proven pharmacological effects that can be potentially damaging in the wrong hands. The Department of Health has particular concerns about Internet traffic in herbs and has placed two on the prescription-only list requiring product authorisation and licensing. They are *tribulus terrestrix*, which raises testosterone levels and is being marketed on the Internet as the herbal alternative to Viagra, and *caulophyllum thalictroides*, which has many uses and abuses, including one as a potential abortifacient.

The only legal means that the Department of Health currently has of protecting the consumer is the product authorisation system. But this can cost £40 million for one drug alone, because it requires expensive studies on carcinogenicity and double-blind control medical trials. Herbal medicines manufacturers, distributors and practitioners argue that the authorisation system designed for synthetic drugs is too rigorous and costly for herbal medicines, which cannot be patented like synthetic drugs. However, Dr

Des Corrigan of the Department of Pharmacology at Trinity College Dublin, points out that the herbal medicines business in Europe is worth six billion dollars annually and can well afford to ensure the safety, quality and efficacy of its products.

In late September, these issues were discussed by the pharmaceutical committee of the European Commission, which concluded that the EU should look at the possibility of assessing herbal medicines in terms of 'traditional use', rather than the standard criteria of product authorisation. This approach is widely supported by people on both sides of the debate.

Frank Hallinan, chief executive of the IMB, attends the EU pharmaceutical committee. 'We are open to discussions on how to solve the problem. This is an evolving and developing situation and we are not fixed in a particular position,' says Hallinan. The IMB has been painted as the villain of the piece by the health food industry, but Hallinan points out that the IMB did not 'go after' St John's wort. It came to the attention of the IMB because someone wishing to manufacture hypericum extract (the IMB will not reveal who) applied for a product licence which requires a product authorisation.

After investigating the herbal medicine's properties, the IMB immediately became concerned that St John's wort, which is effective against mild, clinical depression, would be self-prescribed by depression-sufferers, thereby putting them at risk of not getting the necessary medical help. St John's wort also has side-effects that, in the experience of one psychiatrist who prescribes it — Dr Patrick McKeon of St Patrick's Hospital, Dublin — are as significant as the side-effects of prescription anti-depressants.

The consumer needs to realise that 'natural' does not mean 'safe', Dr Corrigan points out. 'Quality control is important. There have been too many disasters,' says Dr Corrigan. In Belgium, 90 women got kidney failure — leading in many cases to kidney cancer — when they were treated with a poisonous Chinese herb, aristolochia, that had been mistaken for a safe herb, stephania. This happened again in Britain last year, when two people were affected. Measures have been taken to ensure that this could not happen here, says Kerry McBride, chairman of the self-regulating Register of Irish Chinese Herbal Practitioners, which has a record of using medicinal herbs responsibly.

In the interest of protecting the consumer, the IMB and the Department of Health are concerned about unscrupulous cowboys selling adulterated products and using false advertising. In Britain, an Irishman was prosecuted for selling a 'herbal' cream for eczema which secretly contained potentially harmful steroids. Believing the cream to be 'natural', consumers were covering themselves with it from head to toe. In another case, a remedy marketed as natural, contained phenylbutazone, an anti-arthritic synthetic drug that causes aplastic anaemia, a blood disease that can be fatal.

The IMB does not want to put reputable health food stores and herbal practitioners out of business. 'Chasing after herbalists who are doing a reasonable job would not be on our list of priorities,' Hallinan says. Nigel Griffiths of Nature's Way says that all his staff who advise on herbal remedies are fully trained and know when to refer a customer to a medical doctor.

McIntyre explains: 'The health food stores have pioneered the availability of over-the-counter herbal remedies to the public and many have real expertise and integrity, but because there are no regulations it leaves the business open to shenanigans.' In the absence of a coherent European policy on herbal medicines, the public must rely on the honesty and intelligence of sellers practitioners. On 1 January next, health food shops may decide to ignore EEC/6565 by continuing to sell herbal medicines. The Department of Health is understood to be considering prosecutions as a means of focusing the health food industry's attention on the seriousness of the EU legislation. However, the IMB has yet to hire the promised enforcement officers who would go into health food stores and inspect, with powers to prosecute. And so we may have yet another Irish solution to an Irish problem.

THURSDAY, 11 NOVEMBER 1999

Trimble to Deliver his Verdict to Party Today

Frank Millar

The Ulster Unionist leader, Mr David Trimble, has convened a meeting of his Assembly Party for later today at which he is expected to deliver his verdict on the proposed deal to break the devolution/decommissioning deadlock in the peace process.

The indication last night, according to senior party sources, was that Mr Trimble was 'very close' to gambling his political career on the quality of a republican 'commitment' to a decommissioning

process to follow the creation of Northern Ireland's power-sharing executive.

One source said he thought further amendments made yesterday to the draft Sinn Féin and IRA statements — key ingredients in any sequencing process leading to devolution — could be enough to tempt Mr Trimble into a 'back me or sack me' appeal to his ruling Ulster Unionist Council (UUC).

However, Mr Trimble faced the first signs of resistance within his Assembly Party during an initial round of consultations on the shape of the emerging proposals at Stormont last night.

At least two of his 26 colleagues are believed to have told him they do not consider the proposed statements, or the assumed appointment of an IRA interlocutor to deal with the International Decommissioning Commission, enough to meet the party's terms for entering into government with Sinn Féin.

The UUP's deputy leader John Taylor in good spirits at a meeting of the Ulster Unionist Party Council. Photograph: Bryan O'Brien.

Mr Trimble is also planning a face-to-face meeting with his deputy leader, Mr John Taylor, ahead of today's Assembly party meeting, which could be crucial to his final decision on whether to take the package to an emergency meeting of the UUC.

Nervous British government sources last night urged caution and insisted nothing should or could be taken for granted until Mr Trimble's party consultations were complete. But within the party itself there was growing speculation that 27 November has been pencilled in for the UUC meeting.

That in turn reinforced the belief that the Mitchell review might indeed result in a deal which would see the appointment of ministers by the beginning of December.

There were unconfirmed reports last night that one barrier facing Mr Trimble would be removed in the event of an agreement with Sinn Féin, and that Mr Séamus Mallon would seek to withdraw his July resignation as deputy first minister, so removing the need for a re-election commanding an absolute majority of designated unionist votes in the Assembly.

FRIDAY, 12 NOVEMBER 1999

Words Tailored for those Special Occasions

Brendan McWilliams

Any conscientious meteorologist will readily distinguish for you between an umbrella weather word and a portmanteau term. In fact he or she will do it in the course of work a dozen times a day, but sometimes the subtle nuances are lost on hoi largely uncaring and often ignorant polloi. Let Weather Eye explain.

'Precipitation', for example, is a typical umbrella word. It 'covers', as it were, a long and potentially tedious list of quite separate meteorological eventualities, each dependent on a special combination of temperature, altitude, or time of day. The phenomena range from the banal to the sublimely esoteric.

We are all familiar with at least four types of precipitation — rain, drizzle, snow and hail. Rain and drizzle both consist of drops of liquid water, and differ only in the dimensions of the drops. Droplets of drizzle are so fine that no splash occurs when they fall on a surface of water. Snow-flakes, of course, are loose aggregates of ice crystals, while hail consists of small translucent pellets of ice, roughly spherical in shape, and usually around a quarter of an inch in diameter. They can, however, measure two inches, or even more.

But there are other less familiar forms of precipitation. Icepellets are very similar to hail, except that the little lumps of ice are transparent; they are composed of frozen raindrops, or melted and refrozen snowflakes. Granular snow, on the other hand — sometimes known as graupel — is quite opaque, and consists of very small grains of white ice, usually flat or elongated in shape. The most exotic of all is diamond dust, associated with very low temperatures: it consists of small sparkling ice crystals in the form of needles or tiny plates — often so tiny that they appear to be suspended in the air.

To understand a portmanteau term, on the other hand, it is necessary to recall the little rhyme devised by Humpty Dumpty in *Alice Through the Looking Glass*:

> Twas brillig and the slithy toves
> Did gyre and gimble in the wabe …

When Alice questions him on 'slithy', Humpty explains it as a mixture of the two words 'lithe' and 'slimy'. 'You see it's like a portmanteau,' he elaborates. 'There are two meanings packed into one word.'

Two examples come to mind from meteorology. The familiar 'smog' is a combination of the two words 'smoke' and 'fog'. Less widely known is the term 'mizzle', a meteorological portmanteau

Organic farmer Ciaran Duggan and his wife Annette tend their free range Christmas turkeys reared on Highfield Farm golf course in Carbury, Co. Kildare. Picture: Matt Kavanagh.

holding 'mist' and 'drizzle' which aptly describes the kind of gentle precipitation wrung from a moist south-westerly flow of air in Kerry, Cork or Donegal.

SATURDAY, 13 NOVEMBER 1999

The Muse is Often Absent, But You Have to Write Anyway

Cathy Kelly

My writing companion is Tamsin, my golden Labrador, and, as she can shoot lethal, baleful looks at you for hours on end if she hasn't been walked, out of necessity my writing day begins with a two or three-mile trek. Rain, hail or shine, we trudge along, me looking like a yeti in my 17 layers if it's cold. We belt down a meandering country road in Wicklow, stopping to say hello to Joey the pony and feed him an apple. Home, shower, coffee and I'm at my desk rebooting the computer and re-reading whatever chapter I'm working on with Tamsin at my feet. From the study window I can see the mountains and watch the antics of the fat pigeons who look like B52s with their enormous bellies and who waddle around the garden. But once I've started writing, I don't really notice the view anymore; I see what I'm writing, picturing it in my head.

I'm working on my fourth book now and I still think it's incredible the way writing takes over and you sink into a trance. Sometimes, my brain is working so hard that my fingers can barely keep up. I type and type and end up exhausted, happy and dying for a cup of coffee. Then again, on other occasions, it's like pushing glue uphill, and I begin to think of all the other things I could be doing at those moments — even cleaning out the fridge becomes alluring. Naturally, as soon as I stop writing, I decide that I won't bother with the fridge after all.

I listen to music, very low, when I write. My favourite CD is the soundtrack to 'Forget Paris'. It's all mellow jazz with the most fabulously haunting sax version of 'Come Rain or Come Shine'.

Bodybuilder Niamb Colgan struts her stuff after she won the Figure Contest at the OKD I.A.B.O. 'Naturals' Bodybuilding presentation in Liberty Hall. Photograph: Matt Kavanagh.

I've written three books listening to that. I'm getting adventurous now and listen to Brian Kennedy among other CDs but when I get stuck, I stick 'Forget Paris' on again. It's so comfortingly familiar. I'm not normally superstitious but I am hideously so about writing.

When I moved and threw out the old table on which I'd written *Woman to Woman* and *She's The One* in favour of a very nice maple desk, I became terrified that I'd never be able to write another word. Which is where the journalistic training comes in handy. I simply told myself to shut up about the damn desk and write. After working in a busy newsroom for years, you learn how to do that. The muse is often noticeably absent just hours before copy deadline, but you have to write anyway.

I love writing fiction and it's an incredible way to earn a living, but it is still work. You're at your desk for five or six hours, writing, re-shaping, editing, re-editing and hating yourself for not being able to make a particular passage work.

I know when I'm burned out and then I stop, do a word count and write it into my writing diary. Writing a book a year means you have to be ruthlessly disciplined. My diary shows when I've been slacking. Then I reward myself by settling down to read someone else's book.

Never Too Late, Cathy Kelly's third novel, is published by Poolbeg.

SATURDAY, 13 NOVEMBER 1999

At the Disposal of the Archbishop

John Bowman

In the summer of 1947 Seán MacBride seemed poised to make a breakthrough in Irish politics. Fianna Fáil had been in power since 1932 and by then many of its followers were disillusioned that all of de Valera's promises had not come to fruition. Fine Gael was in serious decline and Labour had split into two parties.

Seán MacBride's new party, Clann na Poblachta, was especially threatening to Fianna Fáil: it belittled de Valera for any hints of heresy or pragmatism on the national question; it banged the anti-Partition drum louder than all comers; it was recruiting activists and voters from Fianna Fáil; and in MacBride it reckoned it had the only leader with the charisma, intellect and national record to take on de Valera.

Having prospered at the local elections in 1947, Clann na Poblachta won two spectacular victories in by-elections at the end of October. Among those elected was Seán MacBride.

On the very day of his election to Dáil Éireann on a new republican platform to unite the country and transform politics, MacBride wrote to McQuaid that having become 'a public representative for a portion of Your Grace's Archdiocese, I hasten, as my first act, to pay my humble respects to Your Grace and to place myself at Your Grace's disposal'.

He added that both as a Catholic and as a public representative he would 'always welcome any advice which Your Grace may be good enough to give me and shall be at Your Grace's disposal should there be any matters upon which Your Grace feels that I could be of any assistance'. Furthermore, it was his 'sincere hope that Your Grace will not hesitate to avail of any services should the occasion arise'.

McQuaid quickly acknowledged this 'gracious letter', thanking MacBride for 'the courtesy which

Mrs Phyllis Browne, widow of Dr Noel Browne (centre), with her daughter Ruth Browne (left) and grandaughter Nena Assa in Trinity Library where Mrs Browne handed over papers and other material relating to the activities of the late Dr Noel Browne to the college. Photograph: David Sleator.

you have so promptly shown to the See of Dublin'. Moreover, he would not 'fail to take advantage of your generous suggestion that you are at my disposal for any matters in which you could assist; I should not, however, wish to worry you, unless the good of the Faith were in question. When that occasion arises, I will not hesitate to avail of your services, now so frankly offered.'

Not content with this exchange, MacBride replied immediately, noting that he did not 'deserve the thanks which Your Grace so graciously gives me, for in writing to Your Grace I was but doing what I considered to be my very first duty'. It was 'with no sense of false humility that I say that I shall stand in need of help and guidance in the discharge of my new duties. Accordingly, I trust that Your Grace will not hesitate to call upon me at any time to impart such advice, formally or informally, as may from time to time occur to Your Grace. I know how burthened [sic] with work Your Grace is and accordingly I should deem it a favour if Your Grace did not trouble to acknowledge this note of thanks.'

Any supporters of MacBride who might wish to excuse this rush to ingratiate himself with McQuaid on the grounds that he was a political neophyte fresh from the triumph of a famous by-election victory will find no solace in MacBride's repeat performance after the general election of some months later.

After the February 1948 election results MacBride wrote again: as his 'first official act' he felt he should 'place myself entirely at Your Grace's disposal'. And he would always as 'a Catholic, a public representative and the leader of a party' welcome 'any advice or views' which McQuaid might impart 'officially or informally'.

For a party leader who had excoriated Fianna Fáil for its failure to undo Partition, this was an astonishing letter. MacBride added that should McQuaid wish to discuss any matters, he trusted the archbishop would 'not hesitate to summon me'. He would always 'deem it a favour to be given the opportunity to place myself at Your Grace's disposal'. MacBride concluded this letter by asking for prayers so 'that my colleagues and I may be given the wisdom and light to discharge our duties faithfully as Catholics and public representatives'.

It would be important to note this letter was written in the immediate aftermath of the election and MacBride's reference to his colleagues would be a reference to his parliamentary party that numbered 10 after that election.

McQuaid's instruction to his secretary for the reply to MacBride reads: 'Thank you for courtesy. If there be any matters on which I think you can help, I will gladly ask you to discuss them.' McQuaid would have appreciated that the value of these blank cheques which he had received from MacBride — three such letters within less than four months — was considerably enhanced the following week when it emerged that Clann na Poblachta was to help form a government with MacBride as minister for external affairs and his party colleague, Dr Noel Browne, as minister for health.

And in the third year of that government's life, as McQuaid came to challenge Browne over the Mother and Child Scheme, his confidence can only have been strengthened by having such letters from Browne's party leader in his back pocket.

It is worth emphasising that all of MacBride's letters to McQuaid are handwritten. Since their tone and content are wholly inappropriate for a leader with Clann na Poblachta's roots, policies and membership — or for any party leader, other than one leading an avowedly Catholic party — MacBride may have been taking the precaution that he alone in Clann na Poblachta would see the letters. No secretaries would type them and presumably no copies would be filed in the party's records.

This file in McQuaid's papers does not include any letter from MacBride following the 1951 election — perhaps the trauma of the then very recent

Mother and Child controversy prompted caution on his part. It is always possible, of course, that he wrote the customary letter and that it was not filed or was misfiled.

However, it would not seem to be the case that the absence of a letter in 1951 can be construed as evidence that MacBride had learned any lessons from the Mother and Child debacle which had split — and effectively destroyed — his own party following Browne's resignation as minister.

After the 1954 election — by now leading a party reduced to three seats — he returned to his old form:

'My Dear Lord Archbishop,

On the occasion of my re-election to Dáil Éireann it is again my pleasant duty to place my services at the disposal of Your Grace. It is my aim to serve Catholicism and Ireland to the best of my ability and I shall deem it a favour to receive any guidance and advice which Your Grace may, at any time, think fit to give me.'

The words 'serve Catholicism and Ireland' were heavily underlined by McQuaid — or his secretary — and the letter is marked 'File for reference'.

On the same day, MacBride wrote to McQuaid's secretary, attempting to interest him in one of Noel Browne's election leaflets. It was entitled 'Work To Be Done' and MacBride in his letter outlined his reason for forwarding it to archbishop's residence.

It was 'to draw your attention to the inside pictorial map in which it is apparently inferentially claimed that the new Children's Hospital in Crumlin was initiated and built by Dr Browne'. MacBride added that the hospital was in his Dublin South West constituency and he complained that 'many attempts' had been made to claim it as Browne's achievement.

He concluded: 'My recollection is that the project for this hospital was initiated by His Grace long before Dr Browne was ever heard of. Can you confirm my recollection on this point? If my recollection is correct in this respect should something not be done to let it be known that it was not Browne who was responsible for the erection of this hospital but that it was His Grace?'

This was clearly intended for McQuaid's attention. MacBride would have liked nothing better than an episcopal denunciation of Browne, for whom he now reserved a special loathing — which, it must be said, was reciprocated. But McQuaid had no intention of wandering into this minefield, and especially not at MacBride's prompting.

The leaflet was drawn to his attention. His instruction for his secretary is masterly. 'I have not read enclosed. Better reply that you think it would be more advisable not to worry the AB with the enclosed. At the time of opening [of Crumlin Hospital], it will be possible to make the position clear.'

In his retirement Seán MacBride proved very touchy on the subject of church–State relations. Critics of how his party had handled the issue were accused of giving succour to Ulster unionism. This emerged in a public disagreement between himself and the present writer during the course of a lengthy, live radio interview in 1980.

I had first reminded him that Clann na Poblachta had joined with its colleagues at the first cabinet meeting of that inter-party government in sending a telegram to the Pope expressing their — presumably collective — desire 'to repose at the feet of Your Holiness the assurance of our filial loyalty and of our devotion to your August Person'. Was this not — for a party founded to hasten the end of Partition — an unpromising beginning? MacBride took umbrage. In fact, he had defended the sending of this telegram when the government secretary, Maurice Moynihan, advised against it.

Later I asked him whether the government's handling of the Mother and Child controversy had not damaged its anti-Partition strategy. He insisted that he was treating the Catholic bishops merely as another interest group. The argument turned on whether he had promised to obey or to consult the

The Minister of State at the Department of Foreign Affairs with special responsibility for Overseas Development Assistance and Human Rights, Ms Liz O'Donnell, met with Zaire refugee Henoc Cubuca on board the Tallaght Centre for the Unemployed moby playbus. The mobile creche parked outside the UNHCR conference 'Refugee Women: Victims or Survivors?' to facilitate parents taking part in the conference. Photograph: Matt Kavanagh.

bishops in 1951. I think he thought it unsporting when I quoted his words in the 1951 Dáil debate in which he had insisted that as a Catholic he was 'bound to give obedience to the rulings of our church and of our hierarchy'.

Old politicians' memories are important, but they have their limitations. The contemporary record — or the private hand-written letters in a bishop's archive — invariably speak louder.

In this case McQuaid's archive exposes MacBride's reputation. Are his credentials as a republican a sham? Or is it yet another example of the chameleon in MacBride? F.H. Boland was unimpressed on one occasion when MacBride, having been deferential in a phone conversation with McQuaid, had then spoken contemptuously of him once he had put the receiver down.

Or is it that he was just tops in hypocrisy?

Dr John Bowman is a historian and broadcaster and writer-presenter of the television documentary, 'John Charles McQuaid: What The Papers Say'.

SATURDAY, 13 NOVEMBER 1999

Refugees Have to Stand and Wait as the Crisis Worsens

Kitty Holland

Suliman was in reasonably good spirits yesterday. The 30-year-old Sudanese man, who has 'left everything' to find safety in Ireland, had finally managed to see a community welfare officer. After four days of fruitless queuing he actually got into the Refugee Application Centre in Dublin's Lower Mount Street and actually got an appointment with a doctor.

Things had not gone so well on Thursday when, for the fourth day running, welfare officers were unavailable.

'They treated us shabbily,' he said of his experience on Tuesday. 'I was here for six hours and then they [welfare officers] left, just went out the back, without telling us anything. Just told us to come back tomorrow. Just treated us like we were nobody.'

Elizabeth (33) from Nigeria was more resigned than angry. Standing at the back of the queue on Thursday, her three month-old daughter Stephanie asleep in her arms, she just shrugged that she was 'used to it'.

It's been a bad week for the Refugee Application Centre. As queues grew out of control, two groups of workers withdrew their services, the gardaí were called on several occasions and a community welfare officer was allegedly assaulted by a Georgian national frustrated that he couldn't get accommodation. Everyone was reaching the end of their tether.

While the queuing asylum-seekers could only bear it, on Tuesday the 15 community welfare officers had had enough. Citing concerns about their safety because of the numbers arriving daily, they withdrew over-the-counter services.

While they operated a free phone line their unions, SIPTU and IMPACT, negotiated with the EHB. An agreement was reached that 10 new welfare officers would be recruited and that the Office of Public Works would source additional building space for the centre's work.

Normal services would resume on Wednesday, we were told.

At 8.40 on Wednesday morning it was the porters' turn to kick up. Their union, SIPTU, complained that they were not consulted about their staffing levels. They withdrew their services, only first-time asylum applicants were seen and those with welfare queries were turned away.

Another round of emergency negotiations with EHB management resulted in a promise of three new porters and an increase in 'outreach clinics', in which a porter and welfare officer travel to an area where asylum-seekers are living, effectively bringing the centre to them rather than have them visit the centre.

Normal services would resume on Thursday, we were told.

However, although normal services were provided in the morning, a statement from the EHB at Thursday lunchtime said that 'due to the large number of asylum-seekers who arrived at the unit, staff subsequently had to prioritise first-time applicants for services'. (It was that morning that the alleged assault on a welfare officer took place.)

Yesterday services did finally return to 'normal', i.e. the queue outside began forming late on Thursday night, people faced waits of up to six hours and some who arrived late (anytime after noon) were probably not seen.

Although some 13 new staff are due to start at the centre over the next few weeks all agree that without additional space the queues will continue.

'It's all well and good appointing new welfare officers,' says Ramon O'Reilly, the SIPTU official representing porters, 'but where are they going to put them? There isn't enough space as it is.'

Seán McHugh, assistant general secretary of IMPACT, also emphasises the space issue, saying that the agreement his members came to with the EHB relies on additional building space.

'It won't come together until that happens,' he says.

But how have we arrived at a situation where policy on accommodating the needs of asylum-seekers is driven by crisis?

Jim Curran, manager of services at the centre, says staff are dealing with up to 1,000 people a week, in a centre opened in October 1998 to cope with 500 a week. He explains that while asylum-seekers living in private rented accommodation are dealt with by welfare officers in their local community, those living in emergency accommodation are dealt with in Lower Mount Street.

Because of the housing crisis, more are staying for longer periods in emergency accommodation (currently 2,600). Hence the queues to see the centre's welfare officers.

The sharp rise in the number of people seeking asylum over the past three months could not have been anticipated, says Mr Curran.

This may be the case, says Michael Lindenbauer, liaison officer at the UNHCR in

One a.m. outside the Refugee Application Centre in Mount Street, where people spent the night in wait for the morning queue. Photograph: Cyril Byrne.

Dublin, but it is not enough to assume the rate of applications will continue at the same level. 'You have to have a contingency plan for a sudden increase,' he says.

Planning, says Mr McHugh, has been erratic at best, almost non-existent at worst as regards operating a refugee centre that can cope. He points out that the refugee centre has moved to larger premises three times since January 1997. Each move was precipitated by protests by staff over crisis conditions.

'The situation with numbers was not kept under review,' he says, 'and each time it took a crisis for alternative accommodation to be found.' He welcomes a commitment in the current agreement 'to keep a review on the situation'.

As he himself says, however, the EHB may keep a review on the situation but, unless the decision is made at Government level to increase funding to the board specifically on the asylum issue, 'there's not a lot the EHB can do about it'.

He and Mr O'Reilly also welcome moves to extend the outreach service and to begin housing asylum-seekers outside Dublin. However, Mr Lindenbauer is concerned that such moves will be slow in coming. 'I think there is an enormous will to do it right. The problem is that this phenomenon is new. Dealing with asylum-seekers is not an easy matter and we have to move fast.

'In dispersing asylum-seekers we are looking at structures that are not equipped. Local social welfare officers will have to learn very fast how to deal with asylum applicants; interpreters will have to be put in place; welfare and hospital treatment will have to be devised for the needs of asylum-seekers as normal humans beings in a new situation.'

These are things that cannot be done overnight, he says, and yet they are needed urgently.

'We really need to get everyone around the table, to perhaps establish a task force to tackle the asylum issue urgently.'

He feels the current inter-departmental committee on asylum matters may be too bureacratic.

Most immediately, the centre needs more space. A spokeswoman for the OPW yesterday described the availability of the kind of space the EHB so urgently requires as 'very tight'. Until it is found, tempers may yet fray further, while the queue certainly grows longer.

At least, this week, it didn't rain.

SATURDAY, 20 NOVEMBER 1999

The Day the Music Died…

John Kelly

The Indefinite Article: Two weeks have passed and still the bad taste lingers. A certain shivery unease remains and the terrible flashbacks continue to come — sudden half-remembered glimpses of the nightmare that so dazzled Dublin. Maybe you had the same dream? One where a smug limo cruises the closed-off streets in triumph and everybody in town rushes out to cheer in a ticker tape parade of swirling punts?

And within that limo, there is a figure in a black suit and he is grinning at the ease of it all. He is high on his absolute victory, and he laughs at how eagerly we have all capitulated to such an obviously grotesque charade. With pride, he toasts the death of music and the fact that 'cool' Dublin has turned out to be more of a pushover than he could have possibly hoped.

And then the limo slides up to the kerb and a pair of cowboy boots emerges onto the sidewalk. The shadowy figure remains inside as the crowds surge forward and, one by one, kneel and hungrily kiss the boots. And then, when the leathery legs are suddenly withdrawn, the people whimper and moan and the limo pulls away — heading at great speed back towards the pits of Hell (via The Point).

It is a strange nightmare I know, but I had it two weeks ago — and I was awake at the time. I was watching, from the corner of my eye, the television coverage of the MTV horror and was struck, more than ever before, by the magnitude of its awfulness. And what made it even worse was the fact that this was all happening in our soulful, funky and 'happening' city. Here was tigerish Dublin, proudly licking its paws as the world's capital of banality, exploitation and media excess. Here was something very hard to watch.

And then the real horror struck that maybe this is what we've really come to be expert at — things meaningless, empty and cynical. Of course, the signs have always been there. Let's not forget that we were once a major European power back in the glory days of Eurovision. But even Eurovision was never like this. There was nothing much to laugh at here. It was all far too nauseating to be giggled at and there was a dull defeat in the air. Maybe the bad guys had won? Maybe the people we had always sniped at — the thoughtless performers and footsoldier jocks — did, in fact, rule the world? They had clearly served their master well, and this MTV orgy of nothingness was their grand reward. All we could do was watch in disbelief.

But then, this week, I began to gather myself again. I decided that the answer is simply to stop calling it music in the first place. Because it isn't music. Certainly it employs notes and rhythms, but it's not music. Most of what we saw was the end result of a thoroughly cynical and entirely commercial process. It works like this: the record companies (or enterprising Svengalis) come up with acts, the money is spent, the hack tunesmiths write the material, the material becomes the product, the product is hyped and then the obedient radio and MTV spreads the stuff like slurry. You don't even have to go in for payola any more because everybody so desperately wants to be part of the process that nobody ever challenges anything — at any stage. And the kids, coralled at the front to provide enthusiasm on occasions such as this, take what they get.

I'm setting myself up here I know. There are a several obvious points to fling back at me. Firstly,

Britney Spears at the MTV awards. Photograph: Frank Miller.

music was always a business. Be it Hank Williams, Robert Johnson or Duke Ellington — it was always about money because that's how these people earned their living. But it was the music which propelled the business, not the other way around. So, I'm not saying for a moment that what passes for music in my book is untainted by greenbacks. But, at least, it was music and, at some point, was only about music. The worst of the MTV stuff is never about music — ever. There isn't even a single musical impulse at any point in the procedure.

Secondly, bands and groups have long been manufactured by clever businessmen. The Supremes were a girl band, The Temptations were a boy band — and, in fact, the whole Motown phenomenon was a strictly controlled commercial enterprise. But that said, there was never any doubt about the talent. For one thing, The Supremes could actually sing. And, while Motown was certainly a well planned package, it was also about music. Stevie Wonder, Smokey Robinson — the case rests.

I'm conscious that I sound like every generation before me — giving out about pop music. I sound like I just don't understand it because I'm too old or too square or too something. I sound like I'm tutt-tutting the way people objected to Elvis or Jagger or Dylan — but I'm not.

I'm not outraged by Marilyn Mansun, for example, because he's clearly not for real. Nor am I threatened or challenged by what these new 'stars' are saying because, in fact, they're not actually saying anything. The most profound thing Britney Spears has to impart is her gratitude to 'Jesus Christ and Jive Records'. It's a safe bet that she, for one, is unlikely to change the world.

The worry, however, is that it all seems so terminal. Such is the power of MTV and the rest of the media's eagerness to embrace it, that there now seems no way of stopping it. It's an overwhelming force which excludes anything which presents a challenge. If you don't fit, you won't figure.

That said, however, I've no idea who let the three grown-ups in — but perhaps we can take some heart from the fact that Bono, Mick and Iggy were definitely in the house, mingling and hopefully spreading a little sedition. In fact, that's the least we'd expect from them.

On a further positive note, maybe the backlash has already begun? Maybe that crass display of emptiness a fortnight ago has pushed one too many people over the edge? Certainly, confronted by the full horror of it in our own backyard, a lot of people got very angry indeed. They switched off, they went to bed and they dreamt about a limo cruising the streets of Dublin. They never saw the face who owned the boots but they know well who it was. They say he has the best tunes. But clearly he doesn't — and we must take some comfort in that.

TUESDAY, 2 DECEMBER 1999

Birth of a New Ireland

Editorial

At today's end Ireland will stand as never before in its long political history. The representatives of the people who live on this island, nationalist and unionist, men and women of all religions and of none, have forged an understanding as to how they will live together within the territory they share. On Good Friday of last year that understanding was given form in the wording of the Belfast Agreement.

In the following May it received the approval of the people of Ireland, North and South, Irish and British, in simultaneous referendums. Today, it assumes substance with the transfer of authority to the new executive and the fulfilling of parallel legal requirements by the two Governments.

Future generations of historians may conclude that this was a more momentous day than 6 December 1921, when the Anglo-Irish Treaty was signed. Some of them may find that today was more significant than 6 December 1922, when the Irish Free State came into being. The conclusion of the Treaty and the establishment of an independent State for part of Ireland were incomplete constructions. Though democratically endorsed within the new Free State, they largely banished Northern nationalists from the new definition of Irishness. Simultaneously, unionism began to build another State, with the aim of maintaining the ascendancy of the majority within its boundaries.

The institutions of governance which come to life today reflect a deeper and more complete expression of the democratic processes. Each community and every loyalty has had its say. Every man and woman of voting age has had the opportunity to accept or reject what has been put on offer. It would scarcely be possible to identify a more complete exercise in democracy or one in which a more fair definition of consensus has been applied. The Belfast Agreement was not endorsed by a

Mr Bertie Ahern, the Taoiseach, signs a declaration to give effect to the revised version of Articles 2 and 3 of the Constitution, watched by members of his cabinet and Mr Michael McDowell, the Attorney General (seated right), at Government Buildings in Dublin. Photograph: Peter Thursfield.

simple head-count across the island but on the basis of majority support within each of the two communities in Northern Ireland as well as within the Republic.

A great gulf of mistrust remains and must be bridged. In the aftermath of more than 3,000 deaths and tens of thousands of injuries it could hardly be otherwise. There are those within both communities who yet dissent from this historic compromise. Dissent must be respected, as long as it does not use improper methods to subvert the will of the majority. It has been heartening to hear Ministers-designate setting out, often in trenchant terms, their reservations about the new institutions but going on to accept their responsibilities and to declare themselves the servants of all the people of Northern Ireland. The history of this State can offer similar examples of political dissent being

accommodated successfully within a democratic framework.

But there can be no tolerance for those, on either side, who still claim the right to kill or injure in pursuit of their objectives. That there are yet people so disposed should not be doubted. There remains a security threat and the police and security services in all three jurisdictions face a continuing challenge in the task of thwarting the would-be bombers and gunmen. It would be foolhardy to believe that they may not attempt to strike again or to assume beyond doubt that there can be no further victims of politically-inspired violence.

It is highly unlikely, nonetheless, that such violence, even if it were to occur, would bring down what has now been established. Nor is the present Executive or Assembly likely to be vulnerable to the sort of pressures which brought down the 1974 power-sharing executive. If the arrangements which have come into place this week are to fail, it will be because the IRA refuses to begin the process of decommissioning by the end of February, triggering Mr David Trimble's post-dated resignation and effectively collapsing the new government.

There is little purpose in lecturing Sinn Féin as to its responsibilities on decommissioning for it claims to have discharged these and that it cannot speak for the IRA. This is probably true, for all that there has long been a significant overlap in membership between the leadership of Sinn Féin and the IRA's Army Council. But in his statement of last week, the Sinn Féin president, Mr Gerry Adams, accepted the necessity of decommissioning as part of the peace process. Neither Sinn Féin nor anybody else, therefore, can purport to be taken unawares or not to understand what will happen if, come the end of February, the IRA has not made measurable progress towards putting its weaponry beyond use.

No true democrat will take issue with Mr Trimble if, in those circumstances, he walks away from an arrangement which proves to be hollow and flawed. Mr Trimble has accepted that there may be a period of overlap in which an organisation, wishing to embrace the democratic process, finds that it requires some time to disengage from a paramilitary past. It happened in this State in the spring and summer of 1922. But it must be limited in time. If Sinn Féin is to be part of the new democracy, its sponsoring body — the IRA — cannot retain to itself the right to make war upon other citizens or upon that democracy's own security forces.

The new Northern Ireland executive (clockwise from centre): SDLP's Séamus Mallon, Bríd Rodgers, Mark Durkan, Séan Farren; Ulster Unionists' Sam Foster, Sir Reg Empey, Michael McGimpsey; Sinn Féin's Bairbre deBrún, Martin McGuinness; executive secretary John Semple, and Unionist leader David Trimble sit together for the first time in the new power-sharing Northern Ireland executive at Stormont. Missing are ministers Nigel Dodds and Peter Robinson of the Democratic Unionist Party (DUP) who are refusing to sit in cabinet with Sinn Féin. Photograph: Paul Faith.

On this day we witness nothing less than the birth of a new Ireland. It is an Ireland which rejects the simplistic and majoritarian politics of the past. It acknowledges the diversity of culture, of race, of religion, of identity, which span this island. The arrangements and institutions which now come into place are the product of many years of patient, wearing, sometimes heart-breaking struggle by political leaders, officials, religious leaders, security personnel and activists in political parties, voluntary organisations and groups of every kind.

The faces on television and in the newspapers are those of the known heroes who have won through — Hume, Trimble, Mallon, Adams, Alderdice, Mitchell — and many others. But everyone who voted for this new day — and those who voted against it but who accept the democratic verdict — can claim a share of what now becomes possible in conditions of peace and prosperity. There are literally hundreds of thousands of heroes and there can be more than five million winners in this story.

TURSDAY, 2 DECEMBER 1999

Minister Brings in 'Mother' of all Budgets

Cliff Taylor

Most Budgets have something which grabs the public attention and leads to great heat in the following days.

A few years ago it was the indication — subsequently withdrawn — that child benefit would be taxed. Another year saw a big fuss over property tax. This year, once everyone realises the implications, the big row will be over what the Department of Finance calls the 'individualisation of the standard rate band'.

It does not sound very exciting, but set out in an annex to the Budget documents is a plan to move to a system in three years time where a married couple with two spouses working would have twice the tax allowance of a couple with one spouse working. For the next tax year, the two spouse working couple will move into the higher income tax rate at earnings of £34,000 (E43,171) compared to £28,000 for the one earning couple.

So this year the couple with two earners on an income of £30,000 gains over £1,100 from the Budget, while the gain for the one income couple is around £600.

However, the goal in three years time, as set down in the examples in the Budgetary documents, is that the allowance — or credit — for a married couple with two earners will be twice that for a single earning couple. Taking this year's bands for illustration, the single earning couple moves on to the income tax rate at £28,000, while the two income couple can earn £56,000 before being hit by the higher rate.

The goal of this is to get more married women to return to the workforce. And there is an argument that the single income couple can afford more tax because they do not incur childcare costs.

However, the scheme — as outlined over three years — will be hugely to the disadvantage of those with one spouse remaining at home. It is an effort to attack one of the problems facing the economy — labour shortage — but it does so by introducing an entire new and controversial element into the tax system. It is, surely, unfair to those with one spouse remaining at home — of which there are currently around 100,000.

What else does Budget 2000 bring? It is a package hugely to the benefit of the better off, mainly due to the reduction in the top 46 per cent rate of tax. It has been said before, but is worth repeating. The big problem with the tax system is not the rate at which tax is levied, but the fact that tax kicks in at relatively low income levels and that people move on to the higher income tax rate at relatively low incomes.

The best part of the tax package is that, by increasing the single person's standard rate tax band from £14,000 to £17,000, it means that the single earner can earn a good deal more before becoming liable at the higher 44 per cent rate. The top tax rate will thus not kick in until around the average industrial wage. Married couples with both spouses working will also gain, as their band rises from £28,000 to £34,000.

Apart from this band increase, the income tax measures are disappointing. Having introduced a welcome and substantial rise in tax allowances in last year's budget — and thus aimed the benefits at the lower income earners — this year Mr McCreevy returns to the tried and tested formula of cutting income tax rates. The cut in the top rate, in particular, aims benefits at the higher earners.

There may be an argument to cut income tax rates in the years ahead, but surely the bigger problem in the short term is the relatively low level of income at which people enter the tax net in the first place.

This year's Budget did little to address this issue, with a rise of just £500 in the main personal tax credit and no increase in the PAYE credit. Resources would have been better spent increasing allowances than cutting income tax rates.

In particular, an increase in the PAYE allowance would have been another route to make it more attractive for married women to return to the workforce. He could have afforded to double — or even treble — this allowance, thus giving married women an incentive to return to work, without being so discriminating against those remaining at home.

Anthony McMahon, 2 years, from Drumcondra, Dublin, gets down to business at the annual Christmas Art Holiday 1999 in the National Gallery of Ireland. Photograph: Matt Kavanagh.

Analysis by the Economic and Social Research Institute, completed exclusively for *The Irish Times*, and carried on page 6 of this supplement, confirms that it is the better off in the population who gain most from the Budget. Again, the gains to most welfare recipients are less than the benefits to many taxpayers. Better-off double-income married couples, in particular, will dine out for some time on this Budget. Mr McCreevy insists that it must be seen in the context of a longer-term strategy. However, we are still not told what precisely the strategy is. His first budget cut two percentage points off the two tax rates, thus giving the main benefit to the better off. Last year's package introduced major increases in allowances and also took

The actress and comedian June Rodgers as Mille Ennium hand in hand with Bill Murphy who plays the giant from the festive pantomime 'Jack and the Beanstalk'. Photograph: Matt Kavanagh.

the welcome and reforming step of introducing tax credits.

Credits were heralded as a way of being able to target tax reform at particular groups — but this year the main income tax credits were not the major focus of the tax package. Instead we were back to the old route of cutting income tax rates. However, the move to complete the change to credits this year was welcome, while mortgage interest relief has also been simplified.

The Minister will have plenty of money to spend over the next couple of budgets, according to his economic forecasts. These are based on the reasonable expectation that growth will remain strong. He can thus afford to set out a significant reform programme as part of the talks of a new national agreement.

It remains to be seen whether there will be a big enough fuss about the allowances plan outlined for married people to lead to a reverse in direction. But there is no reason why a new national agreement should not set out clear goals for a tax reform programme over the next few years which would clearly address the remaining issues in the tax system.

MONDAY, 6 DECEMBER 1999

Night of Breathtaking Crassness at the RDS Messiah XXI, RDS Simmonscourt Pavillion

Aidan Twomey

Let us be quite clear: this was a pathetic production of breathtaking crassness. In attempting to popularise Handel's classic, the organisers of this disaster have misunderstood completely the differing impulses of classical and popular music, and made a corpulent mess out of *Messiah*. This had neither the magic of the original nor the energy of good pop.

It failed on all possible terms, most pertinently its own. A *Messiah* for a New Millennium? With singers whose heydays are long past? Performed by a church folk group gone mad? All guitar and tambourine, the cheesiness of the stock pop devices of this quite tasteless arrangement made a mockery of its intentions — this was as modern as the Eurovision Song Contest. For all its pop touches it had less energy than Handel's original, and despite cuts, seemed longer. To make matters worse everything was over-amplified, making the orchestra and choir sound coarse, like being stuck in a lift with the loudspeaker at full blast.

Most shocking of all was that not one of the cast could hold a tune. All night, voices strained to fill parts for which they were not able. The singing seemed as if it had been put through some kind of warble-phone, so distorted was it by tasteless vibrato, designed to cover a multitude of deficiencies.

Nobody succeeded. There were only degrees of awfulness. Worst by far was the dreadful Roger Daltrey. Everything he touched was butchered. Chaka Khan was all over the place. Gladys Knight was just not equipped to sing this music. Jeffrey Osborne came out with least disgrace, a dubious distinction. All this was peppered with the offensively ambiguous double-speak of narrator Aidan Quinn's pointless role. Was he scorning or supporting the *Messiah* story? Who could tell?

The Overture, as is appropriate, set the tone for the evening. After a suitably faithful start, the electric guitars were let loose, never to be restrained again. The whole of the show was summed up in the first number. In the original, the tenor's 'comfort ye' is a special moment as it grows from nowhere. When bashed out in the manner that Osborne did as he groped for the right notes it is as magical as a bucket of vomit; although it seemed positively virtuous as soon as rock dinosaur Daltrey strode on stage to massacre 'Every Valley Shall Be Exalted'.

New depths of dreadfulness were to follow, making even unnecessary gospel *a capella* choruses

seem a relief. And I never again wish to be subjected to a display of such tackiness that greeted the Hallelujah! chorus, complete with thrashing lights, drums and guitars.

The irony is that *Messiah* is one piece that does not need this treatment to be staggeringly popular. Double the disgrace on this execrable performance that it should show such disrespect to the music, the composer and the millions of music-lovers who hold this piece dear. A horrible evening.

WEDNESDAY, 8 DECEMBER 1999

Council Warns Road Protesters of Court Action

Tim O'Brien

Wicklow Co. Council expects protesters who interfered with the council's tree-felling at the Glen of the Downs yesterday to be brought before the courts if they repeat their protest, the county secretary, Mr Bryan Doyle, said yesterday.

Commenting on the council's decision to resume the felling work, which was initially interrupted by protesters in January of 1998, Mr Doyle pointed out that it has now been 10 years since the decision was taken to widen and upgrade the 7 kilometre section of the N11 between Kilmacanogue and the southern end of the Glen in north County Wicklow.

Mr Doyle said the High Court and the Supreme Court had now found in favour of the road and the county council expected to fulfil its plans.

In the past the council has pointed out that Dublin-bound commuter traffic is at a standstill in the Glen from 7.30 a.m. until after 9 a.m. each weekday. The route is one of national strategic importance linking Dublin city with the south-east and the port of Rosslare. It is on Euro-route One, a key European route, the Irish section of which is between Larne in Co. Antrim and Rosslare, Co. Wexford.

The National Roads Authority has said the cost of the work has risen from £18.5 million to £22 million since the protest began. The whole 10-year time frame, it says, is a textbook example of what has caused the much-mentioned infra-structural backlog.

This problem is considered so seriously that a Cabinet sub-committee, chaired by the Taoiseach, is looking into it. A constitutional referendum, and a special division of the High Court to hear planning cases, are among the suggested solutions.

Meanwhile opponents to the Wicklow road-widening scheme say the Glen of the Downs is a nature reserve, a designated Special Area of Conservation and an Area of Outstanding Natural Beauty. If it is not protected from a road widening scheme, it should be, according to the activists.

And if it is not protected, they ask, what is protected?

Others assert that the traffic jams are caused by commuters and observe that the council is proposing to improve the road at a time when Dublin city authorities are attempting to discourage car-commuting. They point to substantial housing developments in the pipeline for north Wicklow and ask how long it will be before the road reaches capacity again. And will another slice of the woodland then be taken?

They point out that the Dublin Transportation Initiative's preferred option is now public transport. There is an electrified rail link to Greystones which is almost complete and much of the traffic in the Glen in the mornings originates in the towns and villages of Kilcoole, Newcastle, Ashford, Rathnew, Wicklow, and as far south as Rathdrum: all of which are served by the rail line, Ashford

An eco warrior blocking the felling of a tree by climbing it at the Glen of the Downs in Co. Wicklow. Photograph: Bryan O'Brien.

being the furthest away from the rail link at two miles.

Clearly the case is an example of the delays involved in the planning system and a decision should have been made sooner but it also highlights an emphasis on road development to the near total exclusion of public transport.

The lesson is that in any traffic management plan public transport has to play a large part.

Opponents of the Glen road say it is not good enough for the council to argue that it does not build railways or operate public transport systems.

Perhaps if the road were seen in the context of a broader transport policy the expensive and wasteful delay ending in confrontation could have been avoided.

SATURDAY, 12 DECEMBER 1999

DIRT Repayment Could Cost Banks Many Millions

Siobhán Creaton and Cliff Taylor

The main banks are now likely to face a tax bill running into many millions of pounds after an audit of their outstanding DIRT liabilities is undertaken by the Revenue Commissioners. On the basis of what the Public Accounts Committee has discovered, the total bill could amount to at least £200 million.

The collection of the overdue tax, along with potentially punitive interest and penalties, is the central recommendation of the report of the Dáil Public Accounts Committee DIRT inquiry, published yesterday. It contains scathing criticism of the banks and the Revenue Commissioners.

It also finds there was no agreement between AIB and the Revenue Commissioners that the bank would not pay its pre-1991 DIRT liabilities. The report finds the opening of bogus non-resident accounts to evade DIRT was an 'industry-wide' problem across the banks and building societies in the late 1980s and early 1990s. It is strongly critical of the boards and management of a number of the major financial institutions and of the Revenue Commissioners, the Central Bank and the Department of Finance for not taking stronger action. It accuses the Revenue of not applying the law equally among different categories of taxpayers.

The report of the PAC subcommittee contains a range of recommendations which will now be examined by the Government. It says that in addition to paying their DIRT tax bills, the banks should be subject to a special levy, of an unspecified amount, to be paid to charity.

It also says money in dormant accounts in the financial institutions should be confiscated and also paid to charity. New legislation would be needed for this to happen, with millions of pounds likely to be lying in such accounts.

The committee has also called on the Government to initiate a review of the operations of the Revenue Commissioners and a separate review into the roles of the accountancy firms which audit financial institutions. The Taoiseach has promised the Government will respond to the DIRT report 'as quickly as possible'. It is expected to be discussed by the Cabinet on Wednesday. The Department of Finance may be asked to catalogue the necessary actions required to implement the various proposals.

The Revenue Commissioners said last night it had already started to review the DIRT liabilities of 21 financial institutions going back to 1986 and had served notice to the remaining 16 that it would be examining their books.

A main focus will be on the likely liability at AIB, the State's largest bank. The DIRT report dismisses AIB's contention that it had an effective tax amnesty with the Revenue on tax liabilities from 1986 to 1991. AIB has said the most it owes in unpaid DIRT is £35 million, well below the £100 million estimate of its former internal auditor, Mr Tony Spollen.

However, if the Revenue can even establish that a liability of £35 million existed in 1991, then the addition of interest under Revenue rules could bring the total bill to at least £120 million, or more if the Revenue seeks to impose further penalties. However, AIB is likely to contest strongly the existence of such a liability. It said last night it was not commenting as it needed further time to study the report.

The liabilities of a number of other banks are also likely to be substantial. The report is also highly critical of ACC Bank, stating it was 'improper' for the bank not to inform the Minister for Finance of a potential £17.5 million tax liability in 1993.

The five ministers for finance who held office during the 12 years were largely absolved of any wrongdoing in relation to the collection of DIRT.

Mr Jim Mitchell, chairman of the Sub-Committee and Mr Pat Rabbitte TD, with copies of the DIRT Inquiry Report. Photograph: Eric Luke.

The committee has categorically ruled out any suggestion of political interference in the collection of DIRT.

TUESDAY, 14 DECEMBER 1999

And Now Live from Newgrange

Dick Ahlstrom

Forget what the calendars say. The real millennium begins next Tuesday, at the Newgrange National Monument in Co. Meath, on the day of the winter solstice. RTÉ will have four cameras ready inside the passage grave to broadcast every moment as the sunlight tracks slowly across the floor of this ancient structure.

Only about 20 people a year can witness this event as it occurs inside the narrow passage grave, but those who have seen it describe it as memorable. 'It really is an amazing thing to see,' said Ms Leontia Lenehan, who supervises guides at Newgrange. 'You do get goosebumps. It is wonderful. It is spiritual, too.'

She described what it was like to be inside the burial chamber at the arrival of the solstice dawn. 'It literally starts off with a tiny sliver of light, like a blade of grass.' It first appears at 8.58 a.m. and for the next six minutes grows larger and brighter, 'a very rich and vibrant shaft of light on the floor'. It shimmers for a time before gradually shrinking and disappearing completely by 9.15 a.m.

She pointed out that the view inside, of stone walls and ceilings, some with ornate carvings, was the same as what our ancestors saw when it was built in 3200 BC. The Newgrange passage grave was 'one of the oldest intact roofed structures in the world'.

Newgrange is one of only three UNESCO World Heritage Sites on this island, testimony to the fact that its stunningly accurate solstice alignment makes it one of the world's oldest known

Sunlight streaming along the pathway into the inner chamber of the Newgrange Megalithic Tomb during the Winter Solstice. Photograph: Alan Betson.

astronomical observatories, predating Stonehenge by about 1,000 years.

It is perhaps the spiritual dimension described by Ms Lenehan and the tenuous connection between those who built Newgrange and those who visit it today that RTÉ hopes to capture with its cameras next Tuesday. The station is leaving nothing to chance, however, and its preparations for the event are firmly rooted in the realities of commerce and showmanship.

It will provide live coverage from before dawn on the 21st, which comes mercifully late, at 8.58 a.m. It also plans to send the images out live over the Internet.

RTÉ has offered the programming to members of the European Broadcasting Union and other television companies. Its invitation has been taken up so far by companies in Denmark, Cyprus, Portugal, Belarus, Macedonia and Bosnia. CBS plans to carry the event some hours later on its 'Good Morning America' programme.

The show, which will run for a full hour from 8.30 a.m., will be anchored by Brian Dobson at the Brú Na Bóinne interpretative centre in the Boyne valley, which covers the Newgrange, Dowth and Knowth neolithic sites. Joe Duffy will be reporting from outside the passage grave and will be supported by the meteorologist Gerard Fleming, who will keep viewers informed if the weather spoils the live show.

RTÉ also has a fallback position if the sun fails to shine next Tuesday, Mr Peter Feeney, who heads the company's millennium programming, said. It has film from last year's solstice when the sun shone brightly and used artificial light during supplementary filming last summer to ensure a dramatic Newgrange experience.

Clearly RTÉ will be hoping to show the real thing, Mr Feeney said. It will have two outside broadcast units committed to the project. 'We are gambling we will get a clear sky,' he said, but they will also have the film 'to show the viewers what they will be missing if it is cloudy.'

The Newgrange visitor services manager, Ms Clare Tuffy, will answer questions from inside the passage grave, and other archaeologists have been lined up to explain its significance.

RTÉ commissioned the Eurovision winner, Emer Quinn, to write a song to mark the occasion. She will perform it live on the 21st at the visitors' centre.

The idea for the first live Newgrange broadcast arose when RTÉ was considering its millennium coverage, Mr Feeney said. 'We would claim that this is the real beginning of the new millennium,' he said.

RTÉ approached the Heritage Service and discovered that Dúchas was planning to approach RTÉ with the same idea. 'We will hope to keep home viewers entertained and watching,' Mr Feeney said. 'The real human drama of the site should still shine through.'

'What an extraordinary achievement,' he said. 'They got it right and 5,000 years later it still works.'

FRIDAY, 17 DECEMBER 1999

President Invokes Vision of a Second 'Golden Age'

Mark Brennock

The end of one millennium and the start of another is merely an arbitrary calendar moment, a milestone among the segments into which we humans divide time for our own convenience.

Yet the President, Mrs McAleese, sought to show yesterday that this arbitrary moment does, in fact, coincide with a period of enormous potential for change in Ireland. She suggested that Ireland could truly be ending one era and entering another.

Above all, she told the massed national politicians of the State in the crowded Dáil chamber that they now had choices to make, and that those choices 'will give our future its shape, its depth'.

Mrs McAleese's address marked the opening of an unusual day in the Oireachtas, one in which

The President, Mrs McAleese, stands to applause from the House, including Ceann Comhairle Mr Séamus Pattison TD, left, when she addressed the Joint Houses of the Oireachtas at Leinster House. Photograph: Frank Miller.

routine political controversies were put aside and political leaders spoke philosophically of the future.

John Bruton, Ruairí Quinn and Trevor Sargent all questioned the headlong rush for economic growth, and wondered where it was leading. The Taoiseach spoke of the need for a caring society, not just a prosperous one. All referred to the need to rebuild faith in the political process after recent revelations of what the Taoiseach called 'instances of untoward aberrations in the high standards of public conduct that we wish to see upheld'.

Mrs McAleese's address was simple but eloquent, reminding the audience of the painful history that had preceded Ireland's economic success, and emphasising the possibilities offered by prosperity and the rejuvenation of politics in Northern Ireland. She invited the Ministers, TDs, senators and dignitaries to dream of the future, to look beyond daily political controversies, to imagine what Irish society could be like and then work to bring it about. 'We get to write a chapter of our country's history,' she said.

She painted a picture of an Ireland 'rich in imagination, rooted in community', free of conflict, sharing its resources at home and abroad. There were decisions to be made that could bring this about and that would result in historians looking back at the approaching era as the time when it was brought about.

We could choose to retain old iniquities and inequalities. We could choose to leave our children a society where 'selfish materialism, shrill begrudgery and apathy' had dulled idealism. Or we could choose to leave them a land of peace, prosperity, equal opportunity and respect for difference. 'The choices are ours,' the President said.

While prevented by the Constitution from intruding into matters of public policy, Mrs McAleese pointed clearly to the key political choices that have to be made. This was the first generation that could choose to eradicate poverty; the first which could choose to embrace multiculturalism and welcome foreigners seeking new opportunities; the first that could build and consolidate lasting peace on the island. Her speech was an attempt to summarise where our modern society came from, what it was now and the prospects for what it could become. Some of her themes were echoed yesterday afternoon when party leaders each made statements in the Dáil to mark the last sitting of the millennium.

John Bruton questioned whether quality of life was rising as fast as gross national product. Ruairí Quinn spoke of 'a growing spiritual impoverishment' at a time of increasing material prosperity. It was a day in which political philosophy made a rare appearance in the proceedings of the Oireachtas.

Mrs McAleese spoke of a 'golden age' she said had existed in Ireland in the middle of the first millennium. It was a time, she said, when newly arrived Christianity had fused easily with existing Irish life, 'growing side by side with the old pagan culture, with no anxiety to obliterate it'. Respect for difference became enshrined in the rulebooks of convents and monasteries.

Now many of the conditions that facilitated 'that former glorious period of our history' were falling into place again.

Lest we get lost in self-congratulation, she reminded her audience of where Ireland had come from. 'Ireland is a First World country with a Third World memory, a memory to keep us humble, to remind us of the fragility of it all, a memory to remind us that too many people across the world wake up each day to lives of sheer terror and dread,' she said.

Our history was 'a litany of hopes raised and then dashed, one lament after another'. Wars, rebellions, plantations and plagues brought awful suffering, culminating in the Great Famine.

Even senior citizens alive today could remember 'when poverty and deprivation stalked the land'.

Grief sprang from the Easter Rising, the War of Independence, the Civil War. Together with 'the forgotten dead of Flanders', each of these events left behind 'the scarring inheritance, the unfinished business of the next generation'.

The new political dispensation in Northern Ireland, the economic transformation and new cultural self-confidence showed we were at a time of profound change. 'The shadows of the past are lifting … the weight of the past is now lifting and opening new possibilities to us,' she said.

The modern successful Ireland still had its problems of inequality and social exclusion that

Rikki Clark of Martinspeed Fine Art Handlers holds up Andre Derain's 'Homme à la Pipe' (1914) during hanging the 'Bassano to Bacon', a commercial exhibition of fine art spanning five centuries at the K Club in Straffan. Behind is Sir Anthony Van Dyck's portrait of Eerryk dePutte. Photograph: Bryan O'Brien.

ensured many people were unable to develop their potential.

She said young people must be encouraged to become involved in public service. However, she acknowledged — without stating it explicitly — the crisis of confidence in the political process that had arisen, particularly from the stream of revelations at the tribunals of inquiry.

A culture of 'righteous accountability' in public life could make us wiser and warier. However, she warned that the revelations could feed 'an uncaring indifference, a cynicism which will erode our capacity to dream and to deliver dreams'.

Above all, her message to the crowded Dáil chamber was that politics can work, can change things, and that politicians and the people can and must choose how society will be shaped. The progress of politics in the North showed this to be true. The forgiveness, generosity, love and compassion of ordinary people, 'who were and who are the very heart and soul of this phenomenon we call the peace process', proved the value of a hopeful outlook.

When cynics said it was impossible and naysayers threatened to make it impossible, she said, the story of these people 'tells us why it is worth dreaming'.

FRIDAY, 24 DECEMBER 1999

Knives Out, It's Christmas

Orna Mulcahy

Christmas dinner. Not the culinary highlight of the year, perhaps, but never mind the food, feel the heat in the kitchen as families sit down to what will probably be their last get-together of the

Three-year-old Sophie Williams home from London for Christmas, is greeted by her grandmother Mrs Ann Grimes, Kells, Co. Meath, on arrival at Dublin airport. Photograph: Eric Luke.

Paula Cuddiby (10) from Greystones, Co. Wicklow, lights her millennium candle with friends on Bray Head at sunset on New Year's Eve. Photograph: Joe St Leger.

20th century. A joyous occasion? Maybe. Great fun? Hmmm. Stressful? Now you're getting there. There's nothing like getting a family around a table to set the atmosphere flaming, faster than a match to brandy. But Christmas dinner is never as bad as you expect it to be, even if the gravy doesn't work out and the roast potatoes are like bullets. It's a meal dreaded up and down the country, but it's often a surprising success.

If you are playing host this year, do get lots of rest beforehand so you're not reduced to tears by not being able to find the melon baller. Don't let everyone go off drinking for hours before lunch, and certainly don't get hammered yourself if you're the one who has to deal with the big, slippery bird. Remember — if you drunkenly drop the turkey, there will be so much grease spilled that someone is bound to slip and fracture themselves on the kitchen floor.

Do take trouble over the food and the table arrangements but don't kill yourself trying to make a gourmet stuffing or a dazzling centrepiece — remember how fiercely traditional people become at Christmas and how curmudgeons have a field day of it?

One guest will love your giant silver twigs as much as you do, another will laugh at them; if you decree dinner by candlelight, your father will complain he can't see what the hell he's eating; if you treat the in-laws to champagne, they'll say it's awfully gassy; and, if you make yourself red in the face from basting the turkey every 20 minutes, someone is bound to remark that it has turned out a bit dry… Then there is the whole issue of presents. Parents should have all the gifts wrapped by now. If not, they had better do it tonight and then NOT forget where everything is.

A dreadful thing happened to friends last year

when they locked everything in the garage and then couldn't, for the life of them, find the key on Christmas Eve. At 3 a.m., there was nothing for it but to saw their way in through the ceiling of a room that connected with the garage. The ceiling was brand new, needless to say, and when the whole ordeal was over, at about 5 a.m., of course they found the key on a hook, under their noses. They had two hours' sleep before starting preparations to have 15 to lunch.

It will be interesting what presents are doing the rounds this year. With the country awash with money, and God knows, maybe even a new millionaire in the family (did your company float this year?) people may have been tempted to go really lavish on the gifts.

Extravagant boxes of cosmetics swathed in cellophane, gift-packs of glasses and champagne, pashminas of every hue, something exquisite from the Polly Devlin sale, or the toy-that-you-can't-get-in-Ireland (bought on that early December raid on New York), not to mention crates of wine and heaps of fresh cream chocolates, will almost certainly feature in some households, but possibly not in yours.

Maybe you feel prosperity has passed you all by. Perhaps it is not one of your lot who has struck it rich, but the guy next door, wee Seán, who was considered absolutely thick as a child but who now gets more charming and interesting with every newspaper report about his meteoric success in computers. Mother might be bitter about this, since none of her many daughters was cute enough to catch him, and none of her sons went into partnership with Seán when all he needed was £5,000 to get going.

Instead, he was snared by a very common sort of a girl who now has a driver, for goodness sake, and the children down for a school in England. Even if expensive things don't feature on your table, they will certainly get talked about at the table — in fact, people will probably talk about nothing else. Prepare to hear a good deal about

house prices and car prices, about the cost of fitted kitchens and ensuite bathrooms, sun holidays, designer sports wear and the latest computer and hifi equipment.

You'll also find people talking about the trouble that young people are having finding a home, the mortgages they have to saddle themselves with, how impossible it is to find things to say when nerves are very likely a bit jangled anyway. Expect a variety of reactions from the light 'look who's talking' to the very heavy — muffled sobs, slammed doors and accusations that no-one understands what it's like to have twins or run a Leonidas franchise.

Most families have spun a complex web of things that can and cannot be said between them, but if there are things that have to be said, then Christmas dinner isn't the worst time to say them. 'I'm the only one who would tell you …' is a handy phrase that can open up any number of frank discussions, be it about how you behaved over Daddy's operation last year, or when you're going to give back the good copper saucepan your wife borrowed two years ago …

Be honest, own up to things, let the guard drop a bit and don't be too hard on each other. And for God's sake, someone, help with the washing-up.

Happy Christmas.

MONDAY, 3 JANUARY 2000

Let us Step with Hope into our New Century

Editorial

And so, we begin an extraordinary journey of discovery into a new century and new millennium. Prophets and seers, rationalists and futurologists, warn of the dangers and speculate upon its likely wonders. Analysts in virtually every aspect of human activity offer predictions and estimates. Let us take most of it *cum grano salis*. Even as we step into the 21st century, it is still difficult to get the weather forecast right.

Yet even the dullest imagination must be stirred by the turning of a millennium. Man fixes his physical existence by the contours of the earth under his feet and by the framework of days which marks his mortal span. When the framework changes as dramatically as now (at least on the Christian calendar) even the most laggard spirit must be moved to contemplate, however momentarily, what lies ahead.

At the end of the 1890s a Victorian academic, imprisoned by the intellectual hubris of the age, declared that the 20th century would be an era without significant advances since all the great discoveries of science had been attained. Such a failure of imagination is unlikely today. For the 20th century has conditioned mankind to the con-

viction — at once uplifting and terrifying — that there are effectively no limits to knowledge.

It has been a century of immense attainment. And yet the human imagination runs far ahead of what has been achieved. It anticipates routine travel to other worlds and an end to the killer diseases of our time. It envisages information management and the application of artificial intelligence at levels to make today's computer systems appear primitive. It expects that the secrets of human genetics will be unlocked with the promise of a greatly extended lifespan for many. It envisages new sources of energy, perhaps through the exploration of other planets.

If the complex and wayward history of the race in the millennium now ending is anything to go by, it seems certain that many of the salient objectives will prove illusory. And amazing discoveries, yet

'Yet even the dullest imagination must be stirred by the turning of a millennium.' Photograph: Dara MacDonaill.

undreamt of, will very likely materialise in their place — much as Columbus set off to find India and stumbled on America instead.

We have knowledge and advantages which should allow us to side with the visionaries and the optimists. As we leave the 20th century, we bring with us great and valuable lessons, learned with the blood and tears of our parents' and grandparents' generations. We know that tyrants extend their grasp when free people abandon their vigilance. Yet, we also know that wars start easily and are concluded with difficulty. We know that modern warfare, in its most terrible manifestation, can destroy the planet. And we know — because we have succeeded in preventing it for half a century — that global war is not inevitable.

We know that the Earth holds limited natural resources and that seas, territories and whole countries can be devastated by abuse of the environment. We know that peoples can starve or die when they are abandoned by their wealthier brothers in the advanced economies. And we know that when the governments of the developed nations come together with common purpose they can prevent such disasters. They can feed the hungry and attend to the sick. They can avert wars and even put a stop to wars which have already begun. We know, if a stable political climate can be created, that even traditionally poor peoples can create self-sustaining economic growth. It is widely expected that the 21st century will see many more nations, principally the Asian countries and much of Latin America, coming to levels of wealth which are now the norm in the Western world.

In short, we know that, in co-operation and combination, mankind can survive and thrive on this planet. There are no objectives which it cannot attain if it truly wants to and if it is willing to recognise the universality of human needs. It is true that we enter a dangerous age. Weapons of mass destruction continue to proliferate. Potentially lethal forces are controlled by nations which are prisoners of extreme ideologies or which consider themselves vulnerable to economic or military threat.

But, in happy contrast with our forebears 100 years ago, we enter the 21st century with structures of international law and co-operation in place which commit us to striving for universal co-operation and accommodation. They may be imperfect and slow. But they can be strengthened and made more effective with even small countries, such as this, playing their role. They must be our best hope for the future and they must be developed and built upon above all else.

Let us step then with hope into this new century. Let us do so with a renewed commitment to the universal brotherhood of mankind. Let us cherish our children and the children of the entire planet. Let us resolve to protect this Earth which nurtures the race and let us determine that there will be lasting peace, justice and sufficient prosperity for all who inhabit it.

MONDAY, 3 JANUARY 2000

Dublin's Century Ends with a Whimper

Róisín Ingle

On Friday afternoon, the winter sun made a valiant attempt to break through the thick white clouds over Merrion Square in Dublin. It never quite made it. More than spectacular sunsets, this was the most apt eve-of-millennium image for Dublin where, compared to the fizz of the global party, the capital failed to shine.

Three days later the millennium-sized hangover has lifted to reveal the dome-sized imagination deficit of those who organised the celebrations in Dublin. It was alright for some. If, for example, you were between 18 and 25, had a ticket to the Merrion Square concert and didn't mind a champagne-free New Year's Eve, then you were, like, sorted.

If, however, you wanted to congregate else-where in the capital to feel a part of what should have been the biggest hooley in Irish history, you were left to make your own fun. Christ Church Cathedral continued as favourite congregation place, but there was disappointment for those who tried something new.

The good-natured crowds who gathered on O'Connell Bridge were offered nothing but inconsistently impressive fireworks as a too-distant backdrop, which paled in comparison to London and Paris.

Whatever the excuses offered by the Millennium Committee, there is absolutely no reason the capital could not have conjured up a world-class extravaganza. In fact, that was exactly what we got on St Patrick's Day last year.

On that occasion, Australian pyrotechnician Syd Howard was brought over to create a quayside firework display set to music, providing a spec-tacular and moving skyfest. Had we attempted to recreate such a spectacle, we could easily have given London a run for its millennium.

But as the clock struck 12, there was nothing to make the crowds feel part of this unique occa-sion. No carnival. No carnival atmosphere.

RTÉ in its post-millennium news coverage didn't even deem the fireworks worth showing, opting instead for the confetti-laden Times Square in New York and sun-soaked Western Samoa.

Meanwhile, the lighting of the bridges on the Liffey left Dubliners decidedly under whelmed. For a start, they were lit five minutes earlier than expected and the promised Mexican Wave of Light across the river never materialised. Instead of being lit in distinct colours, they were mainly covered in an homogeneous green.

'What's happened?' was the bemused reaction of many who milled around the new millennium footbridge without noticing that anything had changed. The biggest cheer of the event was for the rescue boats travelling up and down the Liffey.

'If, however, you wanted to congregate elsewhere in the capital to feel a part of what should have been the biggest hooley in Irish history, you were left to make your own fun.' Photograph: Matt Kavanagh.

Even if you stayed at home there was no escaping what in Dublin at least turned out to be Amateur Night at the Millennium. Inevitably, RTÉ's coverage descended into sub-Jurys Hotel-style cabaret antics with a far from stellar line-up.

Perhaps the biggest indicator that a mess was made of the millennium was the global television coverage. While TV stations showed highlights from all over the world, Dublin offered nothing worth featuring and so it simply wasn't.

In his defence, Millennium Minister Séamus Brennan says it was a conscious decision not to focus merely on the midnight hour for the 2000 celebrations but to make it a wider, longer-lasting commemoration. However, in avoiding the moment, the mood of the masses may have been misjudged and an unrepeatable opportunity missed.

WEDNESDAY, 5 JANUARY 2000

Andrea Corr and the Dostoyevsky Question

Vincent Browne

Speculation on whether in this new millennium intelligent life will be found outside this world, and whether this world will survive its own destructive forces, must be put aside for now to contemplate two of the great issues of our time.

The first concerns the Person of the Year, Dr Tony O'Reilly, and it has to do with concern as to his whereabouts. The second concerns the beautiful Ms Andrea Corr, and it has to do with her earnestness: whether it can survive shocking revelations concerning not just one, but two, of the great literary and intellectual giants she has recently encountered.

First, a story in the *Sunday Business Post* reported that some of the O'Reilly family interests in Independent News and Media were switched from an Irish-registered company to a Cypriot-registered company to avoid capital gains tax here. Dr O'Reilly is not tax resident in this State. But if he is not resident here and if his family interests in Independent Newspapers are not here, where is he and where are his family interests?

Former rugby colleagues recall how he used to disappear for long spells during rugby matches. Perhaps his residency arrangements are another manifestation of how he has deployed his sporting prowess to his financial affairs.

'*The wise old man acknowledged in a radio interview last year that he paid no tax, not just on income derived from his literary work, but also on all income from his journalistic work because of the generous tax indulgence introduced by Charles Haughey.*' Photograph: Dara MacDonaill.

'Ms Corr told the wise old man she rather liked the works of Fyodor Dostoyevsky and said, according to him, that she was especially affected by the quality of compassion in his (Dostoyevsky's) work.' Photograph: Terry Thorpe.

And now to the beautiful Andrea Corr.

As a millennium frolic, the *Sunday Independent* arranged for what they called 'a wise old man' and 'a beautiful young woman' to visit St Kevin's monastic site at Glendalough for photographs. The beautiful young woman was, of course, Ms Corr, and the wise old man was Dr Conor Cruise O'Brien.

The wise old man acknowledged in a radio interview last year that he paid no tax, not just on income derived from his literary work but also on all income from his journalistic work because of the generous tax indulgence introduced by Charles Haughey in 1968. That indulgence was intended to cover income derived from artistic work only, but it has been ingeniously extended in three instances that I know of to include income from journalistic work. This means Dr O'Brien pays almost no income tax and has not done so for decades, which, in the eyes of some, must make him a very wise old man indeed. The photo-shoot had a miserable outcome, in spite of the beauty of Ms Corr and the familiarly defiant jutting jaw of the wise old man. Afterwards, he and Ms Corr shared refreshments and exchanged millennium thoughts.

Ms Corr told the wise old man she rather liked the works of Fyodor Dostoyevsky and said, according to him, that she was especially affected by the quality of compassion in his (Dostoyevsky's) work. Writing last Sunday about his reaction to this confidence, he stated: 'I wondered whether I should tell her of the dark side of Dostoyevsky, which was no less real than his compassionate side.' He continued: 'Her earnestness told me she would be able to take the dark side of Dostoyevsky in her stride without the knowledge of it lessening her admiration for the artist.'

This prompted him to tell her: 'Following the assassination in 1881 of the Tsar Alexander II, who had relieved some of the Jewish disabilities in the Russian empire, the persecution of the Jews was resumed under Alexander III. The chief organiser of the persecution, on behalf of the Tsar, was Konstantin Petrovich Pobedonostsev, and Pobedonostsev's most trusted adviser on the implementation of anti-Jewish policy was Dostoyevsky.'

He claimed: 'Andrea took in this account with close attention and some shock. She will never, I think, see Dostoyevsky again in quite the same light.'

Concluding his account with the beautiful Ms Corr, the wise old man wrote: 'I felt she has the internal strength not to be shaken by a revelation of that kind but be able to put it properly into perspective.'

Ms Corr might find it helpful to put Dr O'Brien properly into perspective by the following information. He was right about the anti-Semitic regime inaugurated by Alexander III following the murder of his father, Alexander II on March 13th, 1881. He was right, also, about the influence of Konstantin Petrovich Pobedonostsev on Alexander III. He was right in the suggestion that there had been an association between Pobedonostsev and Dostoyevsky.

Pobedonostsev had been a contributor to a magazine edited for a while by Dostoyevsky. He was right, too, in suggesting that Dostoyevsky was anti-Semitic, as indeed were most Russians at the time, including the other great liberal writers, Tolstoy and Turgenev. But the claim that Dostoyevsky was Pobedonostsev's 'most trusted adviser on the implementation of anti-Jewish policy', following the assassination of Alexander II, is codswallop. It is codswallop for the following reason: Dostoyevsky was dead.

Fyodor Dostoyevsky died on 28 January 1881, 6½ weeks before the event that sparked the renewal of anti-Semitism occurred. Thus, he could not have had any part at all in relation to the implementation of the anti-Jewish policy or in relation to the implementation of any policy inaugurated by Alexander III.

Yes, there had been some correspondence between Dostoyevsky and Pobedonostsev on the Jewish 'issue' some two years before Alexander II was assassinated. But how, plausibly, could that be bloated into a 'most trusted adviser' relationship some two years later when Dostoyevsky was dead? Anyway, the idea that Dostoyevsky was ever in a position to influence State policy on anything, let alone the implementation of State policy, is absurd.

Can Ms Corr be expected to have the internal strength to put the revelations concerning both Fyodor Dostoyevsky and the wise old man she met in Glendalough properly into perspective? Although she will never, I think, see the wise old man in quite the same light, perhaps her earnestness will help her to take this side of him in her stride, without the knowledge of it lessening her admiration for him.

FRIDAY, 7 JANUARY 2000

Island Breezes are Spiced with Discontent

Declan Walsh in Stone Town, Zanzibar

There can be no secrets on Zanzibar. The capital, Stone Town, is an intimate labyrinth of narrow streets where the people live cheek by jowl. Women share confidences from behind colourful veils, while bearded men twist through the crush on noisy mopeds en route to the mosque.

It is no secret then that beneath the picture-postcard image of azure seas and Arabian mystery, the turbulent winds of political change are again blowing on these enigmatic isles.

Calls for greater autonomy for Zanzibar, which united with Tanganyika to form Tanzania in 1964, are becoming louder and more frequent. While a split is improbable, it is not impossible.

'Zanzibaris are bloody well fed up. We are supposed to be benefiting from the union, but I'd like to see how,' said a Zanzibari High Court judge, Mr Wolfango Dourado. 'Nobody wants to split, but if they go on at this rate they will.'

Discontent on Zanzibar and its sister island, Pemba, also known as the Spice Isles, has been simmering for years. But the death last month of the Tanzanian father figure, Julius Nyerere, who was seen as the 'superglue' that bonded the islands to the mainland, has sparked a fresh wave of debate.

Now the union he defended so doggedly is in danger of coming unstuck. Political opposition has crystallised behind one party, the Civic United Front, which, if it wins next year's election, will press for devolution.

With increasing traffic congestion, the pressure is on motorists to leave their cars at home ... and use public transport. Photograph: Joe St Leger.

'There has always been resistance to the union because it was not based on popular consent. By the nature of being an island, we want to retain our own identity and run our own business,' Mr Ismail Jussa, a senior CUF official, said last week.

Zanzibaris complain that the mainland government interferes where it is not wanted and has neglected the development of the island. Mainlanders, in turn, claim that the 800,000 Zanzibaris are over-represented in the national parliament. But the differences are cultural as well as political. Zanzibar lies just 40 miles off the Tanzanian coast, but in many ways it could be thousands of miles out.

Having been ruled by powers ranging from the Sultan of Oman to the Queen of England, Zanzibaris consider themselves more Arab, Indian and even European than African.

The island has long held an allure of mystery for travellers and adventurers alike. Livingstone used it as a launch-pad for his great African explorations, but despised its thriving slave trade, which saw as many as 50,000 unfortunates pass through in chains every year.

Under colonialism the island thrived commercially, first as a trading post where coloured beads and guns were traded for ivory and gum, and later with the lucrative export of spices, particularly cloves.

Zanzibar was the first sub-Saharan country to introduce colour television and at one point had $800 million in foreign exchange reserves. But in recent years clove prices have collapsed and the economy has stagnated. Tourism, which is dominated by Italian interests, has not met expectations. Behind the veils and quaint facades, Zanzibaris are very unhappy.

Ali Abdulrahman has been working as a tailor in minuscule premises for 25 years. It is not so much a shop as a box that folds out on to the street, with just enough room for a chair and a sewing machine. Earning just 3,000 shillings (about £3) per day, he is tired of the constant grind.

'Every morning I have to get up at three o'clock to fill the tanks with washing and cooking water because that is the only time we have a supply. We are really despairing; we can only stay in this poverty for so long,' Mr Abdulrahman said.

He would be voting for CUF at the next elections because 'this union is not good,' he said. 'We do not get our rights. We want to amend it so there are three states: Tanganyika, Zanzibar and the union.'

Despite the plethora of ethnicities, Zanzibaris speak the same language, Swahili, and practise the same religion. An estimated 95 per cent are Muslim. There is no ethnic hierarchy, and religious tolerance is a matter of local pride. In many ways it is the model Swahili statelet, an example to a continent rent apart by tribal and ethnic division. It should have been the cornerstone of Nyerere's integrationist, socialist vision. Instead, it was a constant thorn in his side.

Nyerere sold Zanzibaris the union, but they never bought into his politics. An essentially mercantile people, Nyerere's now discredited socialist policies were anathema to them. In contrast with attitudes on the mainland, he is not fondly remembered.

'Forgive me speaking ill of the dead, but I can't mislead you that he was a glorious person. He was a ruthless character and we should not let him rule us from the grave,' said Mr Dourado.

A Zanzibari of Indian descent who read for the bar at the Inner Temple in London, Mr Dourado has been an uncomfortable advocate of free speech under successive administrations. He found himself thrown into prison for over three months in 1985 after one particularly unfavourable set of pronouncements about 'the teacher'.

Most recently he hit the local headlines by denouncing the Zanzibari attorney general as a 'bloodthirsty monster'. Mr Dourado was referring to the state's refusal to pursue a trial against 18 CUF members who have been languishing in jail on charges of treason for over two years.

International donors have stalled development programmes for Zanzibar over the issue, and now

Keeping an eye on the past as we move into a peaceful future. Photograph: Bryan O'Brien.

the government promises that it will hold a fair trial by next February. A recent Commonwealth-brokered accord also led to pledges of electoral reforms before next year's elections.

Most of the Zanzibaris to whom this reporter spoke want change and see the CUF, under the leadership of Mr Seif Shariff Hamad, as the vehicle for that change. But the incumbent, Mr Salmin Amour of the ruling Chama Cha Mapinduzi party, who won the disputed 1995 election by a margin of just 0.2 per cent, is unlikely to go easily.

Whatever the outcome, a change in the relationship between Zanzibar and mainland Tanzania seems inevitable. Nyerere once vowed that the union with Zanzibar would be destroyed 'over my dead body'. Those words may yet prove prophetic.

FRIDAY, 14 JANUARY 2000

US Merger Maps out Future for Mass Media

Elaine Lafferty in Los Angeles

'I firmly believe that technological advances in communications are on the verge of significantly altering our way of life. Innovations in telecommunications, especially two-way cable systems, will result in our television sets — big screen of course — becoming an information line, newspaper, school, computer, referendum machine, and catalogue.'

These are the words of a 21-year-old man trying to get a job in an advertising agency 20 years ago.

That young man, Mr Steve Case, did not get the job. In fact, the jobs he did get back then lacked a great deal of visionary thrust, despite his innovations at Pizza Hut; he came up with new pizza toppings, including pineapple.

But this week, Mr Case got the chance to make good on every futuristic pronouncement he has made since then. And there have been plenty of them. As the new chairman of America Online-Time Warner, Mr Case now leads a 21st century company whose diversity and potential impact are being touted as the most revolutionary in modern history.

This year will mark the transition of the Internet from technology to mass-media industry, said Mr Paul Saffo, director of the Institute for the Future, a Silicon Valley think-tank. It was an audacious deal, one which Mr Case initiated after he met Time Warner chairman, Mr Gerald Levin, back in September at a meeting of media and technology executives in Paris. It culminated with several bottles of expensive red wine last Thursday after a five-hour dinner at Mr Case's home in Virginia.

On the face of it, the marriage proposal had much going for it, primarily mutual need. Both companies could bring something to the other. Time Warner was an old-line media company whose first product was *Time* magazine, launched in 1923. Its other 33 magazines include *People* and *Sports Illustrated*. It also owns television stations, including CNN, book publishers, sports teams, music and film studios.

Importantly, it has cable television distribution capability and has been laying a US-wide groundwork for high-speed cable modem Internet access. But the company has had a dismal record trying to break into the Internet. It has been unsuccessful in translating all that content — news and entertainment — onto the new medium.

AOL, for its part, is one of the first Internet companies actually to make a profit, as it did for the first time in its 15-year history in 1998. With 22 million subscribers, AOL is the US's largest Internet service provider. But the future of AOL would be stymied, experts said. Without content and without the highspeed connections — just try downloading graphic-heavy web pages or videos on a 56k connection — AOL would be left in the dust.

Hence the attraction, but the deal was still outrageous. Time Warner is as staid as AOL is volatile. The profit margins of each company are also radically different. On revenues of $4.8 billion (4.6 billion euros), AOL's after-tax profit was $762 million for 1998. AOL, based in Virginia, has 12,100 employees.

Time Warner, based in New York, had revenues of $26.8 billion but its net profit was only $168 million and it supports 70,000 employees.

An Internet company is simply more profitable and less costly to run. One Time Warner insider, predicting the demise of the print magazines in the not-so-distant future, said: 'Remember this figure — *Time* spent $1 billion last year on paper and postage. Figure it out.'

The inference is that delivering news and entertainment via the Web is simply more cost efficient. That perhaps is why AOL appears to be the leader here, having swallowed up Time Warner.

AOL shareholders will own 55 per cent of the new company. Its stock symbol will be AOL. A key player, and one that observers say may be the most pivotal in the next few years, is AOL vice-chairman Mr Robert Pittman, who will serve as co-chief operating officer.

Mr Pittman is largely credited with founding MTV. He is a master marketer, and in his own words, an aggressive expert on consumers' desires.

So, apart from those Time Warner employees who sat at their desks with their calculators this week, tallying up the newly risen worth of shares in their retirement accounts, what does this mean for the rest of us? In the short term, the biggest effect may be on music.

Instead of buying CDs, an Internet user can have music digitally downloaded directly into the home computer. Or, as the user clicks on AOL, he or she can sample music tracks offered by Warner music, then choose to buy the CD and have it shipped.

For those who think digital downloading of music is in the distant future, glance over to those vinyl record albums. Next, think of movies. You click on AOL, and right before you are Warner Brothers movie previews via video. Sample a few, then go to the theatre. In the future, you might be able to simply download the entire movie. Remember that movie 'You've Got Mail' with Meg Ryan and Tom Hanks? It was produced by Warner Brothers with AOL's cooperation.

You might get your news via CNN and Time delivered right to your computer. You will even be able to customise the news you want. If you are not interested in the Kremlin, you won't have to read about it. News delivery will be able to be customised to individual taste, focusing on sport, entertainment, and finance, for example.

Online shopping and television delivery could also be affected in ways that few of us have even considered. And the merger will also put pressure on European Internet and content providers, which are still fragmented by operating on a nation-by-nation basis.

'It fills me with awe and respect — this is the real thing,' Mr Marcus Bicknell, head of European operations for CMGI, a holding company for many Internet providers, told the *Wall Street Journal*. 'It means that you have to get together and get big if you are going to compete.'

The delivery of news, information and entertainment is being consolidated into the hands of just a few companies. Aside from concerns about the monopoly on prices, legitimate questions are being raised as to whether such consolidation of power is a good thing for democracy and freedom of exchange.

Exposure 99

Tom Humphries

Years ago we were taught about Ireland by men who, we were told, did our fathers no harm. Stout fingered brothers with noses full of blitzed capillaries. After lunch they had breath like Bushmills. They told us what we were and where we had come from.

Pen pictures. Ireland was a nation when England was a pup. England's trouble equalled Ireland's opportunity. Boys, we are a great little country. A happy agricultural little nation that just wanted to be left alone boys, to milk cows, eat spuds and sing sad songs about ourselves.

Ciúnas anois. Here's the highlight reel boys. Scholarly. Saintly. Invaded. Hungry. Heroic. Free. There you have it. You know boys, Dev wouldn't give them the ports. Free! And who built America boys? That's right. Paddy worked on the railroads and on the shipcanals and on the highways. Built America and a grand job too. They messed it up but Paddy's not to blame.

That era, the big country men in soutanes and surplices and cassocks, with their good intentions and their bad intentions and their leathers and their prayers and the harm they did our fathers and our friends, that's all fading into history too, part of the pen picture. We got different versions of ourselves from them and from Gay Byrne and between times we made sense of it all.

That time lingered. We all had the same experiences at the same hands. We shared the same national conversation. And then hey presto, like a good marriage turned bad, it was over. Now we are fending for ourselves.

Ireland in 1999; the last glimpse of ourselves before we scurry raggedy-arsed out of the old century. We know where we came from, but we haven't half an idea what we are.

'You'd pay good money to hear George Mitchell at four in the morning with a few malt whiskys on him telling a close friend what he thought of us, having seen the worst of us.' Photograph: Bryan O'Brien.

Religious orders packing their bags. Boom, boom, boom down at the registry office. Charlie Haughey, his reputation gobbled by social ebola, raging through the Four Courts like Lear on the Heath. Stretch limos. Fox hunting. Eco-warriors. On our knees to Puff Daddy and the boys from MTV. Romantic Ireland dead and gone and with Jack Lynch in the grave. Minor British royals giving face to good Irish cameramen. Lordee.

We could never have imagined these images. Even ten years ago we couldn't have conjured them. If we'd known in 1974 what we'd look like in 1999 would we have even kept turning the pages? Would we have dismissed it as farce, or happy ending fairytale tripe or comic disaster. All those poems about bogs and mists and bloody swans? Who knew?

Snapshots of the way we are and where we've come from. You look for the things which give you a sense of us, of Ireland. What's different about here that makes it Not middle Europe, Not Boston, Not Sydney. Or do we want to be different anyway? Did we ever enjoy the smell of burning turf and the sight of winding roads and stone walls. First thing. We aren't glued to the land anymore. We hug the cities, talk up the new tech and live together in small houses on big housing estates that we can't afford. You record our life as we evacuate the century and it is urban life.

Outside our homes apparently there is a blizzard of money. If there is, none of it is sticking to the ground where you live but you are prepared to believe they are up to their ankles in the stuff elsewhere. They keep telling you so anyway.

The Celtic Tiger. Can you see the bloody thing? Can you take it back again? This business of telling everyone how well you are doing, when did that start? We are supposed to be a reticent people, the sort who turn up at a doctor's surgery and when asked how we are, we mutter quietly that we can't complain. Suddenly we have little freckle-faced Donald Trumps running about the place.

Some of us are bruised and scarred from the old world, but the money distracts us like a full moon. It is a national duty to be upbeat. It feels like a mortal sin to put your hand up and say that you don't get it, that you don't understand this tiger business. It's like one of those magic eye pictures. You look at it long and hard but you can't see what everyone else is talking about, so you just nod quietly. So this is the boomtime. Ho hum.

You thought you owned Telecom but then they called it eircom and split it up amongst the folk who could afford a slice. You thought that when there would be money about there would be generosity about too. The richer we get the meaner we become. You wouldn't have a traveller's face or black skin or a refugee's life for all the money in the Cayman Islands. Ireland of the welcomes. Don't take off your coat. You'll not be staying.

The geography of our imagination used to be filled with such wonders as the butter mountain and the wine lake. They have gone, or Charlie and Terry consumed them and instead we have hearings and tribunals, great stockpiles of them. Great mountainous surpluses of the things.

Modern whizz bang alchemy is what they are. Lawyers transformed into millionaires. Witnesses metamorphosed into celebrities. Reporters on the radio all the time translating, interpreting, reviewing. The terrific thing is that we have abolished shame and embarrassment for once and for all. We have come of age. No coats over the heads for these folk, they go the Michelle de Bruin way. Stand up and say you didn't do it. Sit down. Say nothing else.

This is the McCarthy era, except this time the good guys get to ask the questions and nobody gets hurt. Men in suits file through. Raise your right hand, Sir. Are you now or have you ever been a conman? A chancer? A cowboy?

Oh come, come. This agglutination of scandals passes down our digestive system like an ostrich egg passing through the belly of a python. Quite a sight but you could do without it thanks.

Where is the secondary industry? They used to tell us that it was no use to milk cows and gather eggs, you had to make quiches and sell them to people. There was no point in catching fish unless you sold fish fingers. So where are the talking Charlie Haughey dolls (Thanks Big Fella, More Foie Gras there Tezza? Take it in a little under the arms JeanPierre)? Where is the Bumper Fun Book of James Gogarty (hardback with fly cover of plain brown paper), the Ray Burke record (It Ain't Me Babe, It Ain't Me Your Lookin' For), the Ben Dunne Pez dispensers?

These are the cultural artefacts we should be leaving behind so generations hence will remember the time of the funhouse.

1999. Already it has the blurred quality of all the movies we once saw. Abbot and Costello crash My Dinner With André. The canyon between us and those on the silver-screen is greater than it has ever been. On this little island we have created a class of people whom we don't know but whom we watch. A class of stars for us to point at. Their lives don't even overlap with ours.

You are forced to find reasons to be cheerful? Well now that we are just over the cusp of the new era, the quality of daily life all around still bears that happy weathered stoicism that is native to us. And the skies are a little brighter.

Gay Byrne invented sex and Charlie Haughey was the first to master it. Once we gave them both due credit for their achievements in bravely going where no Irishmen had gone before. Now sex is everywhere and with the guilt and the furtiveness and the fear removed we can digest little tabloid scandals with a shrug of our shoulders and not cower under the anticipated blow of a crozier. We can have boybands and gay senators and a taoiseach with a partner. Hardly anybody faints.

1999. Our world was still half full of things that were real. From the departing Donal McCann to the nascent Robbie Keane. The percussive poetry of two hurleys clashing in summer air. The sweet keen of a tin whistle. Some poems, books, songs and dances. We can still find a part of ourselves which is authentic and decent and true.

The good news? We have revived old games, reacquainted ourselves with our language. In the world after Gaybo the most important and creative thing on Irish television is TG4. We have taken the dark cowls off our music. If anything we fancy ourselves. In a world of corporately imposed homogeneity those things are our best shot at sanity, our best hope of being meaningful in the midst of franchise culture.

We still have an environment worth fighting about, worth keeping our little Donald Trumps away from. We're not quite so jaded yet that we don't see the wonder of the world we live in.

And peace. The father of the new era, George Mitchell, did more for us surely than our patron saint. No reptiles ever got dug in like we did in our poisoned prejudices. You'd pay good money to hear George Mitchell at four in the morning with a few malt whiskys on him telling a close friend what he thought of us. What he really thought of us, having seen the worst of us.

He leaves behind a little statelet wherein two tribes are going on a blind date that they aren't too happy about. For those of us in the cockpit of the beery south there is the mild comedy of watching

'You wouldn't have a traveller's face or black skin or a refugee's life for all the money in the Cayman Islands. Ireland of the welcomes. Don't take off your coat. You'll not be staying.' (Queues at the Refugee Applications Centre, Mount Street, Dublin.) Photograph: Cyril Byrne.

northern politics re-invent itself. The factory which manufactured the word NO in every form imaginable for decades is to be downsized as former customers decide what sort of place they want to live in. How do they want to be educated, policed, looked after?

It's a blessing to live in interesting times. Is there a form of biomass conversion anywhere that can turn the lunacy of Drumcree and Portadown and other hellholes into a quiet rational discussion about planning permissions and public park bye laws? What a landmark of political growth it will be when northern politics enjoys its first kiss and tell scandal.

Until then we are left with the old images. One Orangeman standing at the ditch in Drumcree with an umbrella over his head and a sash around his shoulders. Behind him lies a long stretch of wasteland. A picture of gardaí laying out a weapons' stash for reporters. Boys in hoods. Old soldiers remembering. Even from this short distance it looks no different than any other squalid little ethnic war of the old century.

Politicians. Do you know we are still waiting for a good looking one? Looking at Cowen, Bruton, McCreevy et al reassures us about one thing: The politics of the last makeover haven't consumed us yet. We have sufficient of the highly carbonated young men with plenty of fizz but no new flavours. We have moved on from the men in the mohair suits to the all hirsute, all the time new bigger better Labour Party.

We're growing old. Changing. The world doesn't have to put up with our wanton friendliness anymore and less and less do we delude ourselves that the world cares. Who we are and where we have come from? Suddenly that matters less than where we are going and how much it will cost and whether Ronan Keating will be there.

New Year, new century etc, etc. Down the big slide we go. There is no sense of crisis, no national debate, just a little smugness and the slow relentless unravelling of all the old illusions. The

men in suits tell us we are the swooshiest little emperors of Europe, so who cares if we are naked sliding along with our begging bowl under our arse? Who cares what the men in suits have done?

And soon, probably, it will all go wrong. The money will go away. Recession will knock at the door.

'I'm back,' Recession will say gravely, 'and this time it's personal.'

'Come in,' we'll say.

'And take off your coat. Is that Guilt out there sitting in the car? Tell him to come in.'

And in time we'll look back on this wild, weird time and wonder if it ever happened at all. Ciúnas anois, we'll say and clear our throats …

This article was written as an introduction to Exposure '99, *a magazine which recorded, through the lenses of* Irish Times *photographers, Ireland and its people during 1999. Their work formed the basis of a travelling photographic exhibition which toured Ireland during 2000.*

SATURDAY, 29 JANUARY 2000

Diary of Anne Frank a Catalogue of Sad Skies

Brendan McWilliams

As I write it is Holocaust Day, the anniversary of the liberation of Auschwitz concentration camp in 1945. As you may imagine, it is an annual event which receives a great deal more attention here in Germany than in Ireland. And it brings to mind one of the more celebrated victims of that awful era.

As Jews were rounded up in Amsterdam in 1942, 13-year-old Anne Frank and her family retreated to the temporary safety of an inaccessible attic of her father's business premises. There, for two years, eight people lived in claustrophobic, semi-voluntary incarceration.

In what was to become *The Diary Of A Young Girl*, Anne described in moving terms the petty frictions that developed, and analysed the lives and fears and dreams of herself and those about her with a touching honesty.

Unlike other diaries, published and unpublished, the authenticity of Anne Frank's record has never been seriously questioned. Had this been the case, however, its chronological validity, at least, could have been verified by reference to the numerous weather descriptions that, despite the author's isolation, the document contains; the weather described can be compared to the actual weather records now available from contemporary weather maps. Some time ago, meteorologist Anders Persson conducted precisely such an exercise.

On 18 August 1943, for example, Anne describes the weather as 'bad', but says it was 'nice' the day before. Sure enough the weather maps for those days show a ridge of high pressure over Amsterdam on the 17th, to be displaced the following day by a front preceded by freshening south-westerly winds.

On 31 March that year she notes that the weather had been 'cold for some time'; again the charts show that after a depression had passed 10 days earlier, cool northerly and north-westerly winds prevailed for a week or more.

The diary covers the period from June 1942 to summer 1944. All in all, according to Persson, references to 'lovely', 'wonderful' or 'warm' weather occur about 10 times in the text, and 'rain', 'mist' or 'windy weather' are mentioned with a similar frequency. All references, when investigated, coincide with appropriate developments on the relevant weather maps on the dates in question.

In July 1944 Anne wrote: 'I have now reached the stage where I don't care whether I live or die. Whatever is going to happen, will happen.'

And so it did.

Members of the British Army starting to dismantle the observation post in the centre of Crossmaglen. Photograph: Alan Betson.

Shortly afterwards, the family's hideaway was found by the Gestapo, and they were taken to the concentration camps. Anne Frank, aged 15, died from typhus in Bergen-Belsen in March the following year.

TUESDAY, 1 FEBRUARY 2000

Private Safonov does $50m Public Damage

Seamus Martin

A single Russian soldier has, in the space of a few minutes, destroyed more high-tech Russian military hardware than the Chechen rebels have done during the entire war.

The mayhem began when Private Sergei Safonov went out on snow-plough duty at the military air base in Akhtyubinsk, in the Astrakhan province of southern Russia.

His job was to keep the runways clear for the multi-billion rouble Sukhoi 24 front-line bombers which were the airbase's pride and joy. By the time he was finished the runways were clear, but not in the manner in which the authorities intended.

Private Safonov became involved in something of an accident. His snow plough struck a Sukhoi 24 in the middle of its fuel tank, and the jet went on fire. The winter wind which howls across the Steppes at this time of year fanned the flames. Another Sukhoi 24 caught fire, and then a third. Bombs stored at the air base were ignited by the flames, and a further 17 aircraft were threatened.

By the time the conflagration had ended, damage amounting to $50 million had been inflicted, according to the Russian news agency Interfax. Military sources claimed the bill would come to considerably less but would not set a price.

The Moscow daily newspaper *Vremya* was quick to proclaim Private Safonov a hero of the Chechen people in putting the sophisticated bombers out of action. Awarding him this honour, the newspaper issued the following citation: 'In a single day a Russian soldier has destroyed more planes than the Chechen fighters have done in the whole war.'

The Russian military authorities were in no mood, however, for awards and citations. An official investigation is under way, and charges of criminal negligence are expected to be brought against the hapless soldier. The Sukhoi 24, a highly manoeuvrable aircraft, has been used daily in sorties against rebels in the Chechen capital, Grozny.

Two of the aircraft destroyed by Private Safonov were being prepared for an attack on the city. The aircraft, which NATO has codenamed Fencer, is designed for low-level strike missions and has highly-sophisticated TV-guided weaponry.

There were believed to have been some 900 of the aircraft in existence before Private Safonov went to work.

FRIDAY, 4 FEBRUARY 2000

An Irishman's Diary

Kevin Myers

Bonjour, et aujourd'hui je voudrais appeller à votre finer senses parce que je veux aller sur un sponsored walk à Katmandou. C'est pour charité, naturellement. Je ne voudrais jamais visité les Himalayas, avec leur scenery magnifique, leurs vistas ravissant, leurs mountain peaks glistenant beneath le ciel bleu, pour raisons selfish. Absolument pas. C'est strictly pour charité, et rien else. Moi-même, je dread le pense de tous ces uplands glorieux, avec un wildlife second to none — les montagne gazelles, les huge ours, les loups et l'homme abominable, known aux natifs as l'encore-ï. Mais je vais là strictly pour charité, vous comprenez?

An archetypal voyage. Yachts sail up the Liffey past the Custom House, the IFSC and Liberty Hall. Photograph: Frank Miller.

Typhoon Sally

J'aime les charités; j'adore faisant les corporal works de mercy, et lévant la monnaie for les starving enfants de la monde, ou assistant à rehouser toutes les victims d'un earthquake, ou collecting funds pour les pauvres qui étaint clobbered par Typhoon Sally. Cinq ans ago, j'ai decidé a commit moi-même à charités, grand temps. Le premier charité à recevoir le benefit de mes efforts étaint les lepers en le Congo. J'ai decidé sunbather pour les petits enfants noirs qui ont perdus les limbs et les nez et various other odds and ends.

Ce n'est pas possible sunbather properly en Irlande, si je suis allé à Jamaica pour le sunbathing là. C'etais necessaire d'avoir beaucoup de monnaie à payer l'airfare. Comment? Vous avez pensé que je voudrais payer mon own fare, et hotels, et répas, and so on? Come off it; si je vais à tout cette trouble pour les charités, le moins j'expecte est que mes expenses sont couvré par mes sponseurs. Vous

hardly expectez que je forkerai les costs de my own blooming pocket, surement? Soyez reasonable.

Hélas, le mois en Jamaica était rather plus expensif que j'ai eu expecté. Hotels sont très cher là; aussi les répas; aussi les vins fins. Après vingt huit jours browning moi-même pour le charité, avec un peu de windsurfing aussi, et un petit peu de jig-jig avec les filles locales — quel grand bouncy bosoms! yummy! — j'ai trouvé que j'ai eu seulement 13.35 pour les bébé lepers.

Still, on peut fair beaucoup avec 13.35 en Le Congo. Par example, on peut construire un entire city, avec street lighting and mains sewerage, pour en the region 10. Donc je pense j'ai fait OK.

J'ai decidé l'ans suivant que je donnerais le fruit de mes efforts charitable aux residents d'un shanty town en Bangla Desh qui est flattened by un tidal-wave massif. Quel tragedy! Quel horreur! Quel sufferant! Quel sponsorship!

Wildlife

J'ai trouvé beaucoup de sponseurs pour mon effort prochaine, qui était un visite aux Andes. Avez vous eté aux Andes? Non? Eh bien, let me tell you, c'est un grand oversight sur votre part. Les Andes sont superb, avec un wildlife incroyable — les llamas et les pumas et les hamsters (delicieux sur toast) — et surtout, les condors. Magnifique! Vraiment le roi des oiseaux! Et pendant le nuit, mes guides et moi-même would gaze à les étoiles et wonder vers le meaning de la vie. J'ai passé deux mois en Les Andes: quite unforgettable, et tout pour le charité.

Malheuresement, ma visite le n'était pas cheap. J'ai eu raisé un merde-load de monnaie, surtout quand j'ai dit aux potential sponseurs que le monnaie alleront aux petits Bangla Deshis — avec ces yeux brun massif staring at you, leurs winsome smiles, et not a pick on them either. Mais l'airfare à La Paz n'est pas un joke, et pour raisons d'health c'était necessaire restez en topclass hotels. Et quelquechose else.

Les vins français sont tres chèr en Bolivia et Peru; un absolu scandal. Je suspect qu'il y a beaucoup de profiteering going on, Finallement, les guides — j'ai employé cinq — n'étaient pas cheap either. Aussi, ils étaient bone-idle.

Nonetheless, je suis proud à dire que mon sponsored walk des Andées a netté presque dix livres pour les petit bruns enfants de Bangla Desh, orphans sans home, parents, family ou future. C'est agréable penser qu'on a fait one's bit.

Aimez-vous yachting? Oui? Ah bon. Parce que mon next sponsored effort était un tour des grand ports de l'Aegean par yacht, et ce fois, l'argent que j'ai gagné par sponsorship pour mon ordeal gruelling allera aux les victims de Chernobyl — après, of course, j'ai deducté mes expenses.

Berthing fees

Savez-vous que l'Aegean est très cher ces jours? J'étais tres surprisé. Berthing fees sont exorbitant. Biensur, c'était possible couper des costs par restant overnight en ye yacht; mais sur l'autre main, le yacht lui-même a couté un joli penny. Et le crew — cinque blondes qui ont voyagées au naturel: j'ai aimé surtout quand elles étaient en le rigging — ont eu gouts très chèrs. Nightclubs. Champagne. That class of caper. Enfin, nous avons just about broke even; en fait, strictement entre vous and moi, je pense que le trip cost me money. Ah well. C'est le prix de travaillant pour charité.

Et maintenant, je voudrai aller à Katmandou, et je cherche des sponsors. Êtes vous interessé en devenant un sponsor? C'est pour un cause bon, après tout: les enfants aveugles de Somalia. S'il vous plait: est-ce que vous sponsorez mes vacances, oops, I mean my coming ordeal pour les pauvres, par-dessus le Himalayas? Et qu'est-que c'est le difference entre moi et le Romanian qui vend Le Big Issue?

Le Romanian est honnête.

SATURDAY, 5 FEBRUARY 2000

With Time on his Side

Gerry Thornley

He's cocky, which is good, he's gifted, which is even better, and he should go a long way. Yet, in some respects, as the great young hope of Irish back play you wouldn't envy him at all.

With a mere two caps and at just 20, it was hoped that Brian O'Driscoll's speed, low centre of gravity (invariably captured in any picture taken of him), angles of running and good hands would almost single-handedly ignite the Irish back-line in the World Cup. It comes with the territory, perhaps, but talk about a big ask.

A degree of allowance has been made for his youthfulness, but the time-honoured tradition of Irish rugby is that we build 'em up to knock 'em down again, invariably putting the tyros through a mid-career valley before, in some cases, they come again.

Last Tuesday over lunch he admitted he had just been quietly reflecting on some advice given to him in Lens. 'I was told, I won't mention by whom, after the Argentina game that the honeymoon phase was over, which is dead true. Now I'm aware it's certainly time to start performing. There's no more complimentary caps here and there. I need to start working for it right now.'

Ask him if the high expectations on the then 20-year-old (he was 21 a fortnight ago) affected his form during the World Cup, and he says: 'No, no, I can't say it did. It's difficult to explain, because the World Cup flashed by. I didn't think I had the worst game in the world against the Argentinians. Sure I did some terrible things in it. I came off the pitch gutted, but I didn't think I had a shocker or anything.'

Thoughtful in all his responses, that he consented to an interview was a surprise in itself. His previous reluctance to do interviews wasn't down to self-importance, though, merely a conscious desire to dilute the hype which accompanied his fledgling career.

Nor was the reluctance due to shyness or discomfiture. He smiles readily, has an easygoing manner and doesn't seem to take himself too seriously, regularly showing a trait for self-deprecation.

As anyone who has even come within passing distance of the O'Driscoll story will know, his father Frank was the young lad's primary influence. 'Very much so, very much so — there's only one Frank O'Driscoll,' says the offspring with a knowing grin.

Frank, a Clontarf out-half, twice played for Ireland against Argentina, but those were in the days when the IRFU rather arrogantly didn't award caps for such fixtures. In any event, father Frank decided to send his son to Blackrock College when he was 12, young Brian surprisingly having only played soccer and Gaelic up until that point.

'He's cocky, which is good, he's gifted, which is even better, and he should go a long way. Yet, in some respects, as the great young hope of Irish back play you wouldn't envy him at all.' Photograph: Eric Luke.

In his first training session at Blackrock, he was 'thrown into the second row'.

'I must have been all of 4'11". I was minute. I remember we scored a try and I tried to convince somebody to let me take a place-kick. I knocked it over, and from there I was brought up to the A team and then played on the wing. I was fairly quick in those days, I think out of absolute fear of getting caught. Luckily I've toughened up since, eh?'

Not that his schools' career was one uninterrupted success story. Indeed, the turning point, surprisingly enough, was taking a year out of the unrivalled Williamstown Academy and linking up with the Clontarf under-16s. 'That was the best year of rugby ever. We went on tour and we were a good side; we won the league. That kind of gave me confidence.'

At school he flitted between wing, scrum-half and calling the shots at out-half, which he enjoyed the most. He suffered defeat in a junior cup final, was on the bench for the final in his first senior year, and in his final year he hit the upright with a drop goal attempt in extra-time of the semi-final defeat by Clongowes.

His tone becomes more hushed as he recalls the experience. Though he will carry the disappointment through his life, he wouldn't have wanted to do it any differently. 'You see I was a Blackrock boy, so it's a different story. Blackrock love that Cup. The blue and white jersey. You want to own one of those at the start and then after that a Cup medal. There's an aura about that blue and white jersey. There are 190 people in the year and only 15 get one of those.'

For all the scars, O'Driscoll shone, played for the Irish schools and went on to play for the victorious Irish under-19s in their World Cup triumph of almost two years ago. What a contrast in two World Cups.

'When we got to the final I don't think we could have been beaten, because we'd gone through so much. It was a great team and we had this confidence instilled in us by Declan Kidney

that we just felt we could compete with anybody. We had huge confidence in throwing the ball around from well inside our 22. Not a problem. It was just "go out and enjoy it" stuff.

'Friends for life made. You don't forget that sort of thing. Looking at the picture afterwards, with the shield saying World Cup champions, that was kind of freaky, and singing Ireland's Call. If I had to pick one thing that would be it.'

He wasn't long making waves in the senior ranks with the Leinster As, though thankfully he was oblivious to the hopes and the hype. 'I'm probably glad of that. The hype only came with the Australia game, which was a good thing. What you don't know about doesn't faze you.'

He believes his transition to senior rugby was helped by playing at UCD with some kindred spirits, such as Irish under-19 teammates Shane Moore and Paddy Wallace, in the less rarified and pressurised air of the third division.

The highs have been less commonplace with Leinster and Ireland, but there has been more than enough to keep him hooked. Leinster's stock and results have risen in tandem with the arrival of Matt Williams — 'an exceptional coach', whom he puts on a par with John McLean and Stephen Aboud as major influences.

For Ireland, there's been 'the incredible high' of his debut in Australia, the World Cup warm-up win over Argentina, and his first Test try against the United States, brilliantly caught on camera as he balanced precariously inside the dead-ball line while trying to narrow the conversion angle. 'Humphs (David Humphreys) was the only one who appreciated that while everybody else was giving out to me. I actually got a fright myself.'

He admits to being 'perhaps too selfish for out-half', yet against that try-scoring is not necessarily the ultimate. 'I get more of a buzz from creating something for somebody else to score a try. Knowing myself that I've done something good, giving the last pass, having made the break and linked up, that's what gives me the greatest buzz.'

Seasoned internationals often say the second season is the most difficult, though strictly speaking O'Driscoll's championship campaign is more like an extension of a long first. 'I've never experienced Five Nations rugby, so I don't know how much other people know about me or how much I'm going to be targeted as an individual. But I presume it will be very difficult.'

Enough has already happened, though, for the ending of the honeymoon.

He knows that much.

David Trimble takes a question at a press conference. His letter of resignation was unionism's not-so-secret weapon throughout the crisis. Photograph: Bryan O'Brien.

Brave New World in Limbo

Déaglán de Bréadún

There was a similar sense of tragedy in 1974 but not yet the same sense of finality. In both cases a power-sharing executive bit the dust, but maybe this time it would only be temporary. The game was still on and negotiations were continuing: British government sources were confident the show could be put back on the road, although nationalists murmured darkly that London might end up looking foolish for acting prematurely.

It was typical of a confused and hectic day that there were conflicting versions from London and Sinn Féin as to who knew what and when. Reporters struggled to keep up with the fast-developing chain of events.

First the statement of suspension from Mr Mandelson was said to be coming at 5 p.m. As the minutes ticked away, a statement came, but from Sinn Féin, not the Secretary of State. Gerry Adams was heralding a breakthrough, but according to London sources the order to suspend had already been signed. Details of the Adams breakthrough were not immediately clear and shortly before 6 p.m. the Mandelson statement finally came out.

Republican sources muttered about conspiracy. The old alliance of unionists and Britain had connived to bring down the institutions. Meanwhile, London was suggesting that perhaps the suspension order had provided the jolt to galvanise republicans into action so that fancy footwork would be replaced by meaningful action.

The initial de Chastelain report came out, nearly two weeks late but every bit as stark as anticipated. A further report was on its way, but initial reports varied from nothing sensational to potentially seismic.

'Republican sources muttered about conspiracy. The old alliance of unionists and Britain had connived to bring down the institutions.' Photograph: Matt Kavanagh.

Senior sources had suggested earlier that the UUP leadership was anxious to have the suspension order announced in time for the six o'clock news so that delegates to the Ulster Unionist Council would know what was going on.

There was concern lest they should arrive at this morning's meeting at Belfast's Waterfront Hall in a grumpy and confused state. But given the reports of continuing activity after the Mandelson statement and the difficulty even seasoned observers were having reading the game, the sturdy farmers and shopkeepers may be, if not confused, certainly bemused as they take their seats. Over recent days, unionist spokesmen have tried to present the threat of suspension as a relatively minor matter, a bump in the road. The view from the republican side could not be more different: if suspension went ahead after all the progress made with the IRA, the process was probably doomed.

The one basic fact everyone agreed on was that there was no product from the IRA. Nationalists said the IRA was taking a step along the road that would lead eventually from ceasefire to the ending of its campaign. The British government and the unionists remained sceptical. As they saw it, there had been a lot of words and pieces of paper, but how real were the negotiations between Sinn Féin and the IRA? Words in private were one thing but what appeared in Gen de Chastelain's report was what mattered. Recent discussions between the IRA interlocutor and the decommissioning body had been thin on specifics. Republicans in general were accused of lacking urgency in their approach as the hours before the UUC meeting ticked away.

Instead of the sought-after clarity, London was in the dark and the unionists were equally unsure what republicans were at and what their intentions were.

Séamus Mallon pleaded publicly with the Secretary of State not to proceed with the suspension. At the same time he took a swipe at the republicans: his pointed questions to the IRA in the House of Commons, asking would they decommission and when would they do so, had formed the agenda for the assault on the republican position over the past week. There may be recrimination between the two main nationalist parties in the coming weeks.

Fevered activity continued last night but did not seem to be getting very far. A second de Chastelain report began to leak, reportedly stating that IRA representatives had come to see him to outline the context in which they would put weapons beyond use in a manner to ensure public confidence.

A joint communiqué from Dublin and London was awaited which would probably say that these matters could be discussed as part of the review.

Earlier, Dublin had been working flat out for a solution even at the last minute. A plan that was floated, for decommissioning in parallel with demilitarisation, had Dublin's fingerprints on it but insiders said the situation had moved beyond that.

Now the issue was not what the IRA would do on a small scale this week but what spectacular gesture of reconciliation it might be persuaded to make in a year or two. Dublin was getting it in the neck from every side: republicans reportedly felt double-crossed while unionists were said to be going ballistic over suggestions in the press that they could be pressurised to accept a plan initiated by Dublin.

The lean figure of Sir Josias Cunningham hovered over everything and the spectre of the UUC president striding towards the office of the Assembly Speaker, Lord Alderdice, to present Mr Trimble's letter of resignation was unionism's not-so-secret weapon throughout the proceedings.

After all the heaving throughout yesterday and the past few weeks two facts stood out. The brave new world born on Good Friday was now in limbo and the IRA had held onto its guns. Future historians may elicit the names of those who put it about that the IRA was going to decommission on 16 January last. It didn't happen and even mainstream sources in the peace process now believe it will probably never take place.

Longtime observers of the republican scene warn that decommissioning would create the conditions for republican dissidents to prosper and the lives of Sinn Féin leaders would be in serious jeopardy. That is not to say a seismic shift will not take place eventually. But the time is out of joint.

SATURDAY, 19 FEBRUARY 2000

A Lost Generation of Irish Manhood

Conor Brady

The Irish Constabularies 1822-1922 by Donal J. O'Sullivan. Brandon Books, 412pp, £30; *The Royal Irish Constabulary — A Complete Alphabetical List of Officers and Men, 1816-1922* by Jim Herlihy. Four Courts Press, 520pp, £45

Between March and August 1922, the long-familiar bottle-green uniform of the Royal Irish Constabulary disappeared from 26 of Ireland's 32 counties. In the Free State the RIC was replaced by the Civic Guard, quickly re-titled as An Garda Síochána. Within Northern Ireland, another new police force with uniforms, badges, ranks and structures virtually identical to the RIC, emerged as the Royal Ulster Constabulary. Were a time-travelling RIC man to step into a Belfast police station today he would find sufficient continuity of symbols to enable him to feel on familiar ground. Were he to visit a Garda station he would find the opposite — at least initially. And yet, if he were to scratch below the surface, he would also find

A young boy playing on the rocks as the sun sets at Sandycove, Co. Dublin. Photograph: Eric Luke.

evidence of the Garda's linear descent from Robert Peel's 19th century creation.

It is somewhat ironic, as the tide of events carries the RUC towards transformation into a new Northern Ireland police service, that police historians should begin to focus anew on the origins and development of Ireland's constabularies. Donal J. O'Sullivan's *The Irish Constabularies 1822–1922* is the latest addition to a growing body of work in an area of Irish history which has been inadequately chronicled and in which misconception abounds. Jim Herlihy's *The RIC List* follows upon his 1997 publication *The Royal Irish Constabulary — A Short History and Genealogical Guide*.

Donal O'Sullivan, a former chief superintendent in the Garda, charts the history of the Irish constabularies from the earliest days of the county police forces. He writes with the career policeman's understanding of the sinews of a law enforcement organisation, describing command structures, procedures, equipment, pay, allowances and so on. But this is no dry manual. For he also shows himself to be a deeply aware social historian. His focus throughout is on the place of the policeman in the community and he dwells at length on the difficult complexities of this relationship in the particular circumstances of 19th and 20th century rural Ireland.

O'Sullivan is instinctively sympathetic to the lot of the Irish police officer in the British administration. The RIC were among the finest young men that rural Ireland produced at a time of few career opportunities. Because of the two-tier system of entry, the vast majority of the rank-and-file could not hope for promotion to commissioned rank. The ranks were broadly divided along religious lines as well. The great majority of constables, sergeants and head constables were

Catholic while most of the commissioned officers were Protestant. But few of the young country lads who joined had much concept of representing an alien power. When the War of Independence took place they were easy targets for violence and intimidation.

They are now a lost generation of Irish manhood, in the author's description.

In the aftermath of independence many emigrated, some to other police forces, others to employment in Britain or the United States. Those who remained in Ireland were obliged — with their families — to deny who and what they were.

They have no memorial. There is no public record or testimonial of their service. The author presents his book, in some measure, as a substitute for such a memorial. And a creditable one it is. He writes in a strong, narrative style with an eye for detail. He eschews the technique of using footnotes, but skilfully interpolates his sources into the narrative, making for a book which is as enjoyable to read as it is informative.

O'Sullivan knowingly traces the linkages between the RIC and the Garda Síochána. Many of the families which gave the Garda its young men in the 1920s and 1930s were the same as those

Boyd Rankin and Lynne Williams, suppliers of historical reproductions and clothing, take a break from ancient battle re-enactments at the Trim 2000 Hay Making Festival. Photograph: Matt Kavanagh.

which populated the non-commissioned ranks of the RIC before independence. The continuity of service in the police tradition is strong. When the organising committee established by Michael Collins oversaw the creation of a new, armed police force in 1922 it took the RIC as its model.

The Garda's firearms were taken away after a mutiny at its Kildare training depot, but the structures, the procedures, the jargon, the furniture, stationery — even the mattresses of the old force, in some instances, passed to the new. The structure of accountability of the new Garda Síochána also mirrored exactly the British system which it replaced. The RIC was directed by an Inspector-General, appointed by the government which also appointed commissioned officers. In the Garda Síochána the Inspector General was replaced by a Commissioner. But unlike Britain, where local authorities have a say in police matters, Ireland's tradition has always been to run the police as an agency of central government. When the Patten reforms are implemented, the RUC will be accountable in considerable measure to local police boards. The Garda Síochána will be the only police force in these islands under the direct and undiluted control of central government. In this most fundamental way it will carry on the tradition of the RIC.

Donal O'Sullivan's book is an excellent overview of the roots of Irish policing. It might be usefully read by political and administrative figures with responsibility for shaping policy.

Jim Herlihy is a serving member of the Garda. His RIC List is a mammoth achievement which will be a valuable aid to research for anyone who wishes to trace the careers of individual RIC members. Every member's name and registered number is provided, enabling individual service records to be accessed. There are very few families on this island which do not have a connection, in some generation, with the RIC. Mr Herlihy remarks in his introductory notes: 'I have found the bureaucracy of the British Empire to be meticulous in its record-keeping.'

This publication will be the starting point for many a genealogical research project.

Mugabe's Autocratic Rule Gets Shock from Zimbabwe

Eoin McVey

It's difficult to pinpoint why Robert Gabriel Mugabe metamorphosed from champion of democracy to totalitarianism, from Marxist ascetic to uncontrolled sybarite. Power — and far too much of it — was probably a major factor.

But 20 years ago, when the Lancaster House agreement paved the way for majority rule in Zimbabwe and Mr Mugabe proceeded to win the election with a thumping majority, he expressed his unswerving devotion to 'fair and just rule'. He then confounded the cynics by allowing rivals into government with him and pursued a policy of reconciliation with the country's white community which had fought for so long against him.

His confidence in those early days was understandable. His party, ZANU, was drawn from the majority Shona tribe. The opposition was weak and divided. Then Mr Mugabe set about making it weaker still.

The opposition was strongest in Matebeleland, where the indigenous Ndebele tribe supported the rival ZAPU party. The army was sent in and went on the rampage for nearly two years of destruction, torture and murder. Meanwhile, the Prime Minister, as he then was, lectured the population on the merits of justice and the rule of law.

It may have been the unequal merger in 1987 of his ZANU party with what was left of ZAPU, the winning of all but two of the parliamentary constituencies and his elevation to the post of executive President that brought Mr Mugabe to recognise the near totality of his power. That was when the real test of statesmanship kicked in: how would he use untrammelled control and would he put the needs of the nation first?

Unfortunately, the needs of his people seemed far down the list of priorities. Priority number one for the President and his cronies was self-enrichment. Zimbabwe has an abundance of mineral and agricultural wealth. It was regarded, at the time, as a stabilising power in southern Africa when the rest of the region was experiencing great instability. Western donor nations queued to inject capital and investment soared.

But the money spawned corruption, and the road to greed and consumption was travelled at speed. Bribes became commonplace, state contracts and licences were awarded on favouritism rather than merit. The President married his secretary, 40 years his junior, and built her two mansions (one with an illegal loan from public funds) to add to his own two mansions. The First Lady then took up extravagant international shopping with shameless enthusiasm. As the President behaved, so did his flunkies.

The corruption and the flagrant accumulation of wealth by the inner circle rankled with the people, but it was the mismanagement of the economy and participation in the war in the neighbouring Democratic Republic of Congo which brought the country to its knees. Mr Mugabe has defended his extravagant military assistance for President Laurent Kabila by arguing that states must be defended from revolutionary armies, which is a bit rich considering Mr Kabila has no democratic mandate and in many ways is little improvement on his predecessor, Mobutu.

Involvement in the war is deeply unpopular, but Mr Mugabe is unmoved. When two reporters wrote about dissatisfaction with the war they were arrested by the army and tortured. The Supreme Court (still commendably independent) complained to the President about the army's behaviour and asked him — respectfully — to rein it in. He refused and criticised the court for its impudence.

But why support Mr Kabila with the dispatch to war of 11,000 Zimbabwe troops, one-third of the army? Perhaps the reason lies in investments in minerals and timber in the Congo that Mr Mugabe's entourage has made and wants to safeguard, at all costs.

The cost to Zimbabwe has been huge — in excess of £1 million a day. The IMF and the World Bank, already incensed at the move to confiscate white-owned farms without compensation, has demanded that intervention in the war be ended; all aid has been frozen in the interim.

The country is thought to have enough foreign currency to pay for just three days of imports. It will soon be in a situation where it will be sold only what it can pay for in cash. Inflation is running at nearly 70 per cent, unemployment at over 50 per cent and there is a large budget deficit. This is an economy which urgently needs unpopular budgetary measures, but there can be no doubt the inevitable will be postponed, at least until after the parliamentary elections.

One badly needed reform concerns land. Just 50 per cent of the best arable land is owned in huge estates by 4,500 white farmers while millions of poor farmers — accounting for 70 per cent of the population — scratch a meagre living from two or three overworked acres.

But the redistribution must be fair and seen to be fair. Mr Mugabe's gamble on confiscating the lands without compensation has proved a disastrous error of judgment. He thought the domestic acclaim for such a populist measure would outweigh the international and donor community opprobrium.

Unfortunately for him, the needy farmers could remember the first redistribution of land and the fact it went, not to those who needed it but to ZANU cronies, and so they refused to support the referendum proposal. Mr Mugabe got it spectacularly wrong: damned abroad and damned at home.

He has two years left of his presidential term. On Monday he will turn 76. There is little doubt he is staring at his *fin de regne*. Perhaps his last

Niall Toibín on stage. Photograph: Matt Kavanagh.

judgment of significance will be the manner in which he gets off the stage: a dignified exit or an undignified manoeuvring to maintain his rule for as long as possible? Or Yeltsin-like, he may go as soon as he is satisfied his hand-picked choice will succeed him and assure him of a trouble-free retirement.

FRIDAY, 25 FEBRUARY 2000

Moustaches a Loss Leader for Imbibers of the Black Stuff

Frank Kilfeather

Research on Guinness in the UK has found that an estimated 162,719 pints of the drink each year are caught in moustaches, costing drinkers an annual £423,070 in wasted alcohol.

Experts claim the shape, length and density of the moustache all contribute to the volume of wastage. The walrus moustache is probably the most lethal of styles, as it can equate to an annual wastage of £27.48 a year.

Scientists working on Guinness Draught in a Bottle — designed to be drunk straight from the bottle rather than from a pint glass — noticed the phenomenon and called in Dr Robin Dover, one of the UK's leading moustache experts, to explore the full extent of the loss.

Guinness estimates that there are 92,370 drinkers with facial hair in the UK, who consume on average 180 pints a year.

Unfortunately, we have no figures for Ireland. This is strange. After all, it was here that the black stuff was invented and, it must be admitted, it has stood the test of time quite well. A spokeswoman in St James's Gate apologised profusely and said they were not aware of the recent research. She said she had no way of quantifying the loss to Irish people.

However, the moustachioed Irish people I know find absolutely no problem in drinking their pint unimpeded and boast of never losing a drop. In fact, if the truth be told, they would lick it off the floor.

The main Irish complaint — surprise, surprise — has always had a religious angle. A bishop's collar will not be accepted, the head must be closer to a curate's collar.

It all boils down to the actual amount of black stuff contained in the pint in relation to the frothy top. The bishop's collar is likely to be sent back pretty fast: the serving of such a pint is likely to start a riot.

Last month we read that Australian scientists and a US information technology firm had solved the mystery of the gas bubbles in Guinness stout, which appear to defy the laws of gravity by travelling downwards in the glass.

The solution lay in the shape of the glass and surface effects on its walls, which create a circulating current when the pint is poured. While bubbles rise rapidly through the middle of the glass, they move slowly down its sides. The net effect is of upward movement — as dictated by the laws of physics — although the bubbles visible to drinkers through the glass walls are descending.

A few questions remain: how does one get a job as a Guinness researcher? What are the qualifications? Could a journalist do it?

FRIDAY, 25 FEBRUARY 2000

Abuses of Power by Pillaging Politicians

Fintan O'Toole

The course of history has thrown up two different kinds of invaders. One, the most successful, is the coloniser. Colonisers like the Romans or the British move in, gradually extend their control and build long-lasting structures of rule. Their methods may be brutal and their motives may be greed and self-aggrandisement, but the scale of their ambitions is, in terms of both time and place, large. They have the confidence to plan for the long term so, for good and ill, they leave behind legacies that those they rule will never quite shake off.

Then there are the raiders, like the Vandals or the Visigoths. They sweep from the edges of a decadent empire, storming the citadels and putting the complacent old rulers to the sword. But they retain, at heart, a strange sense of inferiority — even though they have seized power, they fear the revenge of the vanquished.

They cannot quite bring themselves to believe in their conquest so they grab whatever treasures they can and carry them back to their domain. They see power, not as an opportunity to shape the destiny of future generations, but as a short-term, smash-and-grab project.

So it is with Irish politics. We, too, have our colonisers and raiders, our Romans and our Visigoths, our Brits and our Vandals. Broadly speaking, it might be said that those who founded the State and sustained it through its awkward adolescence were intent on colonising power. They moved in on the structures of governance with the intention of reshaping them in their own image. Theirs was a long-term, ideological project, driven by a desire to shape the destinies of future generations.

But gradually, the Romans were replaced by Visigoths. As the ideological confidence of Cosgrave, de Valera and Lemass gave way to the uncertainty of life in the global economy, the temptation to see public office as a smash-and-grab raid became, for some, irresistible. Where de Valera wanted to create a timeless Irish spiritual empire, Charles Haughey's ambition was to fill his pockets with loot, cover his traces and get safely home to Kinsealy with his grotesquely inflated self-image intact.

But for some accidents of fate, he might have pulled it off.

More typically, however, the contemporary political bigwig conducts his raids primarily on behalf of his tribe rather than himself. While it is necessary, of course, to keep up the pretence of being a Roman senator, a veritable Cicero, deep down he sees himself as Alaric the Visigoth or Attila the Hun. His job is to sweep into the Chas Mahal, force the snooty civil servants to prostrate themselves in terror at his feet and send some goodies back to the tribal homelands of south Kerry or north Tipperary.

And since he is haunted by the fear that he may soon be expelled from the Capitol, he grabs the booty as fast as he can. This may make the operation rather obvious and unsubtle, but, he reckons, politics is no place for subtlety. Consider, for example, the current Government and its flagrant abuse of the decentralisation programme. The idea of decentralising the offices of State and governmental agencies to provincial towns is a good one, particularly in the present circumstances — with Dublin becoming hopelessly congested it makes sense to move some of the bureaucratic apparatus to towns more in need of an injection of population and funds.

Decentralisation could, and should, be a key part of the spatial strategy that is supposed to be developed as part of the national plan, allowing the Government to make rational interventions in the spread of development.

That, though, is Roman thinking. To the Alarics and Attilas of our present administration, it misses the point. Using Government policy as an instrument for the long-term development of the nation is all very well for the self-important gentlemen in togas, but it makes no sense whatever to the fellow in the wolfskin overcoat with the bloody broadsword in his hand. For him, the point is to grab whatever is going and send it back to the tribal homeland. So, brazenly and without shame, the Government has been regarding the decentralisation programme as a Visigoth regards a villa full of exquisite ornaments. Never mind the artistic value, just rip them out and send them home to safety before they can stop us. Melt them down and haul them away.

We are not, of course, supposed to notice any of this. We are supposed to believe the Minister for Justice, Mr O'Donoghue, just happened to be struck one day last year with the idea that it would be good to decentralise the Civil Legal Aid Board and that by an extraordinary coincidence, the ideal location just happened to be Cahirciveen in his own constituency.

Then, in a series of coincidences so strange that they ought to feature on The X-Files, Mr Cowen discovered, just as he was leaving the Department of Health, that the best place for the National Disease Surveillance Centre would be Tullamore in his own constituency, and Michael Smith had the inspired idea of moving the headquarters of Civil Defence and two sections of the Army's administration to Tipperary.

Presumably, now that he has moved to Foreign Affairs, Mr Cowen will have the brilliant idea of decentralising the Irish embassy to Russia from Moscow to Portlaoise.

The media tends to be indulgent towards such strokes and the Opposition is loath to attack them for fear of alienating the good voters of Kerry, Laois, Offaly and Tipperary. The attitude that underlies them, however, is no laughing matter.

For what these ministers and the Cabinet that has gone along with their actions are saying is that the State and its institutions are essentially the property of individual ministers, to be placed at the service of their careers.

A policy that should be part of a long-term developmental strategy is made subject to the short-term goal of topping the poll in one or other constituency at the next election. Institutions that ought to be part of the emergence of a healthy, independent-minded civil society are being reminded that they can be disposed of at the whim of small-minded politicians.

'The Ballad of Posh and Becks began three years ago but fade-out still seems very far away.' Picture: Peter Hanan.

The public good, yet again, is sacrificed to private ends and the pathetic culture of the raider-politician is given a new lease of life.

SATURDAY, 26 FEBRUARY 2000

The Ballad of Posh and Beckham

The Saturday Profile by Róisín Ingle

If Victoria Beckham isn't careful she may end up being as popular among soccer fans as Yoko Ono was with Beatle groupies when she hooked up with John Lennon. The latest plot line being fed to viewers of this interminable soap opera is that her husband, Manchester United star David Beckham (24), is as henpecked as your average farm yard.

Diehard reds fans fear Posh could be about to do for Manchester United what the anti-Ono brigade said the obscure conceptual artist did for the Beatles.

Beleaguered Brylcreem boy Beckham had a row with his Manchester United boss Alex Ferguson because he missed training to stay at home with Victoria (25) and nurse their sick year-old son, Brooklyn.

Ferguson's ire led to Beckham missing a match against Leeds United. Posh's relationship with the Man U boss has been seriously shaky of late, with Fergie being of the birds-have-no-place-in-footie school. With Posh in the I-don't-give-a-monkey's-about-soccer camp, it was never going to be easy.

She has reportedly moaned about Beckham's salary (a mere £25,000 a week) and his having to commute to Manchester from Hertfordshire, where they are based. Now comes the news that she may be urging Beckham to jump ship for more exotic climes. Or, at the very least, Arsenal. New Man or New Wimp? That, apparently, is the question.

Bizarrely, the fact that a couple worth £35 million between them should desire a lifestyle that doesn't revolve around the hallowed turf of Old Trafford has been reason for concern rather than celebration among commentators.

In recent months the newspaper scrutiny of the couple has taken a slightly more sinister turn. The tabloids, which regularly do little to dispel the notion that all women should be pencil-thin, started to pick at another scab. Victoria appeared in public wearing a red leather strapless frock, her exposed flesh giving new meaning to the phrase good bone structure — we could count every one of them, for goodness sake. Overnight, the anorexia debate, in that responsible Ally McBeal style, had begun.

Wars can start, children can die, but hold the front page if, as happened last week, Posh catches on that modelling is the new pop music and stalks down a London catwalk in sprayed-on hotpants. If her figure gives the impression that she thinks a square meal is a piece of mini shredded wheat then so much the better.

In a week when a documentary was shown about Lena Zavaroni, the child star who suffered from eating disorders all her life and died last year aged 36, this relentless obsession with the physique of a woman, who may or may not be enduring similar anguish, is alarming. But a front-page snap of seven and a half stone skeletal Spice is said to guarantee more than 20,000 more newspaper sales.

Add the golden boots and tresses of her husband to this wall-to-wall coverage and you are really in business. Beckham has had his own troubles and his behaviour — on and off the pitch — has more resonance three days after the death of Stanley Matthews, an old-school soccer player never cautioned or sent off in his entire career.

Beckham's persecution over the last two years has come courtesy of his dramatic sending-off during England's World Cup match with Argentina in 1998 and his spending time with Victoria when he should have been training. For the latter he has been fined at least once by Manchester United. Then there are his sartorial blunders. He wears sarongs and, as Victoria revealed on the 'Big Breakfast', his wife's thongs.

The Beckhams (aka Thick and Thin) live life through a lens, and kidnapping threats are an everyday reality. Because they are rich, photogenic and not the brightest label victims in the world, the Beckhams are members of that curious celebrity breed who are worshipped, targeted and lampooned in equally lethal doses.

For every gushing magazine article there are cruel, obscene and sometimes very funny chants about their love life or even their baby from the football terraces. For every invitation to a glittering showbiz event there is someone (fashion designer Alexander McQueen, for example) who thinks it is uncool to have them at a show.

'2Phat' on Network 2 has begun a regular parody of the couple in the Beckingham Palace series. A recent skit showed Ray D'Arcy dressed up as Beckham attempting to put their dirty Prada, Gucci and Versace gear into the dishwasher. 'Dayvid,' Posh, played by Tracy Sheridan, whines, 'you know you shouldn't mix the colours with the whites.'

They complain about the attention and then hawk themselves and their baby around celebrity haunts like the plastic figurines on the ostentatious wedding cake they cut (with a sword, naturally) at their marital kitschfest in a castle outside Dublin last July.

What really seems to appeal to fans and infuriate those who can't stand them is that while the Beckhams are being touted as the prince and princess of this millennium — they even have thrones in their dining-room — they are more Royle Family than royalty.

Both grew up in the greater London suburbs of Essex and Hertfordshire. His working-class family would sacrifice anything to buy their boy the latest football boots, while she had an unashamedly *nouveau riche* middle-class background. Dad ran a successful electrical wholesale firm and dropped Victoria off at school in a Rolls-Royce.

Victoria Caroline Adams was bullied there because she chose to take dancing lessons when the bell rang instead of smoking behind the bike sheds. Her favourite movie was 'Fame', and as she ran out the gates to escape the taunts of her peers she thought, 'To hell with you, I'll have my day.'

She was the least talented Spice Girl and her best quality was her ability to point her finger and pull a face that made her look as though she was sucking on several pieces of lemon. She is the only one of the group who hasn't released a solo record, and at this stage is more famous for being famous than she is for anything else.

David Joseph Beckham was kicking a ball around as soon as he could stand and left school without passing a single exam. At 11 he had come top out of 5,000 entrants in a soccer skills competition and by the age of 14 he had signed with his dream team, Manchester United.

When they met, Victoria was riding high on Girl Power and he had already displayed soccer genius, scoring against Wimbledon from the halfway line. Now they collect cars, houses, jewellery and clothes to commemorate their love in a uniquely material world.

Ever since David began playing Ken to Victoria's Barbie, Alex Ferguson has reportedly had just one request of his love-struck employee. As manager of the most celebrated crosser (and part-time cross-dresser) in the British soccer world, he wants to see less of Beckham on the front page of the tabloids and more of him on the back.

Some of us just want to see less of him. And her.

Unfortunately for those of us on the sidelines, it's unlikely that the couple will display a Lennonesque ambivalence to this latest media frenzy by growing their hair and going off to live in a bag (unless, of course, the hair is the latest in chi-chi extensions and the bag is designed by Louis Vuitton).

There are, however, some other similarities with John and Yoko, namely, very public declarations of lurve, twee matching outfits, giant photographs of themselves kissing on the wall of their house and the nauseating we-are-as-one mantra.

The Ballad of Posh and Becks began three years ago but fade-out still seems very far away.

MONDAY, 6 MARCH 2000

Three Die in Sunday Afternoon Pier Tragedy

Lorna Siggins

In less sad circumstances it would be a place to go to look at the scenery. With the limestone hills of the Burren to the southwest and Black Head beyond, Tarrea pier on Kinvara Bay has a dramatic backdrop.

It was once one of those secret inlets — a little paradise on the road between Kilcolgan and Kinvara village — but has been 'discovered' in recent years. Yesterday, the Sunday afternoon traffic wasn't out to view the landscape. People came, some with carloads of children, to stare in awe at the aftermath of a simple tragedy.

However, for most of them, by early afternoon there was little to see, apart from idle lobster pots and floats, a digger, and Portakabins erected for dredging work which was due to begin today. Quickly and quietly, the emergency services had taken the evidence away.

Shortly after 1 p.m. a woman had driven up to the pier at speed in a Renault 19. It was a beautiful day, dry and clear with a southwesterly breeze, with the sun casting light around sea cages anchored on the water beyond.

Mr Tony Jordan, a painter and decorator, who lives a mile away in Toureen, was out for a walk. He noticed the car. The tide was coming in at the time.

The woman parked briefly about 10 yards from the pier edge. She got out and walked towards the water. She returned, checked her two children in the vehicle, and drove on. She left skid marks on the gravel as she put her foot down. The car travelled through the air about 10 feet before hitting the water.

'I saw it gradually sinking,' Mr Jordan said.

He raced to a bungalow on a rise nearby and dialled 999. Garda Michael Harte of Gort was one of the first on the scene after the emergency call, logged at 1.17 p.m.

A local diver, Mr Eugene Houlihan, pulled two bodies out, with the help of the Galway inshore lifeboat and the Gort and Galway fire brigades.

The Irish Coastguard's Doolin coast and cliff rescue unit was also called out, but it was all over by the time it arrived. Efforts were made to resus-citate the two, and they were rushed to University College Hospital, Galway, but emergency medical assistance was in vain. Shortly after 4 p.m. it was confirmed that they had died.

A third body, that of a child, could be removed only after the car had been pushed to shallower water, with the help of a local crane company. The child was dead on arrival at UCHG.

Gardaí believe the three occupants had been in the water, about nine feet deep, for the best part of an hour. Supt Paul Mockler said it was a shocking event, and gardaí were trying to establish a cause.

'We were devastated, that something like this could happen on a lovely Sunday afternoon,' Mr Jordan said.

A Gort fire brigade official was visibly upset. He said he had been on the job for 19 years and had hoped he would never have to deal with the death of a child.

Sleeping islands — the Blaskets. Photograph: Pat Langan.

MONDAY, 6 MARCH 2000

A Filthy People Laying Waste to our Environment

Frank McDonald

Let's face it, we really are a filthy people. Because we have no concept of the public realm, we treat any common property — streets and squares, parks and forests, beaches and promenades, and even the pilgrim path up Croagh Patrick — as an open litter bin.

Look at Henry Street and Mary Street in Dublin; as soon as their stylish repaving had been completed, at a cost of £1.5 million, there was chewing gum residue on nearly every slab of granite. And on the very day it opened, somebody got sick on the millennium footbridge.

Walk down Grafton Street any evening and see the huge piles of packaging waste deposited on the street for collection. In many other European countries, notably Denmark and Germany, most of this type of waste would be recovered or recycled.

Temple Lane, where I live, has been turned into Dumpsterville, with at least a dozen large bins parked on the footpaths, forcing pedestrians to walk on the cobbled street. These large wheelie-bins are simply waste magnets, particularly for restaurants dumping food.

Sunflower Recycling used to do a collection in Temple Bar but gave it up as a bad job because it was taking away just 12 bags a week, a tiny fraction of the amount of waste being generated in the area by residents and business premises.

Now, it costs us £2 per bag to have Sunflower collect our recyclables, whereas if we put it out on the street as rubbish it would be taken away free by Dublin Corporation. In those circumstances, a bizarre reversal of the polluter pays principle, it's no wonder so few give a hoot.

The State's new-found prosperity has aggravated the problem by introducing a large element of conspicuous consumption which, inevitably, produces even larger volumes of rubbish requiring disposal. The proportion we recycle is the lowest in northern Europe.

Kerbside, Dublin's only door-to-door recycling collection, is being wound up, partly because of chronic underfunding. Yet the waste management strategy for the capital recommended that 80 per cent of its households should be served by such a scheme.

Nobody cares about the mountain of waste we're creating, or the fact that it's increasing year by year, as long as it's carted off and dumped somewhere else. Indeed, many people only discover the environment as a cause when the problem comes home to haunt them.

The location of new waste disposal facilities of any kind provokes hysterical opposition. The old Nimby (Not In My Back Yard) syndrome has been replaced by Banana (Build Absolutely Nothing Anywhere Near Anything) and Note (Not Over There Either).

Even where waste disposal facilities are run in an exemplary manner — such as South Dublin County Council's highly-engineered landfill site in a disused quarry near Kill, Co Kildare — local people just don't want to know. They would prefer to live with their neat prejudices.

Mr P.J. Rudden, the Republic's leading expert on waste management — whose firm, M.C. O'Sullivan, consulting engineers, has produced many of the regional waste strategies — has been roasted at several public meetings. He says there are signs of change around the country but it's very slow.

'We have to get out there and sell the benefits of an integrated approach to waste management if we are to deal successfully with a lot of misinformation doing the rounds,' he says.

Two years have passed since a waste management strategy for the greater Dublin area was unveiled. It aimed to reduce waste going to landfill to just 15 per cent by switching the emphasis to

'Let's face it, we really are a filthy people.' Photograph: Eric Luke.

recycling and minimisation, with the residue going for thermal treatment.

A site has now been identified for an incinerator on the Poolbeg peninsula in Dublin Bay, near the corporation's sewage treatment plant, now being upgraded at a cost of £200 million. Yet even though nobody lives within 1 kilometre of the place, local opposition is intense.

People in Ringsend, Irishtown and Sandymount won't have anything to do with it, other than waging a relentless campaign against it. They are not remotely persuaded by the fact that Copenhagen's Amager incinerator is much closer to residential areas, with no ill-effects.

It is clearly nonsensical that local authorities must continually find new holes in the ground to fill with our waste; at least with incineration its

energy value is being recovered. And Poolbeg is probably the best site in Dublin for a municipal waste incinerator.

The heat it generates could be turned into electricity, in conjunction with the nearby ESB power station, or used to run the sewage treatment plant. If we were any good at planning, it might also have fuelled a district heating scheme for the entire Docklands area.

It is an integral part of the waste strategy that 60 per cent of the total volume of waste must be recycled, with only the residue being burned. For this to work, waste charges must be introduced in line with the polluter pays principle.

Given that each of us is now producing half-a-tonne of waste per annum, the imposition of charges is essential. Yet in the greater Dublin area, only Dun Laoghaire-Rathdown County Council has had the guts to do this, at a rate of £150 per household per annum.

Dun Laoghaire-Rathdown also intends to move quickly to replace this flat fee with a weight-related charge, thus ensuring that the more wasteful households pay more than those which make some effort to reduce or recycle the waste they produce.

The fact that the £150 charge is being introduced without too much fuss would appear to indicate that public attitudes are changing. Yet in Greystones, Co. Wicklow, it took 18 months to agree on the location of new bottle banks anywhere near where people live.

Repak, the not-for-profit company set up by IBEC three years ago, is dismissed by some as an 'umbrella for avoidance' by industry of its duty to recycle packaging waste. But it will have a budget of £12 million this year, funded by hefty levies on member companies.

Much of this money will probably go to funding new Kerbside-type schemes in Dublin and elsewhere, as well as the company's Greet Dot campaign. Certainly, without a significant commitment to recycling, there will be no public support for incinerators.

As for those who believe that younger people are more environmentally conscious, Bord Fáilte would say that the most litter-strewn stretch of

'And are cleevers or goosegrass forgotten? That sticky plant which adhered to clothes and hair and was so often used in boy versus girl warfare. Childish courtship. And wasn't March for kiteflying? And wasn't it time for spinning-tops?' Photograph: Pat Langan.

road in any Irish town is between the school and the tuck shop.

Sadly, we seem to be raising another generation of litter bugs.

FRIDAY, 10 MARCH 2000

In Time's Eye: When We Were Very Young

These were wonderful days when we were eight or 10 years old. One great thrill was frog-spawn. We collected it in jam-jars, kept it in basins or baths in the garden at home, and also had it in school where in nature study class, we watched the little dot at the centre of the egg lengthen and grow and eventually break out as a tadpole, finally losing its tail and becoming a tiny frog. What happened next? Either the teacher or a couple of the pupils bore the small glass tank away and decanted the whole into a suitable pond. There was a waterworks nearby. Away from school, some of us in the district were fascinated by an old mill-pond which held newts as well as frogs. Lovely, in memory, highly coloured, and a text-book tells us that the males 'develop striking breeding dress'.

Exactly. Nowadays you don't collect frog-spawn without a licence. Why? Are we short of frogs? Well, part of the answer anyway is that moving frog-spawn from place might bring weeds with it which could contaminate, if that is the word, other waters. Anyway, to complicate things, you must have a licence. After some conversation with a friendly voice in Dúchas, this corner received a licence form to fill up. Teachers, by the way, have no trouble in getting permission, so that classroom instruction can continue as it should. By the way, a dog walker tells us that on the Dublin mountains there is, in one busy area, a huge supply of the commodity. Fertile frogs up there.

Bread-and-cheese was another feature remembered from spring, that is, of course, the just-sprouting leaves of the hawthorn. Have they any nutritional or health value? For children used to chew them as they walked home from school.

Now, of course, roadside hedges would carry too much contamination from petrol fumes. In England, Richard Mabey relates in *Flora Britannica*, a massive and entertaining as well as informative tome, how in Leicestershire 'a spring dinner' was made by covering a suet crust with young hawthorn leaf buds and thin strips of bacon, and rolling and steaming it as a roly-poly. The elder is well in leaf now in our parts, and soon we'll be into recipes for the flowers. But, of course, today so many children are ferried to and from school by bus or by parental car that hedges are in no danger of being stripped.

And are cleevers or goosegrass forgotten? That sticky plant which adhered to clothes and hair and was so often used in boy versus girl warfare. Childish courtship. And wasn't March for kiteflying? And wasn't it time for spinning-tops?

SATURDAY, 11 MARCH 2000

Food from a Different World

Elizabeth Field

Every day Hilda Okonmah brings lunch to the staff of a West African grocery store in Dublin's city centre. It might be a fiery egusi soup, thick with chunks of beef and fish and laced with chilli pepper and crushed melon seeds, or perhaps a gentler chicken stew. It might include piping hot gari, the ubiquitous mashed-potato-like 'dunking bread' made from ground cassava, the tropical root from which tapioca is produced. But it always reflects Okonmah's combined homesickness for Nigeria and pride in its expansive culinary heritage where 'when we cook for one, we cook for all'.

No stranger to cooking for a crowd, the tall, statuesque Okonmah was formerly a chef in Lagos and she hopes to eventually open a restaurant in

Dublin. Because there is little written about West African cookery, and its traditions are mostly handed down orally from generation to generation, Okonmah thoughtfully provided a crash course on West African ingredients and techniques for me.

Starting at the grocer's she moved from bags of dried white and brown beans to baskets of gnarled cassava, yam and taro roots, to hairy coconuts, black-spotted plantains, papery white garlic bulbs, dried prawn heads and deep green limes. At home in her kitchen, she demonstrated some typical Nigerian dishes: a super-easy breakfast omelette enlivened with minced chilli pepper, chopped tomatoes, curry powder and thyme, and sweet, velvety-textured fried plantains. Here, large tropical cooking-bananas are simply peeled, sliced, lightly salted and fried in vegetable oil until golden brown on both sides. Then there is the less-familiar fare.

While styles vary regionally, West African cuisine is built on starchy tuberous vegetables such as yams, cassava and taro (sometimes called cocoyam), which are variously boiled, fried or mashed, or dried and powdered and combined with water to form a soft, bland paste. Traditionally moulded into a pillow shape and pinched off with the fingers in individual portions, these pastes are dipped into spicy soups or stews. (It's fine to eat the pastes with a fork and knife.)

The soups can be as chunky and blistering as the gari, and the yam-based fufu pastes are smooth and bland. Okonmah's ogbono soup, for example, combines the heat of chilli peppers with chunks of protein-rich beef and reconstituted dried fish, unctuous red palm oil, slippery okra and nutty-tasting ogbono, the crushed seeds of a mango-like fruit.

Egusi — melon seed — soup starts with the same stock as ogbono, but substitutes spinach for the okra, adds fresh, in addition to dried, fish, and finishes with a cream-coloured, sesame-like purée of melon seeds. There are no equivalents in Western cooking. Newcomers to West African food might wish to approach it by substituting vegetable oil for the heavy-textured palm oil in recipes. Then they can work slowly into the dishes, gradually increasing the heat quotient.

Asked whether she had made any adjustments to her authentic Nigerian recipes to suit Western palates, Okonmah replies: 'Yes. I normally use three or four whole chillis in a recipe instead of the quarter-teaspoon I've used today. They're great for a cold.'

No one knows the exact size of the West African population in Ireland, but government figures estimate the figure to be in the thousands, with a recent rise in asylum-seekers and in resident aliens with work-permits. The immigrant experience is difficult anywhere, but access to native foodstuffs eases the transition. To that end, roughly eight West African grocery stores, stocking provisions imported either via England or directly to Ireland, and at least one restaurant have opened in Dublin in the past three years.

These provide both cultural and social support for African nationals — especially those living outside Dublin, where obtaining native foodstuffs is nigh impossible — as well as a warm welcome for non-Africans seeking information about traditional foodways. At Africana restaurant at 102 Parnell Street, Mary Akin emerges from the open kitchen at the back of her homely, 30-seat eatery, to chat with regular customers and to advise newcomers on menu choices. 'How about beef stew with yam porridge and an order of fried rice?' she advises two Irish women contemplating lunch. She calms their fears about a vegetable soup with pounded yam as being 'bad for your tummy'.

Indeed, the fiery beef stew, served on a bed of bland, tomato-scented mashed yam, is fortifying and tasty, but African diners stare sympathetically as the women grasp frantically for glasses of cold water. The fried rice is a much milder, turmeric-scented dish, accented with fresh herbs, diced onion, carrots, tomatoes and peas, and garnished with fried plantains.

When available, other menu items include isiewu, goat's head stew served in a traditional wooden bowl; spicy peanut soup with boiled rice and beef, chicken or fish; asaro, a mash of yams, prawns and vegetables; couscous and vegetables; stewed chicken; and jollof rice, flavoured with tomato paste, palm oil, meats, vegetables, thyme, nutmeg and garlic. Beverages include Maltina, a non-alcoholic brew made from malted sorghum, conventional minerals, or wine. Desserts are not traditional in West African cookery. Mary and her husband, Stephen Akin, strive for culinary harmony between West Africans and Europeans.

'Some Irish people come here, really anxious to eat hot food,' says Stephen. 'We also serve a lot of French and Spanish people, and we just had a party of Asian airline personnel.'

Acknowledging racism and ignorance in some quarters of Irish society, he nonetheless believes most Irish people are tolerant and that the country is headed for more acceptance of multiculturalism. There is some visible cross-over between African and Irish food sensibilities. A recent lunchtime crowd at the Tropical grocery store on Parnell Street comprised West Africans buying staples along with Irish women examining the shop's display of hairpieces. Both Africans and non-Africans were queuing up for takeaway, Nigerian-style,

'No stranger to cooking for a crowd, the tall, statuesque Okonmah was formerly a chef in Lagos and she hopes to eventually open a restaurant in Dublin.' Photograph: Alan Betson.

baked red snapper and turkey legs, smothered with tomatoes and onions.

'We eat both Irish and African food,' says shopper Patricia Dwyer, clutching a huge, brown yam under one arm. A Ghanaian married to an Irishman, she says her children are especially fond of fried plantains and yam chips. Indeed, the in-store juxtaposition of Alafia Bitters, a Ghanaian health tonic, with jars of Nescafé and knobbly ginger roots portends an expanded culinary diversity here.

'Our door is open,' says manager Paul Lubienga. 'We taste Irish food. Why shouldn't the Irish taste African food?'

SATURDAY, 11 MARCH 2000

Yellow Peril

Justin Hynes

Outside the Jordan hospitality garden in the Albert Paddock two women are in deep conversation. 'Who's that?' asks one, raising an appreciative eyebrow in the direction of the yellow-suited figure who's just emerged from the team's garage.

'That's Trulli,' the other replies, squinting over the top of her designer shades to get a better view of the driver.

'Who's he?'

'He joined them this year. Instead of Damon Hill,' says the girl in the sunglasses.

'Right. He's pretty damn cute, isn't he?' says the first as they prowl closer.

A year ago in the very same paddock, albeit further down this little strip of road where position denotes primacy, Jarno Trulli might have got the same admiring glances from female fans. Chances are though that most would have left none the wiser as to the identity of the then Prost driver. Change the race suit from blue to yellow though and suddenly Trulli is a bit of a star, someone to watch out for. A bit of a contender.

Such is the power now wielded by Jordan in Formula One. For so long the bravest of the also-rans, seemingly cemented into the role of cut-price mediocrity, the Irish team has been radically transformed in the last two seasons.

Last year's best ever finish of third has given them a choice spot in the pit lane, gazing up longingly but not in awe of close neighbours McLaren and Ferrari, and sees them jealously guarding that hard-won territory from big-budget novices Jaguar and a Williams team in the middle of a rebuild in BMW's teutonically perfect image. That new found lustre has also attracted new lucre — a massive deal with German company Deutsche Post that will give the team the financial clout to compete technically with the big two.

These are heady days for Jordan. Gone are the days when the team would field entries and manically celebrate a run into the points. Tomorrow, they will enter their first grand prix of the 2000 season. For the first time, they will go out expecting to win. For the first time, the expectation has a basis in reality.

Heinz-Harald Frentzen, who single-handedly took the team to third place in the constructors' championship as Damon Hill faded into a ghostly shadow of what he had been when earning Jordan's first victory in 1998, is marked down as the man most likely to deliver. He has won before. Twice last year, in France and Italy. At Nurburgring he earned the team its first pole position since the Belgian Grand Prix of 1994. For a time, after his Monza win, and up until electrical failure cost him a comfortable lead in the European Grand Prix, he was being touted as a possible champion. Now, when Frentzen arrives in the paddock heads turn.

But while the expectation of a victory is now a fixture at Jordan and the expectation is centred most fervently on the laconic German, there is one who believes a Jordan win could come from another source. The true believer is Jarno Trulli. And he feels victory can be his.

The President, Mrs McAleese, at Áras an Úachtaráin where she made a live television broadcast to the St Patrick's Day Banquet in Auckland, New Zealand. Photograph: Frank Miller.

'I feel I have a very great opportunity to win races this year,' said the 25-year-old Italian.

'Now that I have a competitive car, I can get the results I always anticipated. I feel that I can compete for the whole championship, and not just one or two races.'

The view is shared by Trulli's new boss, Eddie Jordan, who has already described the former Prost driver as his 'jewel in the crown' and believes the Italian will duplicate the transformation made by Frentzen last year, from talented driver going nowhere to superstar in the making.

Trulli's record in the Australian Grand Prix is, however, far from laudatory. He failed to finish in his last two outings here, but now feels that he has

a chance to make a real impression at the Albert Park circuit.

'I was running third last year before we had a refuelling problem,' he said. 'But I always have a good performance here, if I can finish …'

Reliability is not likely to be a factor in either Trulli or Frentzen's weekend. Despite gearbox niggles, the new EJ10 has proved it can be a real threat to the top two and, with Trulli and Frentzen, the team appears to have its best ever chance of eroding the quality gap that exists between McLaren and Ferrari and the chasing pack.

'This year's car is a lot quicker than last year's. We feel that it is a big step forward. We are closer to the Ferraris and McLarens,' he said before

Keith Wood and a host of golden daffodils. Photograph: Eric Luke.

adding a hasty caveat. 'But we think that everybody has improved a lot and everybody else will be close to the top teams as well.'

Despite the noises of quiet confidence that have been emanating from the Jordan camp since the EJ10 was first used in anger at Barcelona's Circuit de Catalunya two days after its public debut in London in January, getting either Trulli or Frentzen to top step of the podium with any regularity will prove more difficult than last year.

While few would doubt that Frentzen showed remarkable coolness taking the chequered flag at Magny Cours, the 10 points were gift-wrapped by a radically redrawn grid, thanks to precarious qualifying conditions and the appalling weather of race day which saw the German's rival fall by the wayside.

Monza, too, was unlikely to have been Frentzen's had Mika Hakkinen not suffered a rare bout of carelessness as his thumb hovered over the gear paddles. Indeed, throughout the season, Jordan were aided by a series of technical glitches in both McLarens and also by the protracted absence of Michael Schumacher, an absence which effectively removed a certain frontrunner from the equation for five races.

Yesterday at a practice session for tomorrow's race in Melbourne, Schumacher looked like he might be gift-wrapping another big chance for Jordan. The two-time world champion lost control of his Ferrari at a right-handed corner and slid across the gravel before hitting the barrier, having a couple of his own tyres ripped off in the process. Schumacher, however, was able to step away from the cockpit and hitch a lift on the back of a motorcycle to the Ferrari garage and watched the last moments of the session from the pit-wall.

The return of Schumacher and Rubens Barrichello's arrival at Ferrari, coupled with a Ferrari and a McLaren that have so far proved more than capable of meeting race distances, both Jordan drivers are likely to find any ascent to the podium more problematic than last season.

Both will also have to be aware of the threat from behind. Jordan have been firmly in the sights of every team from Jaguar to BAR to Benetton. Yellow has become a highly visible and attainable target.

Jaguar would appear to be the major threat to Jordan's hold on the third garage in the pit and Eddie Irvine, in particular, could be stinging the hornets' tails by Easter and the British Grand Prix.

Eddie Jordan, though, is refusing to acknowledge the challenge of the re-badged Stewart team and has set his sights firmly on breaking into the true top flight.

In the wake of the team's finest year, tough talk has been the defining facet of Jordan in recent weeks, but, starting tomorrow, reliving the high times of champagne and silverware may turn out to be the beginning of a difficult period of withdrawal symptoms.

FRIDAY, 17 MARCH 2000

Enough of Puff's Guff
Puff Daddy & Family

Kevin Courtney

The (allegedly) gun-toting boss of Bad Boy Records, boyfriend of Jennifer Lopez, and best pal of Biggie Smalls brought his entourage to Dublin on Tuesday, and revealed the emptiness beneath all the tough-guy rap and bluster. The successor to MC Hammer's tinsel crown is out on bail on firearms and bribery charges, and free to begin his European tour. All the onstage fireworks, flames and explosions in the world, however, couldn't hide the truth that Sean 'Puffy' Combs is unable to muster up a single original idea during two hours of strutting, preening pyromania.

'Everybody say yeeeahh!' was the refrain of the evening, as Puffy and his homies belted out the vacuous rap clichés, and tossed in the odd tuneless rendition of some long-forgotten 1980s song. With practically zilch in the way of music to offer, Puffy instead went for a pantomime approach, getting the audience to sing along to U2's 'I Still Haven't Found What I'm Looking For' (the actual record, mind, not a cover version), and bringing Bad Boy label artistes 112 and Carl Thomas to provide musical interludes. It was like watching a TV show, with Puffy as the compere, choreographer, producer and sponsor rolled into one.

The Kashmir-sampling 'Come With Me' encapsulated the whole Godzilla-scale folly, while 'I'll Be Missing You', the multi-million-selling paean to murdered rapper, Notorious B.I.G., smacked of showbiz insincerity.

SATURDAY, 25 MARCH 2000

Judge's One-man War on Behalf of Troubled Children

Kathy Sheridan

Denizens of the High Court are inured to it by now: the million-pound injunctions and company wind-ups on Mr Justice Peter Kelly's list, suddenly suspended for yet another tragic child, another story of lost childhood and political neglect.

On 10 March, Mr Justice Kelly did something he had never done before. He directed that a 17-year-old girl should be detained in the Central Mental Hospital, a hospital for the criminally insane. This was despite an expert view that it was totally inappropriate and possibly illegal. Although considered to be a 'very serious' risk to herself and others, the girl is not a criminal nor is she mentally ill.

But he had no option, explained the judge, because of the State's failure to provide appropriate facilities or even a legislative framework to deal with such cases.

The child — who fantasises that her recently dead father will come and rescue her — has since written a few times to Mr Justice Kelly, including poetry on one occasion. Last Tuesday, he read out one of the letters in court: 'You probably think I've gone mad,' she wrote, 'but I have not ... All I want is people who are really going to be there for me, no matter what.'

Yesterday, the nervous-looking, pretty teenager was back in the High Court, five years to the day, ironically, since the 'FN' case, when Mr Justice Geoghegan declared that the State had a constitutional obligation to provide 'as soon as reasonably practicable ... suitable arrangements of containment with treatment' for troubled children.

'The State authorities could have been in no doubt of their obligations in that regard,' said Mr Justice Kelly a month ago, in a swingeing judgment on official promises made to the court. 'It was clear that on no occasion has there been adherence to the timescales indicated to me. In each case the provision of the facilities has been deferred further and further.'

In the meantime, the trail of childhood misery through Mr Justice Kelly's court gains momentum, at a cost of an estimated £50,000 to £70,000 per case to the taxpayer.

Just a few weeks ago, the case unfolded of a 15-year-old girl who went out of control following the death of her mother. After coming under the influence of 'truly evil' people, she was said to have had some 75 sexual partners while working as a prostitute, used her mobile phone as a sex chat line, smoked 40 to 60 cigarettes a day and took alcohol and drugs. In spite of this, she wound up in a State remand centre because there was nowhere better available.

Last week, an extremely disturbed 14-year-old girl with a propensity to epilepsy was ordered to be detained in the acute psychiatric unit of a general hospital. She had almost died after an overdose of alcohol and 20 ecstasy tablets, was allegedly raped after staying out late from a health board residential

'What is also remarkable is that without Mr Justice Kelly's terrier-like pursuit of the authorities, the building work that is finally being advanced might not be happening at all.' Photograph: Frank Miller.

home, and had been diagnosed with a sexually transmitted disease.

What she needed — immediately, said an expert — was a secure residential environment where she could receive appropriate therapy and treatment from suitably qualified staff. But the child's life was in imminent danger, there was no suitable alternative and once again, Mr Justice Kelly spoke of the 'appalling dilemma' in which he was being placed: the State's failure, he said, 'manifests itself week in, week out'.

Just four days before Christmas, another 14-year-old, described by a psychiatrist as 'the saddest child I have ever met', with an alcoholic mother and a violent father who allegedly sexually abused her, and who had tried to kill herself on Christmas Day 1998, was sent to a State detention centre by the High Court. Thus an innocent child who, in

the words of Mr Justice Kelly, 'never had a chance', spent her 14th Christmas in a reformatory.

Shortly before that, a 16-year-old boy with psychiatric and psychological difficulties but with no criminal convictions was ordered to be returned to St Patrick's Institution — a prison — despite the presiding judge's view that his continued detention there was unlawful and the boy's allegation that he had been raped there.

This would have been no surprise to anyone. In 1997, a 13-year-old was warned by Judge Mary Martin that if she sent him there, he would be 'locked up 23 hours a day and raped every night'.

But the Supreme Court had previously ruled that children could be sent there for four to six weeks if there was no alternative. A case is pending at the European Court of Human Rights, arguing that this is in breach of the Convention on Human Rights.

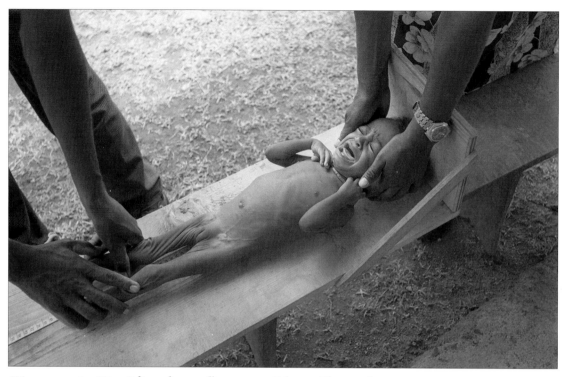

Fifteen years after 'Live Aid' people are still starving in Ethiopia. Photograph: Joe St Leger.

Meanwhile, although the 16-year-old had been in St Patrick's for three months, Ms Justice McGuinness's only alternative was to put him on to the streets, something she was not prepared to do.

His counsel, Mr Gerard Durcan SC, who has acted for many of these troubled children, told the court that all the State and the health board could say was that there might be a place in a State remand centre in two weeks' time. The judge remarked that the boy was now almost 17 years old and medical opinion was that there was only a small opportunity left to help him and prevent him being involved in criminal offences for the rest of his life.

What she said must apply equally to others in similar straits. Court observers who have seen such children leave a court without a residential place often spot the same names four or five years later, only this time on bail applications. The child who wrote poetry for Mr Justice Kelly and wants only

that people should be there for her will soon be 18 and out of his jurisdiction; an adult in the eyes of the State, though one who still poses an enormous risk to herself and others.

What has befallen the two 12-year-old girls (who looked even younger), both on drugs and working as prostitutes? Or the 12-year-old boy, already notorious for violent assaults, drug-taking, absconding and aberrant sexual behaviour?

What is also remarkable is that without Mr Justice Kelly's terrier-like pursuit of the authorities, the building work that is finally being advanced might not be happening at all. While the State sat on its hands, district justices, who for decades had despaired in the face of disturbed children and parents seemingly without rights, at last looked to the Constitution for a solution. No one had thought of it before.

In the early 1990s, judges in the Children's Court began to encourage solicitors to take their cases to the High Court, to vindicate their young clients' constitutional rights. This culminated in Mr Justice Geoghegan's landmark decision in 1995. The State did not appeal. Indeed, within a week, Department of Health officials were dazzling the High Court judge with a raft of proposals regarding residential places.

Two years later, however, confronted with a growing 'children's list' and the fact that any movement in this area seemed to depend on the High Court and not the politicians or the law, Mr Justice Kelly called the Minister for Health to account. The impression left on some observers to those hearings was that to some Department officials, early intervention was the only solution, and that there was little point to developing units when this was a lost generation which would end up in the criminal justice system anyway.

Meanwhile, a heavy burden remains on the judges, says an observer: 'If a judge makes the wrong choice and doesn't detain a child who then goes out and kills himself or somebody else, guess where the accusing fingers will point then.'

'It is no exaggeration to characterise what has gone on as a scandal,' Mr Justice Kelly concluded in a 1999 judgment. 'I have had evidence of inter-Departmental wrangles over demarcation lines going on for months, seemingly endless delays in drafting and redrafting legislation, policy that appears to be made only to be reversed and a waste of public resources on, for example, going through an entire planning process for the Portrane development only for the Minister to change his mind, thereby necessitating the whole process being gone through again.'

The judge then took the unusual step of compelling the Minister to complete two developments, in Lucan and Portrane, within the Department's own specified timescale. Significantly, that injunction is being complied with to the letter, in marked contrast to others around the State which the judge has also set his sights on.

Impressed by the detailed action plan and timescale presented by Health Department officials last April, he consented to an eight-month adjournment to give it time.

But despite the senior managers' group that was set up and some encouraging advances, in no case have the timescales been adhered to.

Furthermore, it had already been decided 'at the highest level in the Department of Health and Children, that as a matter of policy' no undertaking about future compliance would be given to the court.

Faced, then, with the possibility of yet another injunction compelling him to carry out his own plan, the then minister, Brian Cowen — in stark contrast to the rocket-like response in 1995 — took refuge in several technical objections, one of which actually questioned the right of the children named to seek the injunction.

In the face of this and much else, Mr Justice Kelly made the order, 'to ensure that the Minister, who has already decided on the policy, lives up to his word and carries it into effect'.

Even as things stand, the judge concluded, 'it will be fully seven years since the decision in FN before these facilities are in operation. These children and others like them are at an important stage in their development.

'Much can be done for them. Their future lives as adults can be influenced for good but only if the appropriate facilities are available. They have a right to them. They ought to have been provided long before now. It is a scandal that they have not. A great deal of time has been lost. This court can allow no more.'

The saga is lurching to a close but may not be resolved. The possibility is being looked at of taking a case to try to extend a constitutional principle: that if the State does not give the constitutional rights due to a child when he's a child, then it may have to do so when he is an adult.

The implications are breathtaking.

THURSDAY, 30 MARCH 2000

The Things We Wouldn't Say If We Could Turn Back Time

Frank McNally

There may well have been an even more inaccurate military prediction than that made by the American Civil War general, John B. Sedgwick, but his reported last words ('They couldn't hit an elephant at this dist…') are surely the wittiest.

It's a pity he didn't get the joke himself, although at least he has the posthumous distinction of holding the record for the quickest rebuttal of a professional opinion. In the face of stiff competition, too, including a brave effort from one of his contemporaries, General Custer, who celebrated the sight of an Indian camp at Little Big Horn with the words: 'Hurrah, boys, we've got them. We'll finish them up and then go home.'

It's not only the generals who get it wrong, of course. Here's a journalist, 'specialising in the interpretation of international affairs', writing in the *New York Sun* in June 1914: 'It is difficult to discuss the tragedy at Sarajevo yesterday without laying oneself open to the reproach of heartlessness. For while it is only natural to be stricken with horror at the brutal and shocking assassination of Archduke Francis Ferdinand, it is impossible to deny that his disappearance from the scene is calculated to diminish the tenseness of the (European situation) and to make for peace.'

The press is strongly represented in *I Wish I Hadn't Said That*, a revised edition of *The Experts Speak*, first published in 1984 and now out in paperback.

Teed off with politics? Photograph: Eric Luke.

Unfortunately, the age-old dilemma for journalists is that too many qualifications make for dull copy, a situation which gives rise to predictions like the one in a 1995 *Wall Street Journal* editorial, also quoted here: 'Bill Clinton will lose to any Republican nominee who doesn't drool on stage.' But the big consolation for reporters is that it's weather forecasters who make the mistakes people really remember, as the BBC's Michael Fish knows well. In October 1987 he told viewers: 'A woman rang and said she heard a hurricane is on the way. Well … there isn't.' The following morning, Britain was hit by the biggest storm in three centuries, causing what one press agency called 'the worst devastation since the Nazi bombing blitz'.

Most of the great thinkers and inventors experienced ridicule from the experts, but some inspired worse reactions than others. Take John Logie Baird, who in 1925 turned up at the offices of the *Daily Express* touting his invention of television. His visit inspired panic in the editor, who ordered an underling: 'For God's sake go down to reception and get rid of a lunatic who's down there. He says he's got a machine for seeing by wireless. Watch him … he may have a razor.'

The book uses sleight of hand by including, as cases of experts getting it wrong, many entries which were mere lies, or propaganda: from Henry Kissinger denying all knowledge of US involvement in the coup in Chile, to the *Daily Worker* explaining in 1956 that the invading Soviet Army was 'assisting the Hungarian people to retain their independence from imperialism'. And many other entries, especially in the world of the arts, are opinions which the authors might still hold. Who's to say Tchaikovsky, were he alive today, would not be just as irritated by 'that scoundrel' Brahms, as when writing his diary in 1886: 'What a giftless bastard! It annoys me that his self-inflated mediocrity is hailed as genius.'

I Wish I Hadn't Said That is published by HarperCollins at £5.99.

SATURDAY, 1 APRIL 2000

Laughing All the Way from the Bank

Jim Dunne

Falling Eagle — The Decline of Barclays Bank by Martin Vander Weyer. Weidenfeld and Nicolson. 263pp. £20 in UK

Bank history is not the most riveting of topics. Nobody likes banks, and the only way of making them interesting is to describe their ignominious collapse. Barings brought low by rogue trader Nick Leeson is the classic example. Martin Vander Weyer has introduced a new formula: the vendetta as biography. He was sacked by Barclays bank and has now dumped on his former employers to sometimes hilarious effect.

In an early chapter, he pauses to discuss table manners at Barclays. The Victorians had introduced the concept of the fish knife. The Quaker founders of Barclays believed passionately that fish should only be eaten with two forks. One day, the partners of the bank arrived for luncheon in the board room to discover that the table setting included the dreaded fish knives. The general manager with responsibility for catering was summoned and his exile from Britain forthwith was decreed. He was given a choice between Australia and Barbados.

The author's father, who rose high in Barclays — though not, in his son's opinion, as high as he should — was reprimanded for scooping the Stilton from the middle and not, as everybody knows, slicing it horizontally.

The book describes the onerous business of entertaining a visiting Barclays grandee in Hong Kong. He is brought to the Kowloon Club. This is presided over by a mama-san, who selects young ladies to entertain the male customers. Protocol requires that the male inspects a range of talent before making his choice. But the Barclays man from London declares that the first woman will do and takes her off to the Mandarin Oriental, 'one of the few (Hong Kong) hotels which did not allow guests to bring in nightclub tarts'.

It would be misleading to describe this book as a back-to-back romp. A good deal is devoted to Barclays' history and the complex inter-mingling of the founding families. It is interesting, though, to observe that a company could survive managerial incest for as long as Barclays. It had what was known as a Special List, employees marked down for promotion solely on the basis of whom their parents were.

Barclay's great banking innovation was the Barclaycard, introduced in 1966. There are three good things about it, said an enthusiastic branch manager: it scrapes ice off your windscreen, it picks Yale locks, and it gets customers into debt.

The notion of marketing financial services was first introduced in Europe by Barclays. 'Spending a weekend with your family,' thundered one Barclays executive, 'is a missed marketing opportunity.'

Barclays was humbled by its excursions into lending outside its core High Street business. Its investment bank, BZW, devoured capital as the British aspired to have a global presence. It lost a fortune in Russia. In this connection, it is worth casting an eye over the half-yearly results from the Irish banks. Without exception, the profits are made in the domestic business — a point consumers might ponder as alternative banking opportunities present themselves.

The title of this book is a little misleading. Though Vander Weyer may enjoy wreaking some vengeance on Barclays, the bank is still alive and kicking and has a new chief executive, an Irishman from Tralee, Matt Barrett. His track record

Spring in the air. Photograph: Eric Luke.

suggests that nothing very dull will happen around Barclays while he is there.

After a 37-year career with the Bank of Montreal, he tried — but failed — to engineer a merger with the rival Royal Bank of Canada. He resigned and told a newspaper that his new objective was 'to write a bad book, find my karma and grow a ponytail'. (And this from a man educated by the Christian Brothers!) He was head-hunted by Barclays to become chief executive in 1998. His appointment was noted by *The Sun*, not usually exercised by City appointments, under the headline 'the £7 million bonk manager'. The £7 million referred to his remuneration. Barrett had divorced his wife and married a six-foot former model called Anne Marie Sten. He bought her a £50,000 emerald necklace, which she refused to wear. She wanted, she said, a diamond as big as a throat lozenge.

The marriage has not lasted.

Barclays has provided some excitement in its colourful history, and under its new chief executive seems likely to continue to do so.

MONDAY, 3 APRIL 2000

Time Will Make Hero Of Taxing Master

John Waters

Once in a while a voice is raised to restore faith in the capacity of public servants to be more than job-minding automatons, mouthing spin-doctored bureau speak and inane platitudes. Such an occasion was the recent remarks by the Taxing Master of the High Court, James Flynn, in describing tribunals as 'Frankenstein monsters' and 'Star Chambers'.

The immediate response was: What? Did he say that? Here, clearly, was someone with a mind of his own, saying things the dogs in the street knew to be true. It was obvious Master Flynn was

alive, and human. If only, one thought forlornly, we could have more people like this in public life, things — even mad, mistaken or wrong things — could get said, and society might grow a little as a result. This, after all, is the theory of democracy and free speech.

But it was inevitable, given the set-up he was describing, that Master Flynn would be made to eat crow. If his remarks were allowed to stand, other public servants might take to speaking their minds. The true nature of Irish public life, and the mechanisms which propel it in particular directions, would inch further into view. And the many who regard tribunals as expensive, time-wasting charades would begin to understand that they are not alone. The mechanism whereby the retraction was extracted was instructive. Key players with vested interests immediately demanded sanctions. Politicians who gained power by accusing others made solemn statements of their 'concern'. Attacks were launched by journalists whom tribunals have made into stars.

One can observe in the response of the Tánaiste, Mary Harney, the contrived nature of the pressure for sanctions. Ms Harney described Master Flynn's comments as 'clearly offensive' to the Oireachtas and judiciary. But the Oireachtas is not some thin-skinned entity, unable to endure criticism: it is the national parliament, where trenchant debate takes place from dawn till dusk.

Moreover, some of its members agree with Master Flynn.

And while I don't doubt certain judges were offended, I thought we were coming around to the view that judges are over-privileged deities who have been beyond criticism for too long. The notion that judges, who send people down in chains the way the rest of us put sugar on our cornflakes, have a right to be 'offended' by statements devoid of malice or personal imputation is not merely silly, it is retrograde and dangerous.

The public should scrutinise this episode for its important lessons about the public life of this State.

This case exposed the transmission system operated by the engineers of our society: the media are the engine; the Progressive Democrats — a party founded on the principle of appealing to public perception — function as the clutch; and the Government — ostensibly elected by the people and dominated by Fianna Fáil, but in reality run by the transmission system — is engaged to do the will of the true rulers of society.

The wheels move. Once we heard that the (PD) Attorney General had conveyed the Government's 'deep concern' to the President of the High Court, Master Flynn's climbdown or removal was a matter of time.

Let us be quite clear: the objection to public servants speaking their minds relates not to their breaching of codes of silence, but to the content of their views. Only when certain interests are in disagreement with their opinions do problems arise. We saw this during Mary Robinson's presidency when, despite some of her statements breaching the Constitution in spirit and letter, no sanctions were ever invoked. Invariably, she expressed views congenial to the transmission system.

Two months ago, another public servant, Peter Finlay SC, resigned as refugee appeals adjudicator, shortly after making a ferocious attack on the asylum process. He said that he could not serve in a system he did not believe in. But there was no suggestion of Government pressure on Mr Finlay to retract, because there was no media pressure, because the views he expressed found favour with the media: both statement and principled resignation were widely praised.

The classic instance of this syndrome is the case of the now-retired High Court judge Rory O'Hanlon, sacked as president of the Law Reform Commission over comments about abortion and the Maastricht Treaty. Some years later, the State paid Mr O'Hanlon a six-figure sum following the settlement action in which he claimed his dismissal was unconstitutional. When he made his remarks, he came under splenetic attack from politicians and journalists, who accused him of 'undermining democracy', 'scaremongering', and 'insulting the intelligence of the Irish people'.

Mr O'Hanlon is opposed to abortion. His dismissal followed his rejection of a Government 'request' to stay out of controversy. That self-same government (also a FF-PD coalition) remained inert when another judge, Miss Justice Mella Carroll, went public on precisely the same issue by endorsing a statement issued by the Commission on the Status of Women, which made recommendations on abortion in the wake of the Supreme Court ruling in the X case. The difference was that the transmission system agreed with Miss Justice Carroll, whereas it was at variance with Mr Justice O'Hanlon.

Had Master Flynn not retracted, he too might have been dismissed, and in a few years a couple of column inches in the newspapers would inform us that this episode, too, had cost the taxpayer perhaps a million pounds in damages and costs. It is clear that, for all our cant about free speech, we have little space for anyone with genuinely independent views. But as the Moriarty and Flood tribunals meander on, the public will more and more come around to the views expressed by Master Flynn. Time will make of him a hero.

SATURDAY, 8 APRIL 2000

Herbert Park House with ¼-Acre Garden Fetches £5.3m

Jack Fagan

A large detached house at 32 Herbert Park in Dublin 4, bought in 1985 for £182,000, was sold yesterday for £5.3 million. The sum paid at auction for the turn-of-the-century house is easily the highest so far achieved at auction for a Dublin 4 house.

The buyer is a wealthy Irishman with business interests in the US. According to his agent, Mr

Seán Davin, he plans to spend at least another £500,000 on upgrading the seven-bedroom house, which was owned by an American-based couple, Michael and Ann Flynn, who had rented it to the Moroccan embassy since the mid-1990s.

Two years ago another detached house at 36 Herbert Park was sold at auction for £1.56 million. Both stand on a quarter of an acre of gardens.

The record price for a Dublin house sold at auction was set in June 1998 when a British businessman, Mr Terry Coleman, paid £5.9 million for Sorrento House on 1.5 acres of gardens overlooking the coast in Dalkey. He has since been refused planning permission to extend the house.

Lisney, the selling agents for 32 Herbert Park, originally quoted a guide price of £2.5 million but subsequently moved it up to £3 million because of the high level of interest.

Mr Tom Day of Lisney, who conducted yesterday's auction, attributed the high price to the fact that few detached houses have come on the market in Dublin 4 during the past two years, despite an ever-increasing demand from families who want to move close to the city centre to avoid traffic problems.

Herbert Park has become one of the most expensive residential roads in Dublin because of its proximity to the city and due to being on the edge of a particularly well-maintained public park. There was a packed auction room when bidding opened at £2 million. Five people chased the house, offering individual bids of £250,000 until it was declared 'on the market' at £3.5 million. The

President McAleese with Mr Nelson Mandela at a ceremony in Trinity College when they were conferred with honorary degrees from The University of Dublin. Photograph: Eric Luke.

The long, hard climb to the top. Opposition leader John Bruton needs a helping hand. Photograph: Matt Kavanagh.

bidding continued until the price hit the £5 million mark. At that stage, Mr Davin upped the ante with a final bid of £300,000 which brought the auction to an end.

The three-storey house is exceptionally spacious with almost 4,800 sq. ft of floor space, including two interconnecting reception rooms and a breakfast room. One of the seven bedrooms leads to a big first-floor conservatory. The garden includes a purpose-built garage with its own clock tower and basement games room. It could be converted into a mews house because it has a separate entrance off Argyle Road.

A Matter of Time and Space

John Kelly

I might first describe some fanciful writing day. I'd get up at dawn, take the horse for a gallop down to the trout stream, fish for a bit, check on the deer and then return for breakfast at about eight. I'd then retire to my workspace, a converted outhouse at the end of the big field, and settle down.

I'd stay there for an intensive, three-hour stint from nine until mid-day, with no phone-calls, faxes, e-mails or postmen. Noon would be the time to wander back to the house, grill the trout, read the paper and take the dogs (wolfhounds) for a walk up the mountain.

At about two I'd deal with post, faxes, etc., and politely (via my heavy-duty agent) refuse all requests for interviews and readings in awkward places, maybe agreeing to do just a couple, in the US mainly or Rome. The agent would then talk turkey and sort out the details. By three, all the messy stuff is over and it's back to the desk to review the morning's work and tidy it up. If I weren't in writing mode, I might read for an hour or two — time spent at the desk is never wasted —

and then knock off about four, have a doze, eat around eight, cheese and wine in the conservatory and bed by eleven. That's about it.

My reality however is somewhat different. I write whenever I get the chance and even then I'm very rarely in the mood for it. Being busy with other more urgent duties is the complaint of any writer who is not full-time. I have constant deadlines with newspapers and definite obligations to radio, so my day must be planned, first and foremost, around those. Work for which I am contracted and paid must take precedence over any speculative novel-writing or bits of poems.

That of course is the mortgage talking and, at the moment, it talks rather more persuasively than the muse.

Pat McCabe once told me that if I ever actually got to the point where I could devote myself solely to writing then at least I might feel I'd earned it. Certainly I would love to be able to live a writer's life and have a writer's day but in the meantime I just snatch the time when I have it. I write on the DART and over a sandwich. To actually finish *The Little Hammer*, I took a week's leave, headed for France and stuck at it for a solid final week: it was the only way I would ever have got the thing done. It's all a matter of time and space. After that comes the minor consideration of actually having something to write about. But I'll worry about that some other time, if I get a moment.

Stunned Silence and a Blank Stare from Nevin as the Verdicts Sink In

Nuala Haughey

There was a soft knock on the jury room door. The court fell silent, the atmosphere became tense. Then the sombre-faced jurors filed out for the final time and delivered their verdicts of guilt upon guilt.

Catherine Nevin's face betrayed nothing of her emotions as the forewoman's words condemned her to life in prison. There were no swoons, no gasps, no exclamations from any quarter in the packed and stiflingly warm courtroom. Just a stunned silence as the import of the verdicts sank in.

Nevin sat as she had throughout the 42-day trial, bolt upright, her hands on her lap, staring blankly straight ahead. Her sister, Ms Betty White, sat at her side, fighting back tears. Her brother, Mr Vincent Scully, sat behind them.

At one point, he laid a consoling hand on Nevin's shoulder.

At the rear of the courtroom, some of Tom Nevin's relatives wiped the tears from their eyes, the strain and uncertainty of their long ordeal at last over.

More than four years have passed since their brother, a gentle, kind and decent man, was shot at close range by a contract killer at the behest of their sister-in-law, his wife of 20 years.

Then it was the turn of the trial judge to direct harsh words at Nevin, who rose to face her. Her voice breaking with emotion, Miss Justice Carroll told her she had assassinated her husband and also tried to assassinate his character.

When the judge left the court, Nevin's legal team and friends crowded round her. Outside the courtroom in the Round Hall, Tom's brothers and sisters shook hands with friends, relatives, gardaí and journalists. They phoned family and friends on their mobiles to share the news. 'I'm delighted,' said Tom's brother, Patsy. 'I thought it wouldn't happen today after all the waiting.'

'Her voice breaking with emotion, Miss Justice Carroll told her she had assassinated her husband and also tried to assassinate his character.' Photograph: Eric Luke.

Minutes later, Nevin was led to the van which drove her to Mountjoy prison.

Then Tom Nevin's seven siblings emerged to the steps of the Four Courts in the evening sunlight. They stood with their heads high, their pale eyes welling with tears. Dignified to the last.

FRIDAY, 14 APRIL 2000

Revelations Are the Tip of an Iceberg in Squalid Episode

Paul Cullen

I t is, arguably, the most shocking and squalid episode in the history of the Irish public service. Here was a leading bureaucrat in the State's most populous county, a man with more than 40 years of experience, bagging a stream of illicit payments from builders, developers and property-owners — the very people whose business he was charged with regulating.

That George Redmond's conviction is based on tax charges alone cannot hide the enormity of the allegations he still faces. The fact that he failed to declare hundreds of thousands of pounds in secret payments led to the tax charges; the circumstances in which this money was paid may yet lead to far more serious charges.

Perhaps the main tragedy is that all this has finally come to pass now, more than a decade after Redmond retired from his job as assistant Dublin city and county manager, a post which made him *de facto* manager of Dublin County Council. The 75-year-old is now a broken man, in ill-health and, according to his lawyers, 'effectively destitute'.

Redmond's erstwhile pals, the developers he so loved to play golf or have lunch with, are well-insulated from opprobrium or financial punishment with the vast fortunes they acquired through land speculation and rezoning. Meanwhile, the man from Artane has had to sell his family home to meet the demands of the Revenue. Even the £750,000 this raised falls well short of the £780,000 Revenue bill and the £7,500 fine imposed yesterday.

Redmond coveted money, and hoarded it like a miser. In 1988, his investments were worth £660,000 at a time when his take-home pay was just £19,000.

Still, he brought his lunch to work in a sandwich box, and drove a 12-year-old car. He would read the tops of the newspapers in the filling station rather than buy them.

Apart from foreign holidays — his winter tan was ahead of the fashion — it was hard to see where the money was spent. At least, that is, until he was found returning from the Isle of Man last year with his pockets and bags stuffed with almost £300,000 in cash and cheques.

Now that his luck has run out, sympathy is in short supply. Former colleagues recall a tyrannical boss, quick to find fault with his staff, who ran his department with an iron fist.

Even in the witness-box in Dublin Castle, he was tetchy and argumentative on minor points, while at the same time failing to see the moral black hole at the heart of his universe.

If he were to do the State some service now, it would be to reveal fully and openly his dealings with developers, politicians and government ministers, and to explain fully his and their motives. If there ever was a web of intrigue and scandal, Redmond was the man at the centre; he had the knowledge, the information, the connections and the authority to make or break a developer.

Not only did he, in the words of the tribunal, receive an 'extraordinary' number of payments, he was also in close contact with senior government figures throughout the 1970s and 1980s. In particular, he would have had an intimate knowledge of the events surrounding the rezoning of Quarryvale. In 1989, Redmond was summoned to meet Mr Haughey and other senior ministers who were anxious to further the plans of developer Mr Tom Gilmartin to build a massive shopping centre on the site. In the event, Mr Gilmartin's plans fell apart. It was only in the 1990s — after Redmond had retired — that another developer succeeded in getting Quarryvale rezoned.

Redmond has expressed some signs of contrition, but the key question is whether he will now co-operate with the Flood tribunal.

In his explanations so far, the money he got was usually for advice which his friends could have got from the planning department anyway. (So why pay so much for what was freely available?) And it was usually unsolicited, he said.

Only this week, we learned of Redmond's remarkable arrangement with the builder Mr Tom Brennan, by which the builder would send money to the council official. At the tribunal Mr Brennan claimed he would bet his own money on hot tips at the races, then pay over the winnings to Redmond. A harmless little arrangement — until you learn that it netted Redmond up to £50,000 back in the 1970s and early 1980s.

It was also reported that Redmond had an arrangement with the owner of an amusement arcade business. Redmond was a 'sleeping partner' in the arcade business and its owner paid him £5,000, according to an RTÉ report which Redmond later denied.

Redmond says he was given £25,000 from Mr James Gogarty of JMSE, this merely for introducing Mr Gogarty to the developer Mr Michael Bailey.

'If there ever was a web of intrigue and scandal, Redmond was the man at the centre; he had the knowledge, the information, the connections and the authority to make or break a developer.' Photograph: Matt Kavanagh.

Mr Gogarty's version is that his company paid £15,000 in return for planning advice, and another £15,000 in compensation for a consultancy arrangement that never came to fruition.

Then there was the £10,000 'personal thank-you' Mr Tom Roche Snr of National Toll Roads plc allegedly paid to Redmond for his help in advancing the West Link bridge project. Or £2,000 from Mr Liam Conroy of JMSE for his planning help.

These are only the tip of the iceberg. We'll be hearing lots more this year about Redmond's sources of income as the tribunal continues its trawl through the darker reaches of Dublin planning. Is everyone sleeping comfortably?

SATURDAY, 15 APRIL 2000

Maeve's Times

Maeve Binchy

So here we go, my last regular column. I promised myself a year of advising the nation about love, families, life, behaviour and money — now it's over. And my most sincere gratitude to all those who wrote in.

Huge post-bags about anything at all to do with money, much smaller ones about matters of the heart.

Fairly substantial male objection that we were all far too nosy, hands-on and manipulative in the lives of others. They would apparently let everyone run lemming-like to their doom without having even the mildest crisis intervention.

Quite a few older women readers accused me of making up not only these problems but all the answers as well, which presupposes an amazing swansong year of writing myself letters and awarding myself book tokens, while giving real names and addresses.

I was told that I only published letters that agreed with me, which can't be true. Do you remember the time a woman wrote in saying her father didn't want a funeral? I advised her to take no notice of his last wishes and give him a great funeral. Just about nobody agreed with me, but I published a rake of their letters.

I made a lot of friends too, people who wrote in every single month even if only to apologise that they hadn't any real insight about the particular problem in question, but had been giving it thought.

And I got to know, through their letters, some of the wise pupils of Killina Secondary School, Rahan near Tullamore, whose teacher, Stephanie Connor, suggested they deal with Ireland's angst every month.

They took everything seriously, as I wanted people to do, and sent amazing advice about bungee-jumping to cheer up the lonely or depressed.

And of course I believe that the whole thing was a vitally important social *fin de siecle* document, pinpointing exactly how the people of Ireland felt about everything over this past year.

There are ways that I would love to put up for examination the 11 problems that I still have on my desk, including one about soliloquies at funerals, one about telling your female friend that she is growing a moustache and one about how to ask a colleague could you please have the £100 back.

And there are ways that I will miss creeping into Glenageary sorting office, to collect my Post Office box mail, terrified that they might think I was getting literature about rubber or leather fetishes and even more terrified in case there would be no answers to my *Irish Times* problems at all, and nobody would have written in.

But it would have to stop eventually — this worrying myself sick over other people's anxieties, and getting the rest of you to worry too.

So a chronological age seemed a good time to go.

The experts all advise against ever shutting any door too firmly if you can manage it, so the occasional article from time to time would be lovely. It won't be considered a tenor's farewell, if I slide in with the odd thing to say now and then.

And I thought I should stop it while I still had a pulse and was able to get on with things, which was why I asked for this last column of 'Help Yourself' to offer advice about letting go.

The good news is that the jury is no longer out, retirement is the way to go. You just call it different things — like change, or moving on, or relaxing, or progressing. Those are the kind of words you use — instead of anything to do with age, sell-by dates or out to grass.

This time I was very, very proud to collect the huge contents of the PO Box — there were marvellous ideas.

Buy a country house and get horses. Thank you again Tullamore, but if you only knew how terrified I am of horses …

Go to tap-dancing lessons. Yes, of course we all want to. I did try 25 years ago at the London Dance Centre and even bought the T-shirt which we used to mop our faces as we thought the palpitations would never die down.

Learn a verse of poetry every single day. That's a good idea. I'll try next week, but doesn't it take six months to learn a verse of poetry at our age? It certainly takes a year to learn what you should respond with when your partner opens two no trumps, once you've picked yourself up off the ground, and I suppose we could all have coped with that if we had learned it at the age of 10.

Be an extra in movies. Hmmm, I'm not totally sure. I've seen them — it's exhausting — you'd be better off working. The only time I was ever an extra, everyone else went to Make-up and Wardrobe to dress up as a 1950s person, and apparently I didn't need to.

Learn juggling tricks. Well yes, but honestly, where exactly would you do them? I've only recently stopped singing terrifying versions of 'The Purple People Eater' at folk whom I wrongly imagined to be entertained by it.

Write to the Retirement Planning Council of Ireland — it'll set you straight, sending brochures and packages and advising you about its courses. There's also *The Retirement Book* by Anne Dempsey, which it publishes. It is full of info and you can buy it in bookshops or through the Council at 27 Lower Pembroke Street, Dublin 2.

Listen to John Quinn's radio programme, 'L Plus: Living and Learning Beyond 50'. Yes, I tried to do that, but like thousands of others, missed most of it as it was on at a time when we were all still at work. However, they say it will be repeated in autumn at a more suitable time of day. And if you write to John Quinn at RTÉ he will send you the comprehensive brochure, packed with information and addresses.

Go to computer/Internet classes and get control of the thing while you still have the marbles. Yes, fine, but suppose they don't have them in your area?

According to Michael Gorman — who knows about these things — you just get a group of like-minded people together, say 12, and then go to your local adult education centre and ask for a class. You'll get one.

There were hundreds more letters. Positive, reassuring, encouraging and affirming that we are not our jobs, we are ourselves. I have no fear that the summer will hang long and heavily in my hands. Or that the years ahead will be without purpose.

I've seen too many writers caught up in the treadmill of writing books for the mass market who grew old and crotchety having to deliver so many words every two years and tramp around the world promoting them. I've been at festivals, promotions, literary lunches and book signings with them and heard them sigh and groan. This is wrong, that is wrong, the distances in airports are getting longer, the audience out there is getting younger. And the publishers ever more demanding.

One evening last year I shared a platform with a much older writer who had the nearest thing to a nervous breakdown in public that I have ever seen. She sent back the food, kept tinkling her glass

Ruby Walsh riding high. Photograph: Alan Betson.

with her fork to complain that others were speaking too long, bit the head off anyone who asked for an autograph … which was, after all, why she was there.

'This is intolerable,' she said to me over and over. 'Why don't you stop, then, and give up?' I asked mildly. Stop? Give up? It had taken so long, it was so hard to claw your way up to here, how could anyone think of stopping at this point?

I unwisely suggested that she might possibly have enough money now, an understatement of colossal proportions.

'Nobody has enough money,' she snapped. That was the moment I decided to retire, and since that time I have never changed my mind. There is

no lingering regret, because in a way I suppose we all slow down anyway, without realising it.

I look out at the roads in Dalkey that I used to run down, yes run down, to get the train into the schools I was teaching at, or to *The Irish Times* office, and I can't imagine where the energy could have come from.

I see the Number Nine bus when I go back to London and remember how I caught that at Olympia for years at 7 a.m. and got out in Fleet Street for a banana sandwich in Chubbies and into a job which might mean going to any part of the map that day.

Nowadays, going to work is a walk up a spiral staircase to a desk so full of things promised, but not achieved, that the day begins with a monumental sense of guilt.

There has never been time to decide exactly which 80 per cent of the papers and files cluttering every drawer and every shelf should go and which 20 per cent should stay.

Any de-cluttering I have ever done up to now has involved throwing out things like my passport and my letter from Flann O'Brien, while retaining acrimonious correspondence with a dry cleaners 30 years ago about an outfit that had only been worn three times and had now shrunk to a doll's size. A very small doll's size. I don't remember either the outfit or the incident, but out of panic I kept the file.

There will be weeks and months ahead to sort things like that out. Many great happy trips to the dump in Ballyogan Road. There will be journeys without lugging the laptop along, and evenings sitting down in the garden, reading books written by other people instead of sitting upstairs at the desk writing lying faxes to publishers about my own books, claiming they are nearly finished when in fact they are barely begun.

I have this notion that when the phone rings it might be a friend from now on, rather than someone wondering where something promised is. And there could be times when there's lovely sunshine when we might take the DART to Howth for lunch instead of saying that it would take too many hours out of the working day.

I do not believe those who say I will regret it and find myself at a loose end at 11 every morning.

I will not be like a man I knew who woke at 6.30 a.m. every day for two years after his retirement and lay anxiously in bed wondering if the office was in chaos without him.

Nor a neighbour in London who said she was afraid she was very dull, because since she didn't go out to work she had no conversation. Actually her conversation about work had been excruciating, she was far more entertaining on gardening.

I will have another huge novel out at the end of August and of course I have plenty of short stories already written, published here and there, and collected neatly in a big ring file. They can appear from time to time in tasteful collections.

I do not believe that people get sluggish and brain-dead and go round in their dressing gowns when they retire. I think they get better.

Some of my best role models and the happiest people I know are those who have retired and cannot find enough hours in the day to do the things they like doing. They are free from guilt and fuss and are very restful without having actually gone to sleep. I've been looking at them wistfully for about six months now. And it's not that I haven't had a great time at work. I've enjoyed every job I had in four decades.

The days as a waitress, though exhausting, were great; teaching in Cork, though lonely, meant I met a lot of great kids. I had eight years in Pembroke School, Dublin, teaching history, which I loved, and taught my pupils so well that they eventually became my bosses. I taught in Zion Schools, Dublin, met the entire Jewish community, who made me very welcome, and last week I met many of them again in Israel.

At the age of 28 I came as an ageing cub to *The Irish Times*, where everything was, and is, all I could have hoped for in a newspaper. They even let me follow my heart over to its London office when I was keen on a fellow over there, and they let us come back when the fellow and I bought a house in Dalkey.

Publishers in many lands have got my storybooks out there into the shops where booksellers have put them in their windows and people have bought them.

I am more grateful for all this than I can say.

When I was a child I was what was then called a Notice Box — someone who wanted a lot of attention.

And on behalf of us Notice Boxes everywhere, let me say that attention is not always easy to get. So for the very great amount I was able to grab from you all, thank you from the bottom of my heart.

How Dunlop Delivered Bundles of Joy

Frank McNally

Conway's pub is a favourite destination for fathers celebrating happy events across the road in the Rotunda Hospital. Perhaps the odd midwife stops in too.

But the pub was also popular with Dublin county councillors, especially after meetings at headquarters around the corner in O'Connell Street; and thus it was in Conway's that lobbyist

'Asked if the £40,000 had been handed over in the briefcase in which he carried it, he said no: he had taken it out and put it in a plastic bag. "My briefcase was a leather one," he explained.' Photograph: Matt Kavanagh.

Frank Dunlop says he delivered several little bundles of joy to grateful public representatives in 1991.

One weighed in at a bouncing £15,000, delivered in cash at the pub after a meeting in the middle of the local election campaign, and around the time of the first Quarryvale rezoning vote.

The Dáil bar also heard the patter of lobbyists' feet, as a small but healthy £2,000 was handed to another grateful recipient. Some were home deliveries, like the £12,000 given to one of a 'team' of councillors who were working 'hand in glove' with the Quarryvale developers; and the biggest bundle of all — £40,000 in a bag — was handed over in Dunlop's office, to the team's unnamed key player.

It was the most dramatic evidence yet at the Flood Tribunal. Mr Dunlop looked shaken and spoke almost in a whisper at times. But his memory had much improved since Tuesday, when he was asked to 'reflect' overnight; and his reflections were not without humour.

Asked if the £40,000 had been handed over in the briefcase in which he carried it, he said no: he had taken it out and put it in a plastic bag. 'My briefcase was a leather one,' he explained. There was laughter in the gallery then, and also when he attempted tortuously to comply with a direction not to identify councillors' gender. 'He … or she,' he said once, with an unduly long interval, provoking his lawyer to suggest he use the term 'it' instead.

The lobbyist's relationship to councillors was as much anaesthetist as midwife, his evidence suggested, dispensing a range of reliefs according to individual need. Several were administered modest £1,000 sums, after general discussions about the discomfort of election expenses. Others demanded specific amounts, including one with a particularly low pain threshold, who got £20,000 but wanted more.

Mr Dunlop's evidence came in two parts, before and after lunch. The latter portion, taking a mere 20 minutes or so, covered 13 of the 15 councillors allegedly paid. It was testimony that changed the complexion of the tribunal, and the effort of delivering it changed Mr Dunlop's colour too.

Shortly before 3 p.m., he asked to stand down for five minutes. He walked, slightly stooped, into the quietest corner of the hall; and then to a private room. A short while later, counsel for the tribunal said he had been told the witness was 'unwell … and I believe that to be the case'.

Mr Justice Flood adjourned the hearings until 9 May, announcing that the 'highly sensitive' list of names would be sealed in an envelope in the meantime and placed in his safe.

THURSDAY, 20 APRIL 2000

Bribery and Corruption

Editorial

The Flood Tribunal may have started slowly, but yesterday's evidence from public relations consultant, Mr Frank Dunlop, is momentous. Mr Dunlop admitted that he paid £112,000 to 15 Dublin councillors before they voted on the Quarryvale shopping centre proposal and in the run-up to the 1991 local elections.

He says he delivered money to a number of councillors' homes, gave another representative £2,000 in the Dáil bar and no less than £48,000 to another councillor — a 'powerful man' — most of it in cash contained in a plastic bag. Mr Dunlop said he was working 'hand in glove' with a number of the councillors on rezoning the Quarryvale land.

No matter what interpretation is put on events by Mr Dunlop, there is only one word for what went on. That is: corruption. Councillors, elected to serve their community, were offered and accepted what amounted to bribes, in some cases dressed up as contributions to their election costs — to rezone land.

There have been suspicions for years about 'brown paper envelopes' in the planning process. Many of the rezoning decisions of the 1980s and early 1990s were, to say the least, baffling. Media reports, including many in this newspaper, from time to time quoted anonymous sources as saying that cash was often paid to get land rezoned.

Nonetheless, Mr Dunlop's evidence is shocking. The former Fianna Fáil government press secretary and now public relations consultant and political lobbyist, appears to have decided overnight to tell all to the tribunal. No doubt the discovery of a bank account in his name out of which £250,000 was paid around the time of the Quarryvale rezoning, helped to jog his memory.

That a former government press secretary should use his political contacts in such a fashion is outrageous. In time, Mr Justice Flood will have to come to a conclusion on the matter and no doubt he will not mince his words. But the Flood Tribunal still has much work to do. Mr Dunlop told it yesterday that he was reimbursed by the developer of Quarryvale, Mr Owen O'Callaghan, for the money paid to councillors. Mr O'Callaghan has said he is looking forward to giving his side of the story.

The Tribunal will also, no doubt, summon the councillors named by Mr Dunlop and question them on his evidence. They are entitled to be represented and to give their version of events. And the Tribunal will certainly be examining their financial records. It is clear that a number of them have very difficult questions to answer about seeking and accepting very substantial sums.

The full political implications of the evidence heard at the Tribunal yesterday will take some time to unfold. But they will be immense. Political careers will be destroyed. There will be questions about who else in the political and planning system knew what was going on. And the public will become even more sceptical about how politics has operated in this State.

The Flood Tribunal, after months hearing evidence about alleged payments to Mr Ray Burke, has now uncovered evidence of vital public interest in its investigations into Quarryvale. It is a

continuation of the extraordinary revelations — shocking and saddening — by the McCracken and Moriarty Tribunals. There must be shame and anger at how so much of public life was conducted during the late 1980s and the early 1990s.

FRIDAY, 21 APRIL 2000

Remains of Boy Killed in Omagh Exhumed

George Jackson

The coffin of James Barker, one of three boys from Buncrana, Co Donegal, who died in the Omagh bombing in August 1998, was exhumed from the local cemetery yesterday.

His mother, Mrs Donna-Maria Barker, and other relatives accompanied the remains to England last night. They will be reinterred in the grounds of James's former school, St George's Preparatory School, at Weybridge, Surrey, tomorrow.

'Moving James was a very difficult decision for the family to make, but it is the best decision for us all. We must look to the future and James is now on his way home,' Mrs Barker said before leaving her home at Military Road, Buncrana, yesterday after the exhumation.

The exhumation was attended by Mrs Barker as well as by local priest Father Shane Bradley and gardaí and health officials.

'We are not turning our backs on Ireland. We were very, very happy here and James loved the country, but Ireland has had James for 18 months and now we want to bring him home,' she said.

'We moved to Buncrana from Surrey in September 1997 and James had 10 wonderful months here before our world was turned upside down.' James was 12 on 2 August and he died at 6.47 p.m. on 15 August in hospital in Omagh.

'Now all we want is peace of mind, but I think it will be a very long time before we ever get it.'

After the exhumation the coffin was brought to the Barker family home where it was placed in the sitting-room beneath a large portrait of James. Mrs Barker, who constantly touched the coffin, said she could still see her son, swinging off the sitting-room railing, asking her if she wanted a cup of coffee.

'I can see his little side glance, his eyes, his hair, in the corner of the room. His sister Estella takes his T-shirt to bed with her every night; sometimes she takes his dictionary, anything at all that belongs to James.'

Mrs Barker's children, Erin Esther (21) and Oliver-Tristan (5), are returning with her to Surrey to live with her husband, Victor.

Estella (15) will remain in the family home with relatives until she receives the results of her GCSE examinations in August. She will then join her family. After she leaves, the Barker family plan to sell their Buncrana home.

'It is like starting a new life all over again, but that is what we want and what we deserve. We have paid a very high price for our dream to have been shattered.

'James will be buried behind the chapel in his former school because he had very happy times there. It is really what is best for the family now. We all miss James dearly. Time does not heal, it just makes the void bigger,' said Mrs Barker.

The hearse containing the coffin was escorted

Bertie Ahern and David Trimble struggle on with the peace process. Photograph: Eric Luke.

by gardaí to the Derry-Donegal border at Bridgend near Derry, from where it was given an RUC escort to Belfast International Airport.

TUESDAY, 25 APRIL 2000

Vietnamese Doctors Convinced Agent Orange Is Still At Work

Conor O'Clery

In the corridor of a clinic of Bach Mai hospital in Hanoi, bewildered and sad children hang around with their parents in the morning heat. Some wait for fittings of thermo-plastic braces from a prosthetics workshop at the end of the corridor, others to have their deformed limbs gently stretched and massaged by therapists.

All of the children have mental and physical defects and most are almost certainly the victims of Agent Orange. Twenty-five years after the end of the war in Vietnam, during which US Air Force C123s sprayed 76 million litres of herbicides over 14 per cent of the land surface, it is 'Apocalypse Still' for its children.

More than 300,000 children born long after the war are suffering from mental retardation, spina bifida, cerebral palsy, immune deficiencies, liver damage, nervous system disorders, tumours and other cancers, according to Vietnam officials. With its fragile economy, the south-east Asian country lacks the resources to prove the connection between the spraying and the diseases and deformities of children and veterans. But for Vietnamese doctors the circumstantial evidence is overwhelming.

'I know of a woman from the Mekong Delta who had a normal healthy child in 1968, then had three children after exposure to Agent Orange who were all severely disabled and mentally retarded, and two were blind,' said Dr Tran Thi Thu Ha, who heads the clinic.

'They believe it was the war. We don't say that because we are scientific people. But we notice,

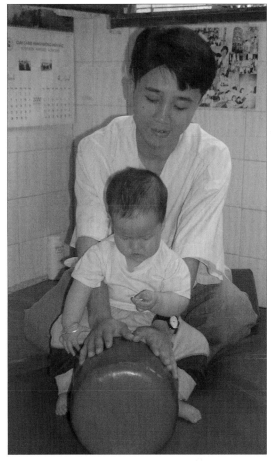

'Twenty-five years after the end of the war in Vietnam, during which US Air Force C123s sprayed 76 million litres of herbicides over 14 per cent of the land surface, it is "Apocalypse Still" for its children.'

especially in families where the father suffered in wartime, that there are more disabled children and children with brain damage.'

While 100 children a day turn up at the clinic, Vietnamese peasants are mostly too poor to make the long journey to Hanoi and undertake rehabilitation courses, said the Russian-trained physician.

'Others come and then they disappear.'

The United States, which has spent more than $200 million on research into the consequences of using Agent Orange for US veterans, accepts no responsibility for the ill effects of Operation Ranch

Hand, which doused trees and rice paddies in the acid and fuel mixture from 1962 to 1970.

One of its by-products is dioxin, possible the world's most dangerous molecule, which has entered the food chain through soil, fish and ducks, according to Hatfield Consultants, a team of Canadian experts who surveyed Quang Tri province in central Vietnam last year.

They found some nursing mothers had levels of dioxin in their breast milk 300 times more than enough to kill a laboratory animal and estimated that it could be decades before Vietnam's rains cleanse the land.

Many Vietnamese believe that if something evil happens, it is because of bad things done earlier in life, and this is an added source of agony to former soldiers who killed in battle.

It is left to individuals like Mr Chuck Searcy, a Vietnam veteran from Georgia, to make amends for America's chemical warfare.

Mr Searcy is the representative in Hanoi of the Vietnam Veterans of America Foundation, which has established two children's clinics there, staffed by four doctors and nine technicians, with some funding from USAID.

'It is very rewarding and gratifying to be back here in a capacity that is moderately helpful rather than destructive,' said Mr Searcy, who spent a year at a US base in Saigon where he heard reports of major spills of Agent Orange.

'I'm not seeking redemption, but I do feel responsible for the destruction and tragedy of the war and America's role in it.'

At the clinic at Bach Mai hospital, which was bombed by American B52s during the Vietnam War, Mr Searcy reflected on the rewards of treating deformities, which would without orthotic treatment leave children able only to crawl.

'You know,' he said, 'it's really wonderful to see a kid beaming with new self-esteem as it walks for the first time.'

Irish Facing New Phase in Lebanon War

Lara Marlowe

How do you wait for an army to retreat? In a week or two — at most seven — Israel's last soldiers in southern Lebanon will withdraw under Hizbullah fire. And the Irish will be in the middle of it.

Lieut Robert Kearney of the Irish 87th Infantry Battalion showed me around his frontline observation post. His men were playing volleyball within the confines of one of their most forward positions. Three sentries were watching the Israelis through binoculars. Be sure the Israelis were watching them.

A few minutes earlier, Hizbullah guerrillas had attacked a nearby 'South Lebanon Army' (SLA) compound, but the Shia movement's heavy machinegun, anti-tank missile and mortar assaults on Israel's militia allies are a daily occurrence here.

Irish troops are barely fazed by the explosions which they so carefully record for the archives of the United Nations Interim Force in Lebanon. When their own lives are endangered — as they were by SLA heavy machine gun fire into another Irish position the previous evening — the response is more angry, but equally impotent.

If Lebanon is on the verge of liberation, the Shaqra position feels like a prison. Irish soldiers are surrounded by 10-foot high gabions — thick walls of crushed stone topped with barbed wire.

Their watchtower faces the Israeli-occupied zone — indeed, one of the volleyball teams has arrived in an armoured personnel carrier from a sister position down the road inside the zone. Giant, scab-like crests — a series of SLA and Israeli compounds soon to be abandoned — dot the horizon, staring menacingly at the small Irish positions.

Afternoon tea and sweet nothings in her ear. Euro MP Patricia McKenna takes a break with her colleagues.
Photograph: Matt Kavanagh.

The young officer from Kilkenny is new to Lebanon, but Lieut Kearney's unit has already seen its share of action. Just seven days ago, Hizbullah guerrillas drove up next to the Irish position. The sentry sounded the alert and the Irishmen went to 'groundhog' — bomb shelters.

The Hizbullah were driving a silver pick-up with a TOW wire-guided missile launcher in the back. 'It made a hissing noise as it went over our heads,' Lieut Kearney said, pointing at the copper missile wire still entangled in the unit's electrical power line. The TOW exploded 50 metres short of its target, an SLA compound on the hillside opposite the Irish.

The Israeli-backed militia usually retaliates against the Irish troops or the villages they are trying to protect. Within the past five weeks the Shaqra position has been hit twice by .5 heavy machine gun rounds. Lieut Kearney showed me a large stone with burn marks that was split by one round. The other left a half-inch hole through the ceiling of one of the unit's billets.

What would happen if one of these rounds hit him? 'There wouldn't be much left of me,' Lieut Kearney answered. At the Haddatha position two weeks ago an entire billet was destroyed. It is the surprise explosions — such as the Israeli Merkava tank round that killed Cpl Dermot McLoughlin while he slept in his Bradchit village position in 1987 — that are most lethal.

When the soldiers of Irishbatt are not on checkpoint, patrol or observation duty, much of their time is spent thinking and talking about the Israeli withdrawal. The pullout — for which the

Lebanese and the Irish have waited 22 years — has already started, with the SLA and the Israelis abandoning several positions. But the bulk of Israeli forces, some 1,500 men, are expected to leave suddenly, some time before 7 July.

UN headquarters in New York has not yet decided what to do. The role of 535 soldiers in Irishbatt will depend on decisions taken by the UN, the Israeli, Lebanese and Syrian governments, and especially Dublin.

If the SLA is not disarmed — one of the greatest dangers — UNIFIL will consider that no withdrawal has taken place, and the Irish and other battalions will stay put. Although no firm orders have been given, the assumption is that in the event of a real withdrawal, stationary units will be transformed into mobile armoured infantry. The Irish soldiers would fan out through the 8 km broad zone separating their battalion from the Israeli border.

You might think that a time of such danger and uncertainty would slow recruitment. On the contrary — there have never been so many Irish volunteers for Lebanon — and most of them have served with UNIFIL before. If you include the men deployed with the Force Mobile Reserve and at headquarters in Naqoura, Ireland has 650 soldiers in Lebanon — by far the State's largest military commitment abroad.

Over 22 years, Irish soldiers have served more than 26,000 individual tours of duty in the area. Forty-four have lost their lives here, the highest

Meals on wheels. 'Most of the volunteers are more than 60 years old and it is not uncommon to have volunteers in their mid-70s delivering meals to much younger clients.'

price paid by any contributing state. That each battalion's flag is sent to Arbour Hill, the chapel opposite Collins Barracks where the dead of the Easter Rising are buried, is a measure of the mission's importance.

Lieut Col Chris Moore, the commanding officer of the 87th battalion, says the 535 Irish soldiers under his command could not be more aware of the crucial moment of their deployment. 'They all feel they are living in historic times,' he said in his office at Camp Shamrock, the battalion's headquarters at Tibnin.

'They are extraordinarily hopeful for the people of southern Lebanon. I first came here in 1982, and I know several generations of local families. We have lived here among the people and suffered with them. The feeling that you're in a situation where history is being made is very strong.'

But as Lieut Col Moore knows well, the history of Lebanon and Irishbatt is as tragic as it is heroic. He is still haunted by the memory of discovering the bodies of three Irish soldiers who were murdered by a colleague on Tibnin bridge in 1982.

The colonel — along with all of UNIFIL — received orders to 'move out of the way' when Israel staged its massive 1982 invasion. In the aftermath, he and his colleagues had to respect UNIFIL passes given to plainclothes Israeli agents who kidnapped Lebanese and Palestinians in the peacekeepers' area of operations.

According to Brig Gen Jim Sreenan, the Deputy Force Commander of UNIFIL and overall Irish contingent commander, the three key dates of UNIFIL's deployment were the 1982 Israeli invasion; the July 1993 assault which the Israelis called 'Operation Accountability' and the three-week April 1996 bombardment which Israel named 'Grapes of Wrath'.

'You had hundreds of thousands of civilians fleeing north of the Litani River,' Gen Sreenan explained. 'These people would never have returned if UNIFIL hadn't existed. Southern Lebanon would have been a free-fire zone. We set up the conditions that allowed them to come back.'

One of the principal fears about Israel's imminent withdrawal is that Israeli aircraft and gunboats will fire massively on southern Lebanon in response to Hizbullah attacks, as they did in 1993 and 1996. Both times Irishbatt sheltered terrified civilians and used its vehicles to transport refugees and wounded.

'Yes, 1993 and 1996 were terrible, dreadful experiences,' Lieut Col Moore said. Could the summer of 2000 be like that again? 'Yes it could,' he answered. But the Irish officer's belief that southern Lebanon may soon regain its freedom seems to outweigh his apprehension about the danger of bad days to come.

'The Israelis have been retaliating into this bloody place for as long as I care to remember,' he said. 'So what's new?'

TUESDAY, 23 MAY 2000

The Square Meals that the Elderly Can't Live Without

Rosita Boland

It's 11.30 a.m. in the bright cheerful canteen of the Little Flower Centre in Dublin's Meath Street, and the day's delivery of 'meals on wheels' to some 40 people is being put into foil containers. The drivers are standing by, waiting to carry the meals out to the parish van, where they'll make an hour-long circuit of the area. On the menu today is chicken drumsticks with beans and mash, and apple crumble and custard.

Cooks Deirdre Flynn and Marie Claxton get paid by the centre, but the three drivers who work on rotas from Monday to Friday are volunteers. Since the runs are at mid-day, volunteers tend to be retired people, who can be available at that time of day. Finding reliable people who are consistent time-keepers is an essential part of the equation: if they don't turn up in time, the meals will either get cold or run the risk of not being delivered.

In the Eastern Health Board's 10 Year Action Plan for Services for Older Persons 1999–2008, the section on meals on wheels notes that among areas of concern are: 'Recruitment of volunteers. Most of the volunteers are more than 60 years old and it is not uncommon to have volunteers in their mid-70s delivering meals to much younger clients. Availability of drivers to deliver the meals is more of a problem than finding volunteers to prepare or cook meals.'

Sister Bridget Phelan is the manager of the Little Flower. 'If someone drops out, I'll do the driving myself,' she says. Drivers Con O'Connor and Willie Redmond are in the centre, and both are modest and candid about their reasons for volunteering. 'The day's too long, you might as well be doing something,' O'Connor says. Redmond adds: 'I'd be bored sitting at home all day.' While they're waiting for the meals to be boxed, they're obviously thinking again about why they volunteer to drive twice a week, since O'Connor turns around, shrugs, and simply says, 'Especially in this day and age …' (This is the same week that George Redmond is telling the Flood Tribunal a few streets away that he cannot afford to eat lunch in town.)

The meals from this centre are delivered Monday to Friday. Sometimes it happens that the people delivering the meals do not get a reply to their knock on the door. They then call back to the centre and someone goes on foot to see if there is anything amiss. Occasionally, people are found dead. More often, they have fallen and cannot get up, and the people who deliver meals on wheels are the first to notice. Sister Phelan reckons that 80 per cent of the people who receive meals on wheels in their area are living on their own.

In Britain, various local bodies are currently experimenting with a new tack on providing meals for the home-bound elderly. Devon County Council has a scheme in which a month's supply of frozen meals is delivered in one go. Microwaves are provided. The argument is that people will then be able to eat at whatever time of the day suits them, and it cuts down on the logistics of rotas for cooking and delivery.

Silverton parish councillor Jean Roach has organised a petition of protest, saying that old people do not like change and that they would lose the regular human contact the old system involved. A similar frozen-food delivery system is in place in the north-east of England, and there are also plans to introduce it in Scotland.

At the Little Flower, cook Marie Claxton doesn't like the sound of frozen meals delivered monthly. 'This might be the only contact people would have with anyone else,' she points out. 'They could possibly not see anyone for the rest of the month.'

In the Republic, meals on wheels is provided by a number of different organisations. The health boards provide some, but not all, of the meals. A jigsaw network of local groups do the rest of the work, mainly on a voluntary basis. This *ad hoc* network varies from county to county, hence accurate figures for the number of meals being delivered is difficult to ascertain.

The Midland Health Board, for example, delivered some 99,994 meals last year, in 13 different areas of its region, to 486 people, but was unable to supply a complete set of figures for volunteer workers. The largest area was Co. Longford, which had 180 people in receipt of meals, and the smallest was Mountrath, which had just one person receiving a meal. Elsewhere, the South Eastern Health Board delivered some 155,000 meals; the Southern Health Board delivered 293,392 meals; the Eastern Health Board some 1.2 million meals; the Western Health Board 6,610 under its community nursing scheme; and the North Eastern Health Board 89,000. No figures were available for the North Western Health Board.

Once the meals have been loaded into the parish van, Sister Phelan and myself go on foot to the Oliver Bond Flats to meet some of those who are expecting meals.

May Coulter, who does not go out any more and is very hard of hearing, has been getting meals for two years. She sits at the table, the foil containers arranged neatly in front of her. Her favourite meals are beef, cabbage and potatoes. When she hears it's chicken today, she rubs her hands together happily. 'Lovely! Lovely chicken,' she croons, looking down at the as-yet-unopened foil container.

Tommy Grogan, who will be 82 this year, has been living in his current flat for 68 years. He, too, has been getting meals for some two years, ever since spending a six-week stint in hospital with a disorder connected with malnutrition. He had not been eating properly, got double pneumonia, and

spent 11 hours lying on the floor of his flat before being found.

'I'd be lost without the meals,' he says, perching on the couch of his tidy little living-room. He doesn't have a particular favourite, because he likes everything. Usually, he eats the meal as soon as it arrives. When he hears about the microwave system in use in parts of Britain, he grimaces politely. 'I'd miss the people coming every day, the jolly people. Of course I would.' He also says that he wouldn't be sure of his ability to use a microwave. 'I don't use the big part of the cooker — the oven — ever. I just use the top bit, the rings,' he offers.

At present, people pay a subsidy of 65p for their meal every day. The EHB's 10 Year Action Plan makes the point that 'all of the organisations considered that the current subsidy of 65p per meal is insufficient'. Yet the organisations still manage to prepare simple meals which are nutritious and

Women murdered in Ireland are remembered. Photograph: Joe St Leger.

varied. On the weekly menu at Little Flower recently, in which each day's meal is different, was: ham, sprouts, mash; chicken Kiev, carrots and mash; roast beef, turnips, mash; coddle, mixed vegetables, mash; corned beef, cabbage, mash. Desserts included apple tart, rice pudding, and trifle. According to Rita Fitzsimons, who has been delivering meals on wheels for all of 23 years, stew and coddle are the long-term favourites.

The meals on wheels service is available to all older people, regardless of their means, but it is usually availed of only by those who are less well off, according to Regina Buckley, who is the director of public health nursing in the Eastern Health Board.

She's aware of the microwave policy in parts of Britain, but sees problems with it. 'Would people defrost the meals properly? Would they cook the meals for the right length of time? There would need to be a lot of education given about that.

'I think meals on wheels is an invaluable service, and I'd like to see it extended to seven days a week,' she says. While the service runs Monday to Friday in most urban areas, in rural areas, it's often less. Buckley sees challenging times ahead for the meals on wheels service here. 'It's getting harder and harder to recruit volunteers,' she points out regretfully.

THURSDAY, 25 MAY 2000

Anti-Terror Exercise Wrecks Sydney Olympics Venue

Johnny Watterson

One of the venues for this year's Sydney Olympics has been left in partial ruin after an Australian Defence Force team, conducting a mock anti-terrorism exercise, took to their job like aspiring gold-medal wreckers.

Doors were kicked down, windows smashed, walls flattened and carpets damaged as the anti-terrorist squad stormed through the new Aquilina softball stadium, leaving it looking much like the Hogan Stand after the cranes had moved in. The bill for damage is estimated at tens of thousands of dollars.

A spokesman said the crack force had been given permission to conduct the hostage-recovery exercise, and the £17 million stadium would be restored to its original glory 'by the close of business' today.

'We use purpose-built buildings but we needed to offer something that the troops hadn't seen before,' the spokesman said. 'This sort of training is the most sophisticated that can be undertaken. It's a dangerous job.'

However, the exercise did not please some local residents, who first knew about it when they observed Black Hawk helicopters swarming in the sky for the mock attack. The defence spokesman said the force had tried to notify the residents about the exercise but 'could not letter-box all local areas'.

'We have to think in terms of realism,' he said. 'It's no good saying, "There's a door, we would normally break it down but on this occasion we'll just put a cross on it and pretend we've done it". We have to do these things for real.'

Not wishing to appear bent on destruction, a Defence Force spokesman said later a repair team was busy rebuilding the site.

The cost of repairs was incorporated into the overall cost of the exercise, which will come out of the New South Wales state budget, a spokeswoman added. 'For every exercise of this nature there is a damage control team always available.'

Élite forces have staged counter-terrorist exercises throughout Sydney for the last month. So far, all the other Olympic venues remain intact.

Such exercises are not unique. In the early 1980s, a special police unit practising the rescue of a hypothetical kidnapped foreign dignitary burst

into a room in Melbourne's Sheraton hotel, confronted the terrified occupants and dragged the man away. The only problem was, they stormed the wrong room, and had 'rescued' an innocent tourist.

SATURDAY, 27 MAY 2000

PDs Sucked Back into the Culture from which They Fled

Fintan O'Toole

It was one moment of madness, a single lapse in a long career of upholding the law of the land. He had interfered in the proper punishment of a drunken driver, thus frustrating the course of justice.

Everyone who considered the case said that his actions were entirely untypical, and that he and his family had paid a very heavy price for an action from which he had derived no personal benefit.

His defenders said he was 'the victim who had lost the most'. Surely, it would be right to draw a line under the whole affair and give him a second chance? But the judge in the case of Garda Sgt James Cunningham, which came to court just three months before the Sheedy affair became big news, felt that the law must be upheld.

He accepted that when Sgt Cunningham had stopped a doctor from taking a urine sample from a drunken driver, he had acted on the spur of the moment. He accepted, too, that the loss of his career was already a great hardship to the sergeant and his four children, but 'an attempt to pervert the course of justice was a serious matter', made all the more so by the status of the defendant as a representative of the State and the law.

A suspended prison sentence of nine months was necessary to uphold the integrity of the justice system.

The former Supreme Court judge Hugh O'Flaherty, who also interfered improperly with the case of a drunken driver, was fortunate to have, in the present Government, more merciful judges. Yet even he must have been astonished at the extraordinary rehabilitation of his reputation.

A little over a year ago, he was in disgrace and the Minister for Justice was telling the Dáil of the 'serious charges' that had been levelled against him by the then Chief Justice. By last Tuesday, his actions had been downgraded by Charlie McCreevy to a mere 'mistake', and by Wednesday, he had become, for at least some in Fianna Fáil, not a sinner to be forgiven but a saviour to be venerated.

Fianna Fáil senator Camillus Glynn told the Seanad that Hugh O'Flaherty was, quite literally, a new Jesus Christ. 'He has been treated disgracefully and I do not believe he did anything wrong. He compares with a similar great man, the good man from Nazareth who was crucified.'

In the light of such rhetoric, merely sending Mr O'Flaherty to the European Investment Bank with 1½ times his Supreme Court salary seemed insufficiently devout. Lavish shrines are the least of what he is due. The reality, however, is rather different. There was, indeed, a blood sacrifice but Senator Glynn picked the wrong martyr. It was not Hugh O'Flaherty who suffered to save mankind, but the Progressive Democrats who suffered to save Hugh O'Flaherty.

By going along with a gesture that can only be regarded as a deliberate reminder of the continuing impunity of the ruling élite, the party destroyed the very basis of its own existence. In a week when the decision of Des O'Malley and Mary Harney to split from Charles Haughey's Fianna Fáil should be surrounded with a halo of vindication, the PDs allowed themselves to be sucked back into the political culture from which they had fled.

Mary Harney's self-confessed failure to understand how offensive the appointment of Hugh O'Flaherty to a plum job would be was in itself astonishing, but even by Wednesday, when she broke her silence on the affair, it was still possible for Mary Harney to salvage something from the debacle.

Even while accepting that the appointment would have to go ahead, she could have distanced herself from Charlie McCreevy's flagrant rewriting of history in his Dáil defence of the appointment and at least acknowledged that Hugh O'Flaherty's actions in the Sheedy case had been both serious and wrong.

Instead, she parroted McCreevy's words about a 'mistake' and 'a second chance'.

She must have known how disingenuous Charlie McCreevy's speech had been. In the course of a mere five sentences, the Minister for Finance managed three times to be subtly economical with the truth of the Sheedy affair. He told the Dáil for a start that 'the Chief Justice, Mr Liam Hamilton, in his report on the Sheedy affair, acknowledged that Mr Justice O'Flaherty only became involved in this case in a spirit of humanitarian interest'.

This is, indeed, almost a direct quote from the Hamilton report — but the key word 'only' has been added to the quotation, implying, crucially, that the judge's actions in raising the Sheedy case with the Dublin County Registrar took the form merely of a humanitarian inquiry. The report, however, goes on to suggest that Mr Justice O'Flaherty must have known that the registrar would in fact act on his queries.

Charlie McCreevy continued his apparent summary of the Hamilton report with the sentence: 'And yet what he [O'Flaherty] did left his motives and actions open to misinterpretation.' This, again, is almost a direct quote from the report. It is however merely one part of a sentence which carries a much more serious import than the Minister's quote suggests: 'I also conclude that Mr Justice O'Flaherty's intervention was inappropriate and unwise, that it left his motives and action open to misinterpretation and that it was therefore damaging to the administration of justice.'

The Minister's editing transformed a very serious lapse into a mere matter of optics.

Charlie McCreevy went on to say that, after all, Hugh O'Flaherty 'did the honourable thing and resigned'. Again this is literally accurate. But it leaves out the vital fact that Mr O'Flaherty resigned only after the Minister for Justice had taken the unprecedented step of informing the judge that proceedings to impeach him were about to begin. The crucial difference between a guilt-stricken decision to go quietly and resignation under threat of being ignominiously fired was glossed over in the Minister's bland formulation.

The reality is that Hugh O'Flaherty and the other two protagonists in the Sheedy affair — Judge Cyril Kelly and County Registrar Michael Quinlan — were fortunate not to find themselves the subject of a Garda investigation. As Sgt Cunningham discovered last year, attempting to interfere with the due process of law is a 'serious matter'.

We know, indeed, that at an early stage in the unfolding of the Sheedy affair, a criminal investigation was actually considered.

The Department of Justice report on the scandal notes: 'On 15 March 1999, the DPP phoned the Secretary General [of the Department] about the case and asked in particular whether a Garda investigation was under way. The Secretary General explained that no such investigation was under way as we had no complaint of criminal conduct. The director agreed that a criminal investigation would have been premature.' That judgment was based on a proper reluctance to do anything which might prejudice a judicial review of the Sheedy case which was then pending.

However, the issue of a criminal investigation remained alive. On 31 March 1999, when it was still not clear what had happened in the Sheedy case, the Minister for Justice contacted the then Attorney General David Byrne 'in relation to the appropriateness of making a complaint to the Garda Síochána concerning the manner in which the Sheedy case was listed, now that the judicial review proceedings had concluded. The Attorney advised that there was not sufficient basis, at that time, to refer the matter for a criminal investigation, and that any decision whether to make a complaint to the Garda Síochána should await the outcome of the judicial and departmental inquiries.'

By the time both of those inquiries were completed, however, the three protagonists in the affair had resigned and the notion of possibly referring the case to the Garda was dropped.

It may well be, of course, that a Garda investigation would not have discovered any grounds for a criminal prosecution. Not only was there no such investigation, however, but the Oireachtas Joint Committee that was meant to inquire into the affair abandoned its hearings when Hugh O'Flaherty refused to appear before it.

Mary Harney must have known, therefore, that the suggestion that Hugh O'Flaherty had been unjustly pilloried was, if anything, the opposite of the truth. Had she pointed this out, even while reluctantly supporting the appointment, Mary Harney might have put some distance between her party and Fianna Fáil's breathtaking decision to endorse the culture of impunity for 'people like us'. Instead, she gave credence to the damning political equation that Fianna Fáil plus the PDs equals Fianna Fáil.

It was a sad end to a party whose primary appeal was its adamant refusal to play along with cute strokes, dodgy deals and the creepy ethos of looking after your own. If PD now stands for Play Dumb, it is difficult to see a future for the party.

If the point of the O'Flaherty appointment was for Fianna Fáil to send out a message to those who might be troubled by tribunals that moral indignation is just a passing phase, the humiliation of a party which was once capable of expressing such indignation must have been a delightful bonus. Tribunals and PDs, the message said, come and go, but Fianna Fáil's loyalty to the faithful will go on forever.

Bertie Ahern gets in a few words before the tide turns. Photograph: Bryan O'Brien.

SATURDAY, 27 MAY 2000

Gay? More Like Delirious

Eddie Holt

Beaming a cheesy smile that surely flashed 'lock up your sons', Walter Liberace camped it up more than a troop of boyscouts. In spangles, fur and feathers, the ivory-flashing ivory-tickler didn't just look gay — he looked delirious. Yet his fans were overwhelmingly female or, to be more politely specific, as a voiceover said, 'women of a certain age'. That age certainly had nothing to do with the first flush of youth. But still, to millions, Liberace remained a heterosexual sex symbol.

'Reputations: Liberace — Too Much of a Good Thing is Wonderful' stripped away the elaborate cloak of deception. Once 'the highest grossing entertainer in America', the state took possession of his body after his death in 1987. The opening scene showed a hearse, filmed from a helicopter, travelling across the desert from Los Angeles to Palm Springs. In the coffin (alright then, 'casket'), the shrivelled remains of Liberace were about to undergo an autopsy. The coroner's examination showed that the star had had AIDS.

The stark 1980s equation of AIDS equals homosexuality or IV drug use or unfortunate victim of a blood transfusion no longer holds. Even so, though that point should have been made, it seems incontrovertible that Liberace contracted the disease through engaging in sex with men. But to come out of the closet, he would have had to admit to perjury and would have alienated practically all those midwestern matrons of a certain age. In a typical showbiz psychodrama, the real Walter Liberace was sacrificed to his surname-only stage persona.

Back in 1956, Liberace visited Britain. Homosexuality was still illegal there (until 1967) and the *Daily Mirror* was not only lively but literate. Its renowned columnist Cassandra (William Connor) wasn't impressed with the ostentation of Lib or his gig. 'He is the summit of sex — the pinnacle of Masculine, Feminine and Neuter. Everything that He, She or It can ever want,' he wrote. 'This deadly, winking, sniggering, snuggling, chromium-plated, scent-impregnated, luminous, quivering, giggling, fruit-flavoured, mincing, ice-covered heap of mother love is the biggest sentimental vomit of all time.'

Well now, that's axe-man criticism as florid as the target of its attack. Risky too. Liberace sued. The case attracted huge coverage. 'Are you a homosexual?' the judge asked the fragrant Walter. 'No, sir.' Had he ever indulged in homosexual practices? 'I'm against the practice because it offends convention and it offends society.' So that was that then. Cassandra lost the case and Liberace won damages of £8,000 (with costs of £27,000). The closet was padlocked, nailed shut and sealed after that particular performance.

But in the 1980s, Liberace's final lover, Scott Thorson, let it all hang out. A former 'dog-handler in the film industry', Thorson was instructed by Liberace to undergo plastic surgery to remake his face in the pianist's image. So he had chin implants inserted, work done on his cheek bones and his nose reshaped. From the surgeon's well-stocked medicine cabinet, Thorson developed an addiction to cocaine and muscle relaxants. Eventually his drug habit grew so bad that he was evicted by force from Liberace's Los Angeles mansion.

Hell hath no fury like an evicted man sculpted in his gay lover's image and likeness. Thorson sued for palimony. Still, Liberace denied everything. In the meantime, he too visited the plastic surgeon. Thorson recalled the doctor working on Liberace's face while snorting cocaine and drinking vodka. 'The guy ruined Lee's face. He left horrible scars up through his hairline.' The job was allegedly so badly done that Liberace used to sleep with his eyes open. People who saw this often thought that he had died.

There was something creepy about this tale. The autopsy, the plastic surgery and the open-eyed sleeping were a part of the creepiness, of course. But there was a sense, not of a remodelled Frankenstein, but of a soulless vampire behind the fancy cloak and trademark candleabra. What it must have been like to be Liberace — permanently in denial, permanently on guard and permanently acting — can scarcely be imagined. To his army of matronly fans, he was America's brightest star. To most critics, he was the man who stripped the class out of classical music.

Recent reappraisals have cast Liberace as pre-figuring glam rock. Certainly, there are obvious parallels between him and say, Elton John. But 'glam castrated classical' is a dodgy genre and, even allowing for the obscene cheesiness of Liberace on stage, there was always something pathetic, something more eerie than mere showbiz, about the artifice of his act. In fairness though, he was a creature of his very certain age. The US of the 1950s wasn't likely to be receptive to a gay man 'coming out'. Showman Liberace understood this and castrated his true identity along with the music. The best 'Reputations' in some time.

SATURDAY, 27 MAY 2000

Mumba One

Tony Clayton-Lea

Here comes an *Irish Times* public service warning: within the next 12 months the Irish pop music contingent will completely rule the world. Just look at the respective successes of The Corrs, Boyzone, B★witched and Westlife and wonder at not only the commercial potency of cheap music, but how the masses are sucked in by white suits, jig-pop and cover versions. Well, we can now add another name to the growing pile of, er, Hiberno hip hop pop: Samantha Mumba. There is a difference, however, between the Corrz and the boyz and the girlz and this particular girl. The difference between Samantha and the stretched, smiling faces

'The difference between Samantha and the stretched, smiling faces of the elder generation of Irish pop stars is that she's the nearest thing we have to a genuine R&B pop star.' Picture: Peter Hanan.

of the elder generation of Irish pop stars is that she's the nearest thing we have to a genuine R&B pop star.

A Billy Barry kid from the age of three, it's only over the past couple of years that 17-year-old Samantha has been going out and nabbing individual auditions. She stopped stepping out with the Billy Barry team at the age of 15 when she clinched her first lead dancing/singing/acting role in a show called 'The Hot Mikado', a revue based on the songs of comic opera duo, Gilbert & Sullivan. Bye bye, then, to semi-pro imitations of Riverdance, Madonna and Michael Jackson, and hello to welcome-to-the-real-world of rehearsals. 'It was a ball and set me off on the path to where I'm on now,' says Samantha. 'I had to have an American accent, which I pulled off without any real problems.'

The American accent is all the more surprising when you take into consideration that Samantha is from Drumcondra, on Dublin's Northside, with an Irish mother and a father from Zambia. Her parents are now separated, and her father, who has been an Irish resident for almost two decades, has experienced more verbal abuse in the past year than ever before. Although Samantha is inevitably as pretty as a model, it was her American accent that got her into this pop lark in the first place when, during work in a pantomime, she heard that Louis Walsh, Boyzone and Westlife's Big Kahuna, frequented the Dublin nightclub, Lillie's Bordello. A little bit cheeky, a little bit shrewd, a large bit courageous …

'I was 15 at the time, and I knew I wouldn't have been able to get into the club by myself,' says Samantha, 'so I went with my mum, and pretended I was an American R&B artist. My American accent went down a treat! So I was sailed on into the VIP room, where Louis Walsh was sitting. I didn't pounce on him there and then, but we ended up swapping phone numbers. He phoned my mum the next day, and he introduced me to a few record companies. I picked the one I got on the best with. The rest is pretty much history.'

Samantha is adamant that she is not going to be a one-hit wonder. Although a mere stripling in comparison to her Irish counterparts, she seems aware enough to appreciate the scarifying obsolescence factor within pop music. Hence the decision to focus on the steady European and American markets, rather than the fickle British region. Her influences are the best in latter day R&B: TLC, Fierce, Honeyz, Sister2Sister and Destiny's Child. She says she loves Whitney Houston and eventually wants to veer away from her current love of commercial R&B pop.

'I'm starting off with the commercial R&B pop side of things at the moment. I enjoy it and it suits the age I am. Eventually, I suppose I might grow into straightahead R&B material, the kind that appeals as much to mature kids as adults.'

Samantha sees as her obvious rivals in the female pop market the likes of Britney Spears and Christina Aguilera. 'There's more than enough room for me to slot in with what's happening. A lot of the tracks on the album have a slightly different edge. My music is very in your face and all about attitude. Britney and Christina are blond, blue-eyed American sweethearts. I'm going for a totally different angle. The only common link is that we're all girls.'

What of the way in which seemingly perfect pop careers, initially so hyped, garlanded and acclaimed (just where did Kerri Ann go to?), can go down the tubes without so much as a by-your-leave?

'I'm taking everything a day at a time,' says Samantha in the sensible tone of a girl who knows that eating carrots can make her see in the dark. 'It's one thing Louis Walsh told me — you have to stay grounded. Once you lose your head, it's an illusion, it's over. I'm lucky. I'm doing something that I'd pay someone to do, but now I'm being paid to do it. It's a complete bonus. As for Britney and Christina — I admire them but we're completely different.

'It can go wrong so suddenly, especially when you start believing your own hype. Of course, you've got people saying everything is brilliant, but my main job at the end of the day is to make sure the music is right. I'm here to do the music, dancing and performing. I love performing and I want as many people as possible to hear the music. You can take the compliments but it doesn't mean to say you have to believe them yourself.'

Wise words indeed and, frankly, admirable. And as if this wasn't good enough, strong rumour (bordering on the truth, actually) has it that David Bowie has taken an interest in our Sam. Mister Ziggy Stardust is currently in line to direct the video for her second single, 'Body To Body'. It's a song that just so happens to contain an officially-approved sample from Bowie's 'Ashes To Ashes'. But don't tell anyone we told you that. Remember, Mumba's the word.

Sinn Féin Minister Hangs Looser Than Flags

Frank McNally

Martin McGuinness was standing in front of his departmental headquarters in Bangor, telling reporters how the further development of the peace process would be a 'huge challenge' for everyone.

'You're a scumbag, McGuinness,' shouted a woman from the other side of the fence, underlining in her own way the Minister of Education's point. Mr McGuinness remained calm, however, as Sinn Féin constantly advises. Bangor is not a strong republican area, to put it mildly,

'Arriving for work in an old Ford Granada, [Martin McGuinness] found the lamp-posts around Rathgael House bedecked with union flags, Ulster flags and the purple standards of the UVF.' Photograph: Dara MacDonaill.

and the locals weren't expected to throw him a party.

He already had evidence of their feelings. Arriving for work in an old Ford Granada he found the lamp-posts around Rathgael House bedecked with union flags, Ulster flags and the purple standards of the UVF. Flags are commonplace in the North, but these were new or at least freshly laundered. There wasn't much wind yesterday, but they were so well starched they nearly stood up by themselves.

The Minister took this in his stride, too. He recalled a time when the RUC and British army presence at IRA funerals had caused great upset to the relatives. Gradually, the families came to realise that the military presence was a tribute to the deceased. That's how he felt about the flags — he would take them as a 'compliment'.

Sinn Féin was taking everything as a compliment yesterday. Earlier, in Stormont, Mr McGuinness heard his party president, Gerry Adams, accept more backhanded praise from unionists.

On the one hand, he suggested David Trimble should apologise for the canine analogy in which he suggested republicans were not 'house-trained'. On the other hand, he took the remark as 'an admission from Mr Trimble that Sinn Féin does not roll over at the behest of unionism'.

Then, before you could say 'Down, boy!', Mr McGuinness showed that if there was patronising to be done, Sinn Féin could give as good as it got. He had 'a beautiful grandson', he announced, who'd been attempting to walk for the past two months, and faltering. But last Saturday, the day of the Ulster Unionist Council meeting, the child finally 'let go of the furniture'.

Lest anyone was missing the moral of the story, Mr McGuinness continued: 'He's moving forward to embrace a new future for himself, and that's what unionists need to do. They need to let go. They need to lighten up, and to move forward and be decisive about the future.'

Chinese Shoot Corrupt Politicians

Conor O'Clery

The 'degeneration' of the politician happened because he 'fell victim to the temptations of women and money, and took advantage of the power endowed by the party and the people to make personal gains'. Sound familiar?

This was not a judge at one of the Dublin Castle tribunals but a disciplinary commission of the Chinese Communist Party, commenting recently on Mr Cheng Kejie, a deputy chairman of the Chinese parliament. Unlike his soul mates in Ireland, Mr Cheng cannot hope to brazen it out; he can only expect a bullet in the head. In China they shoot corrupt politicians.

Last month the former deputy mayor of the southern city of Guigang, Li Chenglong, was executed after accepting cash donations (in red envelopes) for handing out jobs and construction contracts. Two months ago a former deputy governor of Jiangxi province, Hu Changqing, was shot by the state for taking bribes, becoming the most senior official to be put to death in 50 years.

Chen Xitong, the corrupt mayor of Beijing, barely escaped with his life. He was jailed in 1998 for 16 years; his deputy, Wang Baosen, committed suicide. In China they also shoot officials and businessmen caught up in sleaze, or put them away for long prison terms.

On Saturday Shen Weibiao, the 32-year-old manager of a Bank of China branch in the city of Shaoguan, was executed for the white-collar crime of diverting funds for his own use.

Yesterday Mou Qizhong, once known as China's richest man, was sentenced to life by a court in Wuhan for foreign exchange fraud. Instead of a lengthy tribunal to mull over his complex billion-dollar transactions, he got precisely one day in court.

Iran's Prime Minister, Sayyed Hassan Nasrallah, marks a new beginning. Photograph: David Sleator.

The forms of corruption are depressingly familiar.

Mr Cheng allegedly first accepted an envelope of cash in 1992 for lowering the price of redevelopment land, and then took kick-backs for issuing building licences at low prices.

He also had a mistress, a married woman named Li Ping. He was secretly videotaped with her at a Macau casino, which may have been his real undoing. The possibility of being shot has powerfully concentrated his conscience. Mr Cheng has since offered to return all his illegal income to the nation.

A novel idea!

The official *People's Daily* said the arrest of Cheng showed 'there is no hiding place for corrupt elements in the party' and they would be shown no mercy in an all-out attempt to clean house.

The party's image is crucial to its survival. If it gains a reputation as nothing more than a club for corrupt officials, the one-party system loses its legitimacy.

The prospect is annihilation in an upsurge of unrest. The punishment of a high official is clearly meant as an example to the party and the people alike.

'The Chinese have learned from their history,' said Mr Seán O'Shea, a director of the Beijing-based consultants, Reid and Associates, who is originally from Westmeath. 'The tolerance level for corruption has to be much lower in China because of the propensity for any such activity to swiftly become a challenge to basic social order, whether under the emperor or the party.'

Tough punishments seem popular in China, which has the highest rate of executions in the world. There is an utter lack of public sympathy for apprehended officials.

In contrast to Ireland, where wealth and power are admired and the 'untouchables' belong to the élite, class divisions are only now beginning to emerge in China, and the rich are envied rather than esteemed.

Deng Xiaoping said a decade ago that it was glorious to be rich, but the suspicion is deep-rooted that fat cats can get rich only through corruption.

There is a golden circle of sorts in China. No senior officer of the People's Liberation Army has ever been prosecuted, despite widespread reports of military involvement in large-scale smuggling.

Hundreds of government officials are said to be caught up in a gigantic smuggling racket in Fujian. But since it reportedly implicates high officials in Beijing with Fujian connections, a news blackout on the investigation has been imposed.

With the Premier, Zhu Rongji, dedicated to smashing corruption, it is a precarious circle to belong to. When starting his anti-corruption campaign two years ago, Mr Zhu said he had 100 coffins — 99 for corrupt apparatchiks, and one for himself if he failed to fill the others.

There is an obvious parallel in the growth of corruption in Ireland and China. In both countries money began seeping to officials and politicians when the economy started to take off. In China the opportunities for embezzlement multiplied more quickly, as state assets were privatised and banks continued to make up losses.

'Ten years ago there wasn't half as much corruption in China,' said a Chinese economist. 'Go back 20 years and there was almost none. There was nothing to spread around and public assets were of little value.'

Now it has reached endemic proportions, and the sums are huge. Embezzlement from state funds in the first half of 1999 totalled 20 billion yuan (£1.7 billion), according to the government's conservative figures. In the same period, according to the *People's Daily*, 120 billion yuan of state funds, one-fifth of tax revenues, were 'misused', a term which covers many sins.

But no one in China need fear a public tribunal — only the executioner's bullet.

TUESDAY, 6 JUNE 2000

Movers and Shakers

Katie Donovan

You arrive in a strange town, and knock on the door of a certain house. There's a handshake, a few questions. And hey presto, you're in. Sounds ideal, doesn't it? This is what happens if a Mason travels and knocks on the door of a Masonic lodge in a strange town. It is a ritual centuries old, dating back to the origin of Freemasonry as a craft guild of stonemasons.

In medieval times, stonemasons were illiterate. They showed a new boss in a new town their qualifications for the job just by being able to shake his hand in a certain way. They met in temporary structures (hence the term lodge) adjacent to the building site. If one of them got injured or killed on the job, the others looked after his wife and dependants.

Freemasons still wear aprons as part of their ceremonial garb, a tribute to their forebears who wore leather aprons to protect their clothes from the rigours of the trade. Stonemasons' tools — such as the compass and the square — still have symbolic resonance in the rituals of the monthly meetings. 'We are taught that all our dealings with others should be square — a fair deal for both parties,' says Michael Walker, grand secretary of the Masonic Order in Ireland.

'We like to hold on to our traditions but we are not a crowd of fuddy duddies,' adds Selwyn Davis, a Dubliner who has been a Freemason for 30 years. Freemasons who were clearly far from being fuddy duddies have included Benjamin Franklin, Oscar Wilde and Clark Gable.

The Grand Lodge of Ireland is about to celebrate its 275th anniversary; 1,500 members from as far afield as Jamaica and Sierra Leone will attend the celebrations in Ireland starting with a concert tomorrow night at the NCH and followed by a gathering in the RDS on Thursday. There are 700

Masonic lodges in Ireland and 150 abroad which are affiliated to the Grand Lodge of Ireland. The Grand Lodges of Ireland, England and Scotland are the oldest in the world.

Nowadays there are about 33,000 members in Ireland, North and South, from plumbers to Church of Ireland ministers and Catholic priests. Contrary to popular belief, the Order is not 'a middle-class Protestant club' says Selwyn Davis who is chief executive of the Edmondstown Golf Club. Davis, a Jew, joined the Freemasons 30 years ago. He is

now chairman of the Metropolitan Board — meaning he is the leader of the 36 Masonic lodges in Dublin, an annually elected post.

'We are non-religious and non-sectarian,' emphasises Davis. 'There is only one stipulation, that whatever you are, Muslim, Hindu or what-ever, you have a belief in a Supreme Being, in your own God.'

Freemasons are not allowed to discuss religion or politics at meetings. 'It is unfortunate,' says Davis, 'that people tend to confuse the Freemasons

Making hay while the sun shines. Photograph: Matt Kavanagh.

with the Orange Order, perhaps because of the recurrence of the word "lodge" in the two organisations. There is no link whatsoever between the two.'

There was never a policy of excluding Catholics, says Barry Lyons, assistant grand secretary and librarian with the Order. Lyons is Catholic, and has never experienced any sectarianism: 'The organisation was up until recently predominantly Protestant, due to self-imposed withdrawal by Catholic members. In the 19th century, there was a Papal Bull decreeing that the Freemasons (and other secret organisations, with more conspiratorial elements) were off-limits for Catholics. It meant that prominent Catholic Freemasons like Daniel O'Connell had to pull out.' Daniel O'Connell described the Freemasons as 'philanthropy unconfined by sect, nation, colour or religion', notes Michael Walker.

What sort of people join? Freemasons, says Selwyn Davis, tend to be 'doers'. They are typically married and settled, and are most likely to be 'pillars of their church or community'.

Charitable concerns are paramount. The Freemasons donate £1.5 million per year to 2,500 dependants. These are the wives and children of 'deceased or distressed brethren'. 'We help put children through school, and we have sheltered housing projects for the elderly,' says Michael Walker. The Freemasons' charity work also includes raising £500,000 to purchase nine minibuses for Alzheimer day-care centres.

OK, the Freemasons seem squeaky clean on all counts so far. But what about the fact that women still aren't allowed to join? 'The order was founded by operative stonemasons,' says Selwyn Davis. 'Can you see ladies hauling stones?' But nobody, male or female, hauls stones nowadays, and the order is still all-male. According to Michael Walker, 'We don't get serious inquiries from women.'

In Britain, although the United Grand Lodge of England does not accept women, there are several lodges that are women-only and one, the Co-Masons, which is mixed, but 'they are not officially recognised by us or by the United Grand Lodge of England,' says Barry Lyons. 'Until there is a groundswell of objection from the younger members, this men-only policy won't change. I don't know why, but the older men prefer it the way it is.'

Women play an important role in fund-raising and social events, points out Selwyn Davis: 'We enjoy their support. I don't think they feel excluded. It's like I don't feel excluded when my wife goes off to her Mothers' Union meetings. Live and let live.'

'Men like to be members of clubs,' says Michael Walker. And the Freemasons certainly offer their members an exciting aura of secrecy. In the old days, says Davis, the secrecy came largely from the fact that the Catholic Church disapproved of its members joining. Nowadays, members are much more open about being Freemasons.

The purpose-built Victorian Masonic Hall in Molesworth Street is open to the public during the summer. Here you can see the Grand Lodge Room, where every December the grand officers are installed. On the floor is a chessboard style carpet, the black and white squares symbolising the good and evil we encounter in life. Symbols abound, from the cut and uncut lumps of stone (signifying the moral transformation ahead of new candidates) to the gold stars on the blue ceiling (symbolising the fact that early Masonic meetings took place outdoors). There are painted scenes of the construction of King Solomon's Temple, which is the origin of the symbolism of Masonic ritual.

In spite of all this talk of openness, the veil descends when it comes to divulging the exact nature of these rituals to outsiders. Monthly meetings take place behind closed doors guarded by 'tylers'. Ceremonial aprons and collars are worn, and the stonemason's tools are laid on the 'altar'. 'We parade in, in the order of the officers of the lodge,' says Selwyn Davis. 'The master opens the lodge in a stylised form, using beautiful old-fashioned English. It's like a play.' Meetings involve more prosaic elements such as the secretary's minutes, and a dinner afterwards. Subscription is between £30 and £50 a year, plus whatever the dinner — which, in Molesworth Street, is provided by caterers — may cost (not more than about £10).

As for the famous handshake: 'I'm obliged not to tell you what the handshake is,' says Selwyn Davis. 'It's an interconnection of various knuckles and joints,' says Barry Lyons, vaguely. 'I've never seen it used outside of meetings. A more obvious method of recognition outside of meetings would be a tie or a ring.' Initiates — entered apprentice

Freemasons — go through three degrees of membership, each of which involves a different handshake.

Freemasons' reluctance to reveal themselves continues to invite speculation that they have something to hide. 'The Freemasons are outlawed in Pakistan, because it is seen as a subversive organisation,' says Selwyn Davis. During the early 1990s, there were allegations that the Freemasons were infiltrating the RUC. Michael Walker has said that the large number of Freemasons in the RUC was probably because the Masonic lodges were some of the few places an RUC man could socialise in a safe environment, secure in the knowledge that his Masonic brethren would support his wife and

Mr Philip Hamell, Chairperson of the Euro Changeover Board of Ireland, at the announcement that every household in the country will receive a summary plan for the changeover to euro cash from 1 January 2002. Photograph: Dara MacDonaill.

family if anything happened to him. 'I suspect there are still quite a lot of RUC members, but there are also a lot of gardaí,' adds Barry Lyons.

Concerning the Stalker inquiry, Walker has said that he thought it 'highly unlikely' that any Masonic influence played a part in ending the mission of the former deputy chief constable of Manchester: 'Neither Sir John Hermon nor Sir Hugh Annesley are, or ever have been, Freemasons,' he says. 'The allegations were proved baseless.'

Although Freemasons speak fervently about how moralistic their organisation is, that does not mean it is immune to a few bad apples. The late John Furze, the senior figure at the Cayman Islands end of the secretive Ansbacher Deposits operation (used to defraud the Irish Revenue of millions of pounds from the 1970s to the mid 1990s), was a Freemason. According to the Masonic constitution, 'The use by a Freemason of his membership to promote his business, professional or personal interests is forbidden. A Mason's duty as a citizen must always prevail over any obligation to other Freemasons, and any attempt to shield a Freemason who has acted dishonourably or unlawfully is strictly forbidden.'

'We have procedures for dealing with un-Masonic conduct,' says Davis. 'It has happened that members have been suspended and expelled.'

In the 1970s there were allegations in connection with unsolved bomb attacks in Italy that secret service agents, clandestine Freemasons (members of the P2 Masonic Lodge), mafiosi and right-wing extremists were conspiring to destabilise Italy to provoke a coup. Renewed 'P2' activity was reported in 1992 and connections between the mafia and Freemasons were openly acknowledged. 'We don't recognise the Grand Orient of Italy,' says Michael Walker. 'They are, we believe, involved in politics. Italians find it hard not to be. They are political animals.'

The appeal of Freemasonry in Ireland seems to be its exclusion of politics: 'Everyone is equal, it's

very fraternal, and it's very relaxing to be away from the outside world,' Selwyn Davis concludes. Years ago, when Michael Walker went through the trauma of redundancy from his job in a fertiliser company, 'the only place I found peace and support was at Lodge meetings'.

WEDNESDAY, 7 JUNE 2000

Ruling Ends Nine-Year Battle To Block Sale

Joe Humphreys

They were never really wealthy, but they always enjoyed a comfortable living at their 19th-century Georgian home on two acres in Blackrock, Co. Dublin. Now the Blackall sisters, Eileen (88) and Rose (81), face financial ruin. 'They are literally penniless now. For a family used to money that's hard to take,' said Mr William Blackall, a nephew.

'It's terrible to see them end up this way. The house means so much to them. It's not just a property. It's something real and tangible to them. It's where they have lived all their lives. Rose herself was born there. They can't imagine being without it.'

Mr Blackall visited his aunts yesterday afternoon shortly after news broke of the High Court ruling ordering the sale of Marino Park to property developers for £400,000, a fraction of its current market value.

Since being evicted from the house two years ago, the sisters have been living at their cousins' home in Blackrock. Now bedridden, they were unable to travel to the Four Courts to witness what seemed to be the final chapter in a nine-year legal battle.

'They were devastated when they heard the news,' said Mr Blackall. 'Eileen was just sitting silently on the bed, and Rose, I've never seen anyone so white. They were both too shocked to speak.' Barring any further legal moves, yesterday's ruling is the end of the women's struggle to block the transfer of their home to Chessington Ltd.

They jointly own the house with their sister-in-law, Ms Iris Blackall, the widow and administrator of their brother Gerald's estate. The house had been owned by the Blackall family since 1917 when it was purchased by the sisters' father, the Nationalist MP, Tomas Blackall.

In 1995 Judge James Carroll in the Circuit Civil Court ordered the sale of the house amid a dispute over wills. It was bought by Chessington for £400,000.

Two years later the case came on appeal before Ms Justice Laffoy in the High Court. She affirmed Judge Carroll's order and granted Ms Iris Blackall liberty to apply to the Circuit Court for an order giving her possession. Four months later Judge Carroll granted that order. The Supreme Court upheld Ms Justice Laffoy's ruling.

In the meantime, the sisters had been served with an eviction order which was enforced by a sheriff in October 1998.

Following many unsuccessful revisits to the High Court, the case came back to the Circuit Court where Judge Liam Devally was asked by Mr Brendan Maloney, who had been given carriage of sale of the property, to order the execution of a deed of conveyance to the purchaser.

In a ruling which effectively nullified the contract of sale, Judge Devally found that all parties, including Chessington, were aware that only 12.5 per cent of the deposit on foot of the purchase contract had been paid and that no one had requested payment of the outstanding deposit.

He believed that by allowing years to pass before even tendering the deposit the developer was in fundamental breach of Section 31 of the contract of sale.

The case returned to the High Court last February when Mr Justice Finnegan was asked to finally decide whether a valid contract was in place and whether the sale should proceed.

In his judgment yesterday, Mr Justice Finnegan said that, while there was a breach of the conditions for the sale, the contract for sale remained in existence.

But the legal meanderings may not end there. Relatives of the sisters were last night examining the possibility of an appeal to the European Court of Justice. 'We will try to get an injunction on the sale pending a hearing in Europe,' said Mr Blackall.

Legal sources said, however, that the European Court would be unlikely to entertain such an appeal unless an issue of EU treaty law was at stake.

Since their eviction, the health of the sisters has declined dramatically. Eileen has suffered a heart attack and has undergone two eye operations, leaving her with only partial sight. Rose has been in and out of casualty on at least four occasions.

'It's terrible to see them end up this way,' said Mr Blackall. 'It's like in the past few years they have lost everything.'

What little remuneration the sisters will get for their home, now valued at between £3.5 million and £4 million, is expected to be whittled away by mortgage charges and legal costs.

SATURDAY, 17 JUNE 2000

On the Bus, the People Look, Spit Bile and Talk About Us Sponging, Stealing their Jobs

Kathy Sheridan

The pretty 22-year-old sits across the table in her comfortable home and describes what growing up in south Co. Dublin was like: 'The number of times I was called a Paki, a nigger, a mongrel, a mixed breed ….' Her mother's eyes flicker. The daughter continues, with a wry laugh: 'Well, I know for a fact that I'm not from Pakistan. And I'm definitely not a nigger.'

Her mother looks dazed. 'They called you nigger …' she says slowly. 'You never told me that.' Several times over the next few hours, Dr Mary Toomey would repeat those words, disbelievingly: 'They called her nigger … She never told me that.'

To a populace still reeling at the implications of a near-fatal attack on the (white) father of a mixed-race family in Dublin's Pearse Street last weekend, it's hardly startling stuff. Aoife Toomey has no obvious wounds to show for being the child of a mixed-race marriage. No-one has stabbed her, or stood outside her home yelling abuse or urinated through her letterbox.

She is a relaxed, stylish young woman who will shortly have a Trinity politics degree to add to her good fortune as the cherished only child of professional, middleclass parents. In a few weeks, she will marry Matthew, a white, all-American boy, and they will settle in the US.

The wounds only show when she mentions the children she hopes to have: 'Everyone thinks I'll come back, but I will not. I'm getting ready to start my life 3,000 miles away in a place where I don't stand out at all. I refuse to feel ashamed of being Eurasian. Here, I am expected to apologise for it, to be thankful and humble and less visible. So I will not bring children up in this place. I'm not whingeing. That's just the way it is.'

'Where or when has our leader, Bertie Ahern, come out and condemned racist attacks and attitudes, openly, vociferously?' Anti-racist demonstration, Dublin. Photograph: Frank Miller.

The wounds run deep. Casual abuse and naked contempt at personal and official levels have marked the long, slow erosion of dignity and identity. Now, the pain and sense of betrayal are manifest in Mary Toomey. A woman of presence and accomplishment, she married Barry Toomey, an Irish engineer, against the will of her parents, high caste Tamils in what is now Sri Lanka. Later, she would ring with good news (another book commission), but to add: 'All afternoon, I have heard my mother's voice — "You are forgetting … You are selfish … My grandchildren will not belong anywhere". I now see that she was right.'

Mary Toomey came to Ireland in 1967 to do a PhD in ecology at Trinity College. 'I brought educational assets into this country. The natural sciences were virtually unknown here and biology was being introduced in the schools, so the Department of Education had me teaching teachers from Louth to Kerry.'

In a Co. Wexford village after Mass on St Patrick's Day in 1968, she was inundated with lunch invitations. 'They wanted to touch me and I remember joking: "I'm afraid I cannot part with this tan". I never once felt uncomfortable.'

She was commissioned to write the first biology textbooks for schools; was headhunted to work at universities; was offered a job by UNESCO (the UN's education and science organisation), to travel across the world, to talk about science education. 'I turned it down. I chose to live in Ireland because I loved it …'

She is fiercely proud of her Tamil heritage. 'We have frescos, culture, carvings, going back to the 5th century BC. In 1963, 90 per cent of the Sri Lankan population were literate and education was prized as the jewel, through every caste. Fourteen per cent of the budget was allocated to education, which was free right through from primary to university.'

It's not a boast, just a pointed reminder that a 'lily-white' skin is no indicator of learning or accomplishment (and certainly not in Ireland, where a new international survey shows a quarter of all Irish adults are functionally illiterate); that asylum-seekers and even economic migrants ('now made to sound like dirty words'), might have something to contribute, even to smug Ireland; that the next time someone like herself fetches up at Dublin airport, immigration officials there might see more than 'a little brown woman' standing before them and dispense with the ritual humiliations.

'Two of the hottest new designers at London Fashion Week are Ugandan Asians,' adds Aoife. 'These are the people Enoch Powell made his famous "rivers of blood" speech about, yet the success story of Ugandan-Asians in England is amazing.'

The faces of women cleaning the toilets at British and French airports — once invariably Asian or African — are now mainly white again, they remark. 'Doesn't that prove something — that where refugees and economic migrants are allowed to work, they will work their hands to the bone and their children do particularly well?'

In her world travels to give lectures and promote her gardening and plant books, Mary is recognised and welcomed at many airports. But not Dublin: 'Every time I come back to the airport, it's always the same. No whites in front of me will be stopped. But I will be stopped, and the question, always, will be: "Where are you coming from?" That's before they look at the passport.' (The question is relevant to asylum-seekers who, under European law, must be processed in the country of first resort.)

Aoife — again with the wry laugh — recalls how after a European trip last year, she and Matthew arrived back at Dublin.

'I got into the EU channel and Matthew, being American, into the non-EU channel. I should have been through well before him. But the guy stopped me, looked at me, and asked how long I had had citizenship. He hadn't even glanced at my passport, which has my place of birth — Dublin — written down. Eventually he muttered something that didn't sound polite and let me go. The irony is that Matthew, a non-EU citizen, had been waved straight through.'

Mother and daughter are no 'pinko-liberals' in favour of an open-door policy. They are all for proper procedures and controls. Aoife, bound for a new life in the US, sees nothing wrong with the stringent vetting procedures both she and Matthew must undergo. 'You should see the paperwork … Even Matthew has to supply his tax records for the past four years. Then there's my history — whether I was a spy in 1945, or a member of the Communist party, or a neo-Nazi; or whether I have body-piercing or tattoos. And we'll both be finger-printed and our photographs taken, which must show our right ear and our right side.

'And irrespective of whether he and I stay together, he will be legally responsible for me for seven years … But I have no objection whatever. I am asking to be allowed to live in their country after all. The important point about it all is that it's even-handed; I am treated no differently to anyone else who is going to the US. And it has all been handled with total courtesy, in a way that never compromised my dignity or sense of self.'

Mary nods in agreement. 'Of course, people must ask questions. But where are the Irish smiles? What has happened to Irish courtesy? Why must they be so stone-faced?'

To Mary, official stone-faces are not new. Roll back 10 years to when she approached a Department of Justice official to seek a study visa for her 17-year-old nephew. 'I will never forget that girl who treated me with such contempt …' she says, her voice trailing off. 'I then made an appointment to see somebody in charge. I lost my dignity, my pride, my arrogance as a high-caste Tamil … I pleaded for a two-year visa, I said I would be paying his fees, that he would be going to a private school, that it wasn't in my culture to ask for hand-outs — and to this day, we never have sought handouts, in spite of three redundancies of my husband.

'I got the visa, through tears, beggings, pleadings. I had to do that and yet I am a citizen. I could not bring my mother here, who was found in a refugee camp. There was no procedure to bring a blood relative into this country. Why, as a citizen, can I not do this?'

Compare this with Canadian procedures, where Mary's older sister was able to sponsor another sister and she, in turn, another. And where a brother was able to sponsor her mother.

And now, Mary is 'climbing the walls' wondering how her relatives, affluent holders of American, Australian and Canadian passports — one an immigration official in Canada, another a lawyer — will be treated when they arrive in Dublin for Aoife's wedding.

When her nephew, a Canadian passport holder, arrived in Ireland a few years ago to help out in a family crisis, he was 'pushed aside, left standing there, until the whole line had been processed, being watched by everyone and treated with contempt. Are they too going to be deprived of their dignity?'

Mary and Aoife can tell stories about racism in south Dublin to equal any in a country village. There's the anonymous woman who has been ringing Mary for three months now (and whose voice she recognises), with the same bleak message: 'There's no room for foreigners in this country — you must get out fast.'

The 'anonymous' girls from Aoife's old convent school who used to ring her with the same racist abuse. The couple sitting opposite her and her friend on the bus, who looked directly at her while spitting bile about a son who couldn't get a job, 'yet here's all these coloureds, taking jobs, sponging off the government, and they can hardly speak English'.

Into Aoife's lucky bag fell not only a strong father but an enlightened teacher. Niall MacMonagle, an English teacher at Wesley College, Dublin, to which she moved in fifth year, introduced her to thought-provoking writings, such as Maya Angelou's poem, 'Walking in my Skin'. In Wesley, she also absorbed the lessons of Nigerian students whose arrogance 'oozed' from them and made her realise that she wouldn't have to spend the rest of her life 'apologising for being Irish — and having to explain why I'm not a lily-white Irish girl'.

Yet, she's getting out — a decision that saddens her mother beyond words but one which she well understands. Mary will simply never vote again: 'The TDs we elected to represent us have not taken care of their citizens. They have let me down.'

Letters written to TDs and ministers (the latter about Aoife's treatment at Dublin airport), produced no response. 'In the North, they expected Gerry Adams and Martin McGuinness to condemn IRA atrocities, and to use that word,' says Mary. 'What's so different about this? Where or when has our leader, Bertie Ahern, come out and condemned racist attacks and attitudes, openly, vociferously?'

She believes like many others that the choice of language by politicians is crucial. As Sister Joan Roddy noted this week, the contrasting welcomes given to Kosovar refugees on the one hand and to asylum-seekers on the other, suggest strongly that people take their cue from the Government.

'Ireland has lived in this cocoon,' says Mary, 'and had this begging bowl mentality. And now we've emerged with an up-side-down begging bowl. Are we educating a whole person through our education system? If so, how can any normal, educated human being take pleasure in humiliating another?

'I had hoped that my child and grandchildren-to-come would have a sense of belonging in Ireland, but that has been removed from my confidence. Therefore I don't want them to come here. Why would I? To see them stopped at the airport and asked "Who are you?"

'My ashes shall be thrown into the sea, for the simple reason that I do not belong anymore. Ireland built me as a person and I am very, very

thankful, but now they are robbing me of that. I do not regret a moment of my life here but the question is: do I belong here anymore?'

SATURDAY, 17 JUNE 2000

LockerRoom

Tom Humphries

It's Tiger Woods' world. We just live in it. On Friday evening they announced that it was too dark to play any more golf at Pebble Beach. Wishing, as he says, to finish up on a good note, Tiger Woods holed a simple 35-foot putt for a birdie on the 12th hole and called it a night, walking off the green looking tired. I was there at the time, feeling tired. Jesper Parnevik was there too, looking as if everything he knew was wrong.

Then Tiger put his face, his views, his logos on TV for a while and afterwards came to the press tent for a 20-minute yakkety-yak with the intelligentsia during which he discussed everything from Jack Nicklaus to the LA Lakers to his remarkable eight-under-par score after 30 holes of the US Open. I sat and listened and looked passably intelligent myself.

Then, at sometime after 10 p.m., Tiger headed to his hotel where he performed his ablutions and had something to eat. I headed to my hotel and did the same. I am Tiger Woods I told myself.

Then at 4 a.m. Tiger Woods got out of bed, (perhaps by means of levitation we just don't know). He performed even more ablutions, had some breakfast and headed to the driving range. He was working at the driving range at 5.15 a.m. He was on the putting green with Butch Harmon at 6 a.m. He finished the last six holes of his second round by 10 a.m. I know this because I saw the highlights on telly when I woke up at 10.30 a.m. I am not Tiger Woods.

Jesper got up early too. Finished the last six holes of his second round and caught the next bus

David Norris dances for Joy-ce. Photograph: Matt Kavanagh.

to Palookaville. Look out for him running amok in a McDonalds or something. In all, Tiger Woods played 24 holes on Saturday. He finished up 10 shots ahead of the bunch of losers who comprise the best golfers in the world, ranked two through to John Daly. Amidst crowds, bigger and richer than those which followed Moses, I watched as much of Tiger Woods as I could. I nearly finished up in intensive care. Give him this. The kid has got shots. The kid has got stamina.

At times in the past few days, watching Tiger Woods play the US Open at Pebble Beach was like watching a great maestro sing Puccini at La Scala. It elevated anyone who wasn't a pro golfer. It was the perfect confluence of talent, arena and challenge. Enough there to make us giddy but too much subtlety there at that exalted level of performance for most of us to understand.

Too much for Colin Montgomerie anyway. Lordee but what a dreary old moanie minnie Mrs Doubtfire is. As if not attending the memorial ceremony for Payne Stewart (who was famously generous to the buxom Scot) wasn't embarrassment enough to heap upon himself, the old trout bumbles into the press tent on Saturday morning and announces that surely the gods do conspire against him in matters meteorological.

Then he goes out and partners Ernie Els for the afternoon. Els shoots the best round of the day whilst suffering the company of the hapless baboon from tropical, windless Troon. Either all weather is local or Monty ain't Tiger Woods either. Anyway we came to praise young Caesar not to bury big Monty. We were talking about perfection.

On Saturday afternoon at 5.30 p.m., Mr Woods finished the first nine holes of his third round. He pointed a sand wedge at the catering tents and turned all mineral water therein into wine before walking to the 10th.

Why not? He was nine shots ahead of the rest of the field at that point and the battle had become Tiger Woods versus Pebble Beach. The course, a great and beautiful warrior itself, had already whipped all comers. The average round for the day was 77.2 shots.

Woods went toe to toe though, his knowledge of the physics of golf truly makes this the sweet science. It took a mistake to put that in perspective. On Saturday morning, during his six-hole preamble to the day, Woods' drive on the 18th went for some surf and turf action and he filled the television screens of Mr and Mrs America with some salty curses. Alleluhiah! Cut him and he might bleed.

On Saturday Woods got through the first nine holes of his afternoon session in 35 strokes, or level par. Only Ernie Els and Pádraig Harrington did better. Woods' score was the more remarkable only because it contained a triple bogey and a bogey, the first punches which Pebble Beach had landed on Tiger Woods all week. His recovery from those misfortunes was so extraordinary that in the press tent afterwards we asked if could put our hands where his wounds had been. Just to be sure.

There were times when he slapped Pebble Beach around as if it were a rented sparring partner. He stripped the old giant of its austere dignity at times. On Friday, the sheer temerity of a 205-yard seven iron from the rough on the sixth fairway to the elevated green ahead had to be seen to be believed.

From practice to trophy time his week was filled with such jewels. The eighth at Pebble Beach is a wonder of the golfing world, a dog leg which breaks right, the gap being filled with the beckoning blue Pacific of Carmel Bay.

Jack Nicklaus, this old codger who used to be Tiger Woods, said once that if he had one shot to play before death (or before dinner, who can remember all this stuff) one shot on any hole in the world, he'd pick the second shot at the eighth at Pebble Beach.

The hole calls for a little brinkmanship from the tee. Knock your drive towards the edge of the cliff and then whip your second courageously over the sea towards the stingy little green on the far cliff and you'll be fine. Of course, the ball should stick to the green the way a bad name sticks to a dog.

Woods devised something different, pushing his drive to the right, so perilously close to disaster that rescue services could do nothing. Then he'd whip it over the waves trading the tougher lie for the simpler approach to the green and a birdie chance each time. Lots of ooohs as we follow his drive, lots of aaaahs as he sticks for his second.

In the end all of us followed him on procession and homage. It was that kind of US Open — one man performing at a level that we could scarcely understand, one man planting the flag of Tigerworld on the highest summit at Pebble Beach. All bow.

One man. He Tiger Woods. He da man.

TUESDAY, 27 JUNE 2000

Clinton and Blair Greet Scientific Triumph

Kevin O'Sullivan

As announcements go, it was out of the ordinary; almost simultaneous press conferences throughout the world — Washington, London, Paris — as scientists and politicians marked a day unprecedented in the history of humankind.

The peace that unexpectedly broke out between two rival research teams attempting to unveil their version of the human genetic code was sealed by President Clinton, who declared: 'Today we are learning the language in which God created life.'

He was joined via satellite link by the British Prime Minister, Mr Blair, who heralded 'the first great technological triumph of the 21st century'.

Some commentators said the draft versions of the entirety of human DNA, courtesy of the Human Genome Project (HGP) and Celera Genomics, a private corporation, was the biological equivalent of landing a man on the moon. This 'book of life' may be the most important scientific

advance since the Apollo lunar landings, but its significance is far greater.

For it will soon amount to 'the complete set of biochemical instructions describing how the human body is made and maintained', once the HGP tidies up its working draft during the next two years and Celera clears up some anomalies in its map.

The totality of the work will transform medicine beyond recognition, albeit later rather than sooner. New drugs will be developed for previously untreatable diseases, and ways found to replace or repair faulty genes.

Treatments will be tailored to an individual's genetic make-up and doctors will be able to predict

Comedians Ren Hicks and Johnny Vegas combine their talents on Parliament Street, Kilkenny during the Murphy's Cat Laughs festival of comedy. Picture: Matt Kavanagh.

the future of their patients with much greater certainty.

Some cancers will be eradicated. In the latter half of the century inherited diseases may be eradicated by knocking rogue genes out of the gene pool.

But it may not be as simple as this, as other research shows many genes may be involved in some diseases, and be part of a complex interaction with their environment.

In the meantime, determining the exact meaning of a vast amount of information — the equivalent of a new foreign language with some 50,000 words — is the primary task, and a frenetic search has already begun to identify the 'active' rather than the 'junk' genetic components; the ones that are pivotal in human health. The most vexatious issue — who owns the human genome? — remains largely unresolved.

The human genome race exposed the tension existing between publicly-funded research and 'for-profit' science. The HGP is a collective involving 16 different institutions from six countries, led by the US and Britain. The publicly-funded consortium has operated since 1990, committed to making its data freely available for the good of science and humankind. But in 1998 the brilliant maverick, biochemist Dr Craig Venter, surfaced.

His objective was to patent genes and sell the information to pharmaceutical companies with a slogan 'speed matters — discovery can't wait', and armed with the most advanced DNA 'sequencing' technology available. Before fast computers, a DNA sequence 12,000 bases long — the equivalent of a relatively small amount of genetic material — took more than a year to assemble. Supercomputers changed everything. Three years ago working out a 12,000-base sequence took 20 minutes. Today it takes just one minute. His company, Celera Genomics then said it would be the first to unravel the human genome. Relations with HGP soured last year after negotiations on collaboration broke down and acrimony dominated the race up to earlier this month.

It was not just about being first but also the quality of research and whether it would be freely available. A pact on a joint announcement emerged as the immensity of their endeavours was eventually allowed dictate. Political pressure and Celera's acceptance of commercial realities played a part in defusing the confrontation.

The gold-rush, none the less, has begun with two US biotech companies seeking rapid commercialisation of the information, not withstanding the HGP's team determination to have the genome available free of charge. Millennium Pharmaceuticals is forming an alliance to develop gene-based treatments for inflammatory diseases such as arthritis and multiple sclerosis, while Human Genome Sciences is to start clinical trials of a protein which activates the immune system to fight infection.

Dr John Sulston, director of the Wellcome Trust-funded Sanger Centre in Cambridge, where a third of the genome was sequenced, said the point in human history had been reached 'where for the first time we are going to hold in our hands the set of instructions to make a human being' — with obvious philosophical implications for the way we think of ourselves.

He added: 'I for one didn't want my genetic information to be under the control of any one entity, any one corporation. We had to fight, sadly. On the other hand I was proud to do it. It hasn't been easy, but today we are announcing a number of announcements which mean that the fighting is over.'

Both the HGP scientists and Celera used similar techniques to sequence the genome but applied them differently. HGP used blood and sperm samples combined from several anonymous donors. Celera placed an ad in the Washington Post, selected 30 men and women, and used about 10 of them — humans are about 99.9 per cent the same genetically, and their collective work will eventually explain how that 0.1 per cent makes each individual unique.

TUESDAY, 27 JUNE 2000

Harney's Difficulties Delight Opposition Parties

Denis Coghlan

Mary Harney has egg all over her face … again. Hugh O'Flaherty hadn't even booked his air ticket for the European Investment Bank, courtesy of Fianna Fáil and the Progressive Democrats, when she was being blamed for preventing Charlie Haughey getting a fair trial.

It was wild. On the one hand, the Tánaiste was too soft with Fianna Fáil; on the other, she was too hard. She just couldn't get it right. And the more Ms Harney tried, the deeper the hole grew.

Her difficulties brought understandable delight to the Opposition parties. John Bruton put the boot in with gusto. Having failed to get the Dáil to discipline the Tánaiste last May, when she had lost the run of herself and called for Mr Haughey's jailing, he demanded vindication.

Judge Haugh's ruling had serious legal implications, the Fine Gael leader thundered, and there had to be political accountability for what had happened. In that regard, Ms Harney was for the high jump. 'Looking at the matter objectively, it is hard to see how the Tánaiste's position is tenable,' Mr Bruton intoned.

You could almost hear the headstone being chiselled. Ms Harney had a heavy political responsibility to discharge because of her Cabinet membership. And neither she nor the Government had taken sufficient steps 'to diminish the publicly damaging effect of her original remarks'.

They were all out of step except Johnny Baby. Revisiting the scene of his Dáil motion, the Fine Gael leader attempted to suggest that more was less: that a Dáil censure motion involving Ms Harney's views that the former Taoiseach should be jailed — because of disclosures before the Moriarty tribunal — would actually help him get a fair trial.

It was as startling as Judge Haugh's ruling that Mr Haughey could not get a fair trial and therefore should not be subjected to a criminal prosecution by this State. At some future and unspecified time such a course of action might be possible. But not now.

This was the judge who initially refused Mr Haughey's application to adjourn all charges until after the Moriarty tribunal reported, but then offered the former Taoiseach 'additional safeguards'.

Judge Haugh felt Mr Haughey should have these mould-breaking protections in the interests of a fair trial. All potential jurors were to be questioned on whether they had any relationship with Mr Haughey, with Ben Dunne, or any involved companies or potential witnesses.

On appeal from the DPP the 'additional safeguards' were rejected by the High Court. But the 'fair trial' battle continued, with Mr Haughey's legal team quoting a range of defamatory material from RTÉ, the newspapers and a planned political

'Mary Harney has egg all over her face … again.' Photograph: Peter Thursfield.

meeting. Then, with only days to go to the hearing, Ms Harney put her foot in when the Moriarty tribunal disclosed £8.5 million had been paid to the former Taoiseach. We know the outcome. The Director of Public Prosecutions and the Attorney General are now considering a judicial review for the High Court. Ms Harney is holding her peace. And Bertie Ahern is saying as little as possible.

But Derek McDowell gave it a lash. Having refused to support Mr Bruton in his last Dáil motion on the issue, the Labour Party spokesman was again ploughing his own furrow. The judgment would cause serious public concern, he said, because after three years, Mr Haughey had still not answered charges arising from the McCracken report. If a jury trial was not possible, then the case should be referred to the Special Criminal Court where three judges sat without a jury, he said.

Support for the Tánaiste came in nasal Limerick tones. Des O'Malley wasn't hiding what he thought about the judgment. The alleged prejudice, he said, appeared to be considerably less than the McArthur murder case of 1982, when Mr Haughey had said the Garda had got 'the right man' in circumstances where the identity of the accused was at issue. The trial had gone ahead.

Freedom of expression could not be overlooked, he said, when the accused was a former Taoiseach and a well-known public figure.

SATURDAY, 1 JULY 2000

The King of the New French Tribe

Michael Walker

Pele talks tomorrow. The greatest player ever to grace the playing fields will hold a press conference before Euro 2000's final in Rotterdam, at which he will name an all-star team of the tournament.

It will be a crass marketing ploy by some credit card company or other, no doubt, but it is also something every fan does. Across the Continent debates will rage, yet there is one thing that can be guaranteed: the name of Zinedine Zidane will be first amongst his equals.

If not on every single list, then the non-believers should be put in a room with a video of how Zidane controls a spiralling football, how he rolls the ball under his foot as he glides past the opposition, how, when he needs to be, he is hard, and how, when he is given the chance, he takes it. They will soon believe.

Scoring from the penalty spot should be the most straightforward task in the game, but how often it is that we see famed players miss. From Chris Waddle, Roberto Baggio through to Raul, Jaap Stam and Frank De Boer, big names miss big penalties. Not Zidane. On Wednesday night in Brussels Zidane wrapped his right foot around the ball with total knowledge and authority. If there were nerves, they did not show. The ball hit the back of the net at an acute angle and with velocity. Victor Baia, the impressive Portugal goalkeeper, went the other way, fooled completely.

It was the last kick of the match, the pressure was on. Zidane delivered. It was a golden goal all right.

And then Zidane set off, all 6 ft 2 in and 13 st of him. One arm in the air, broad smile on his face, a regal celebration. What was also noticeable was the smile on the faces of his team-mates. Not only were they delighted Zidane had scored the goal that took them through to the final, they seemed genuinely pleased for Zidane himself. They clearly love Zizou as a man as well as a footballer. As Arsenal's Patrick Vieira said: 'He is my hero.' Swoon.

But it is easy to see Vieira's point. Zidane may be the eminent footballer at this tournament, the World and European Footballer of the Year in 1998 and the scorer of two goals in a World Cup final, but his on-pitch disposition is far from egotistical. Defeated, deflated opponents always treat him with special affection. The arrogance displayed by lesser players is not an affliction from which

Judge Donnchadh Ó Buachalla arriving at King's Inns for the inquiry into his handling of the transfer of a pub licence into the sole name of Catherine Nevin after the murder of her husband. Photograph: Bryan O'Brien.

Zidane suffers, and it cannot be easy to be so modest when you know that on the night of France's World Cup victory the hundreds of thousands who crammed onto the Champs Élysées chorused 'Zizou, Zizou'. It was the love of a nation.

In the days that followed that July 1998 success France was overwhelmed by sociologists talking of the country's renewed sense of self-discovery. The football team, they argued, said much about the ethnic reality of modern France. Players born in Guadeloupe, Ghana and New Caledonia were prominent, others were children of Armenian, Polish and African parents. Together they conquered the world in the name of Les Bleus.

Arsene Wenger, not a figure prone to exaggeration, said: 'France has a mixed history and the most recent is a history of losing. The country was exploding a little bit with different tribes of immigrants. Then suddenly you win the World Cup with a team made up predominantly of immigrants. It changed the whole political process. It gave the country the feeling they could win with different people from different countries mixed together.'

The king of the new French tribe was Zidane. Born in the Algerian quarter of the rough and ready port of Marseilles in 1972, Zidane was the son of two of the city's many Algerian immigrants. But he was passed over by his local club and still seems hurt about it.

'Of course I adore Marseilles,' he said before Euro 2000. 'It is my town, the place where I was born. It is the club that I always supported, the club I watched from the stands when I was small. Enzo Francescoli was my favourite.'

Instead Zidane was spotted by a scout from Cannes playing in a game in Aix-en-Provence. He was 14, but even then had the velvet close control to stand out. As the scout, Jean Varraud, said: 'A unique touch on the ball.'

From Cannes Zidane moved to Bordeaux where he met Didier Deschamps, Bixente Lizarazu and Christophe Dugarry, although considering his talent it was late, as a 22-year-old, that Zidane was first capped for France. It was against the Czech Republic and France were 2–0 down when he came on. Zidane immediately scored twice.

People, particularly Italian people, began to pay attention. By the time Euro '96 came around Zidane was on his way to Juventus, just as the previous great French playmaker, Michel Platini, had done a decade earlier.

Yet arriving at Euro '96, Zidane had only 10 caps and disappointed to such a degree that World Soccer magazine put him down as the 'French Flop' of the competition. 'Flat, laboured displays,' they said, although they conceded that the car crash Zidane had been in prior to the tournament could not have helped.

The man himself said: 'You've got to be tough in your duels. I've the advantage of being big and solid in my legs, but I must work to be less susceptible to knocks, to fall down less often.'

Two years later, prowling the green fields of France with a lion's grace, Zidane had learned to stand up. The fleetness of foot was there for all to see, as of course were the goals against Brazil.

But France, despite becoming world champions, were not the team they are now, and Zidane was not the player he is now. Zidane now has a recognised strike-force to play behind and supply.

He turned 28 last Sunday and feels he is at his peak. Strong, lithe, quick, intelligent, Zidane has everything. Sergi, only an observing substitute for Spain last week, when asked after what he thought of Zidane's performance, replied: 'Gobsmacked'. That, at least, was the translation.

They have lined up to sing of Zizou at Euro 2000. 'He's playing football from another planet,' said Lilian Thuram. 'It was still a pleasure to watch Zidane,' said the Denmark manager Bo Johansson after his side's 3–0 defeat. 'He constructs play like nobody else,' said the Portuguese full-back Dimas. And from Edgar Davids, a Juventus colleague: 'Simply training with Zizou inspires me.'

From the man in the middle there is not so much. Zidane talks with his head down but plays with it up. One day, he said, he would like to play in Spain. He will not stamp his gifted feet in the manner of others when the time comes to leave Italy. Nor will they be glad to see the back of him, even if he orchestrates a French victory tonight. They know a player when they see one in Italy. They understand the privilege of watching a man like Zinedine Zidane. Pele must, too. When he reads out his list, ZZ will be top.

WEDNESDAY, 5 JULY 2000

Irishman's Diary

Kevin Myers

There are many creeds in Northern Ireland, many sects, infused with tribal animus and regional memory. They all have their heroes and their foes, which they gather to revere or to curse in the strange covens of that place. But there is a seldom-mentioned sect which cures those it recruits of all sectarian taint. It blesses with the magic wand of enthusiasm and personal loyalty, and its brotherhood are bound by rules which are barely a century old.

Their church is the workshop, their communion host the carburettor, the communion wine the cylinder oil in which they spend their days. They might be illiterate in politics and history, and their vocabulary in ordinary English less comprehensive

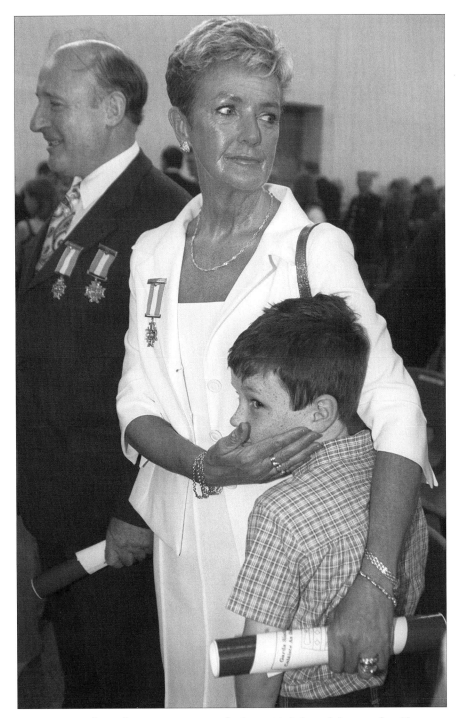

Ms Anne McCabe, widow of Detective Garda Gerry McCabe with her grandson Eoin McCabe (7) and Detective Garda Ben O'Sullivan, after the Scott Medal Awards at the Garda College, Templemore. Photograph: Peter Thursfield.

than that of an average 10-year old Swede. But what they know, they are experts in; and their understanding of the dialect and liturgy of the internal combustion engine is as exhaustive as the College of Cardinals' mastery of the complexities of Thomism.

Joey Dunlop was their pope, their moderator, their archbishop, their pastor. Like all binding religions, this creed's hold on its adherents is quite mystifying to outsiders; but as with all great religions, outsiders could see and be impressed by the effect that it had on those who worshipped within its rules. And those who gathered around the dismembered engine parts of Nortons, BMWs, Kawasakis, BSAs, were bound by an enormous loyalty to one another, and to the secret scripture of their creed: the motorbike manual.

The internal combustion engine has a remarkably ecumenical effect on those drawn to its influence, and its loyalties are curiously regional. Cork, for some reason, is one such area where worship of the motor-car is very powerful. Henry Ford's family were poor Protestants from Cork, and Ireland's most distinguished car magnate, Sir Patrick Hennessy, was from an equally poor Catholic background. You must go to the opposite corner of Ireland to discover an internal combustion engine culture as strong: to Antrim, and the tiny, hill-locked communities where the particular form the worship takes is in an obsessive dedication to the species of beast first created by Gottlieb Daimler 115 years ago.

North Antrim has a reputation for sectarianism, not least because it is the heartland of Paisleyism. Yet the complexity of loyalty, the subtle nuances of local tolerance and respect within a broader picture of what to the outsider seems like intolerable bigotry, means that even the most divided communities find an everyday modus vivendi. Differences are concealed; strategies of language are invented to avoid points of conflict. People agree to differ by not talking about their differences.

But that is not how the brotherhood of the motorbike conceal their differences. Simply, there are none. All those Herbies and Wilburs and Wesleys, the Seanies and Seamies and Paddies, with their spanners and their wrenches and their oil-saturated overalls and with fingernails which haven't been clean in 10 years — they have found their grail of commonality, and not merely are they not participants in the sectarian conflict of the past 30 years, they are so absorbed in the mysteries of the poppet valve and camshaft that they are barely aware of the sectarian gale which has been howling outside their garage doors for so long. Philip Allen and Damien Trainor, murdered in the Railway Bar in Co. Down two years ago, were fine examples of the carburettor innocence which has managed to survive amid so much death.

That was what made the local tributes to Joey Dunlop so very striking. Normally, when such an eminent person dies, testimonials refer to 'both sides of the community'. Not in Joey Dunlop's case; there was only one community, which worshipped around engine block and crankshaft: small town working class, highly skilled technically and conservative in its ways. Its members have their dinner in the middle of the day, they drink alcohol sparingly or little at all, and their few non-motorbike conversations will probably be conducted in a singular and largely incomprehensible variant of Lallans.

They know their own community, and their own community knows them, and they are content that it is so. That their heroes are the most technically skilled, physically courageous sportsmen in the world is beyond doubt. Their incomprehensible addiction to speed unites them as it eliminates all subsidiary difference. There is neither east nor west, border nor breed nor birth when motorcyclist meets motorcyclist, though they come from the ends of the earth.

Every TT racer knows of the certain annual cull in his profession, sudden death or terrible, life-shattering injury. Were racers drawn from a higher social bracket, as grand-prix drivers are, Joey

Dunlop would long ago have been Sir Joseph Dunlop, and he would not have owned a wee bar in a North Antrim village but would have been a tax exile in Monte Carlo, with long-legged blondes simmering gently beside a blue swimming-pool.

But he was in fact Joey Dunlop, of Ballymoney, Co. Antrim, the greatest sportsman Ireland has ever produced, not merely five times world champion in the most terrifying sport of them all, not merely world leader in his sport for 30 years, not merely such a technical genius that he understood the witchcraft of his motorcycles' carburetion better than Honda's experts, but a kindly gentleman of Olympian modesty. Those who worship in the church that Joey Dunlop led will wipe a tear or two away with oil-impregnated hands, say not a great deal, and will return to their poppets and their cams. That was Joey Dunlop's way. It is their way too.

Two nuns help each other as they climb up Croagh Patrick mountain during a pilgrimage near Westport in County Mayo. Photograph: Reuters: Ferran Paredes.

FRIDAY, 7 JULY 2000

New Party to Try for 15 Seats in General Election

Miriam Donohoe and Geraldine Kennedy

The launch of a new political party is at an advanced stage of preparation by one of the two barristers responsible for the establishment of the Flood tribunal. It intends to contest 15 constituencies in the next general election on a broad policy platform, including anti-corruption.

Mr Colm MacEochaidh who — with Mr Michael Smith — offered a £10,000 reward for information on land rezoning corruption which ultimately led to the resignation of Mr Ray Burke and the establishment of the planning inquiry is behind the new party.

It is understood that Mr Smith, who is national chairman of An Taisce, is not associated with the new initiative.

Mr MacEochaidh, together with some of his supporters, feels that a new party could win votes with recent opinion polls showing a huge backlash against the Government and other established parties following sensational revelations at the Flood and Moriarty tribunals.

Mr MacEochaidh told *The Irish Times* last night: 'I'd rather not comment at this stage.'

It has been confirmed, however, that the new party aims to have a broader platform than anti-sleaze issues. It is planning to offer a 'new perspective' to voters and is now preparing detailed policy positions on transport, education and housing.

It will also seek to challenge the focus of the National Development Plan and the expenditure of millions of pounds on roads rather than on

'Lily Bud', a British Bulldog watching the Annual 12 July Orange March through the streets of Enniskillen. Photograph: Alan Betson.

public transport. It believes that the State has dropped down the league in education and is seeking to set new priorities. It will also concentrate on the housing crisis and is expected to be strong on conservation and environmental issues.

Mr MacEochaidh has been involved in several high-profile, environment-related court cases and many of the new party's supporters are expected to be drawn from the environmental lobby. He represented some of the Glen of the Downs protesters.

The Irish Times learned yesterday that tightly-controlled discussions and soundings have taken place in recent weeks about the establishment of the party. It is understood several potential candidates have been consulted about the idea. It is not clear, however, whether Mr MacEochaidh intends to be a candidate or to be a facilitator in the party's establishment.

It was not intended to formally announce details of the party until near the next election when it was planned to have a full fanfare launch with candidates.

Mr MacEochaidh and Mr Smith offered an anonymous reward of £10,000 in 1995 through Newry solicitors Donnelly, Neary and Donnelly. They took the action after Garda investigations in 1974, 1989 and 1993 failed to pin down corruption rumours. Within weeks, 30 people had contacted the firm.

It could not be confirmed last night whether the new party intends to concentrate its candidates in Dublin constituencies or to contest the 15 marginals around the State.

FRIDAY, 7 JULY 2000

Drumcree and Duty

Editorial

Every year on Armistice Day — 11 November — a diminishing number of veterans of the First World War gather and remember with quiet dignity the sufferings and sacrifices of those who gave their lives in that dreadful conflict. That powerful desire to remember, amid prayerful whispers of 'Never again', was the motivation behind the building of the Cenotaph in London, and the thousands of similar war memorials erected throughout the world since then.

On Sunday, a memorial service to those who fell at the Somme will be held in Drumcree Church of Ireland parish church in Portadown. What quiet dignity will accompany this service? Very little, if the past six years are anything to go by. More ominously, the thuggish displays of recent days in Drumcree and the rioting elsewhere in Northern Ireland may yet be a harbinger for much worse to come.

What responsibilities befall those in positions of influence in this circumstance? For those of a Christian persuasion it is surely to act, and counsel others to act, in a manner befitting the message of the Gospel, Christ's message to love one's enemy. Precious little sign of that coming from the hill overlooking the Garvaghy Road.

The Orange Order maintains it is not responsible for what others do while campaigning in support of its demand to walk down the road. It refuses to talk either to the Parades Commission (established by parliament) or the chosen representatives of the Garvaghy residents. It has adopted what many will regard as a grotesque position: its members cheer the antics of a notorious terrorist from the Shankill Road but refuse to seek peaceful accommodation with Catholic co-inhabitants of Portadown.

This annual display of hatred and intolerance, focused on the parish church of Drumcree, has also done severe damage to the image and standing of the Church of Ireland itself. Some of this damage is self-inflicted. Last year, the synod, the church's parliament, took a step forward when a letter was sent at its behest to the Orange Order seeking assurances about its conduct at the church. The Order did not reply.

IRA prisoner, Brian Arthur, is greeted by well wishers including his son Declan and wife Paula leaving the Maze Prison after serving seven years. Photograph: Matt Kavanagh.

The synod then asked the Drumcree vestry, the parish's ruling committee, to withdraw its invitation to the Order to attend the annual service. Neither the rector nor vestry replied to the letter. This apparent contempt for the church's own democratic institution had no consequence: at this year's synod, Drumcree was barely mentioned.

On Monday last, a group of men, describing themselves as from the 2nd Battalion C Company of the UFF Shankill Road marched outside Drumcree church and later fired volleys in a Protestant housing estate in Portadown. One day later, the Church of Ireland Primate of All Ireland, Dr Robin Eames, issued a statement which, while appealing for restraint, not alone failed to condemn the UFF incident, it did not refer to it at all.

Dr Eames has unique authority — moral and actual — when it comes to Drumcree: not only is he the head of the church in Ireland, he is also bishop of the parish. The wider community on this island is entitled to expect robust leadership from the senior members of a church which to date appears incapable of preventing itself from being used by people whose credo is hardly Christian.

On Sunday, in other parishes up and down this island, members of the Church of Ireland will say Morning Prayer. Many will recite the Third Collect, the collect for Grace. It urges the Lord to help them 'do always that is righteous in thy sight'. Is it righteous to abuse neighbours of a different religion? Is it righteous to disobey the law, to throw acid at the police, to stone them and spit at them? Is it righteous to hold 'I am not my brother's keeper?' If it is not, that message needs to be proclaimed aloud. Leaders of the Orange Order and Church of Ireland should fulfil that proclamation as we enter this weekend of fear.

MONDAY, 10 JULY 2000

Torture Case Girl Homeless Despite Being In Care

Padraig O'Morain

The 16-year-old girl whose father was jailed last week for torturing, raping and mutilating her and her mother has nowhere to live and spends her days on the streets although she is in the care of the Eastern Regional Health Authority, it has emerged.

Father Peter McVerry SJ, the priest who works with homeless children, said the case highlighted the urgent need for an independent authority to help children and teenagers who had nowhere to live, and for this function to be taken away from the ERHA.

He said the case had 'sickened' childcare workers horrified at the ERHA's failure to provide a stable, therapeutic setting for the girl, her brother and her mother. Sources contacted by *The Irish Times* say it highlights the need for an investigation into the way the ERHA and its three health boards manage social work services.

The ERHA said it could not comment on the cases of individual children in care.

Last week, the Dublin man who raped and tortured the then 14-year-old girl and his wife was jailed for 15 years at the Central Criminal Court. The court heard the mother and daughter were chained to a wall for weeks at a time and refused permission to go to the toilet or to take a shower.

The girl's father slashed both their faces with razor blades, a screwdriver and a saw blade, leaving them scarred for life. He stabbed them with a spike which he kept for punishment. He raped his daughter 24 times and forced her into oral sex. There were several bouts of torture during which he mutilated them and told them they were going to be killed. Their ordeal only ended when they escaped in 1999.

Father McVerry said that instead of placing the family in a stable, therapeutic setting, the health authority had allowed three deeply traumatised people — the mother, daughter and brother — to drift.

Last week the girl told the court that she still suffered flashbacks and could not form a normal sexual relationship.

The Irish Times understands the ERHA is considering placing the girl and her brother in a house. It is also understood to be in the course of offering counselling to the girl. Father McVerry said this was a reaction to the embarrassment caused by the exposure of how the authority had failed the family, that it was too late and was no substitute for a proper therapeutic setting.

It is understood the girl presents herself to the ERHA's 'out of hours' service every night to seek accommodation and an emergency bed is provided for her. Even during last week's court case she had to seek emergency accommodation. Every morning, she has to leave her emergency accommodation and return to the streets. The girl is said to have serious problems and is considered by childcare professionals to be in grave danger from those who prey on homeless and disturbed children.

Sources say the case illustrates a difficulty faced by childcare workers in getting a comprehensive response from what they see as a top-heavy management structure. Earlier this year, the Eastern Health Board was transformed into three area health boards — each with its own management structure — under an overall authority.

Father McVerry said the recent report of the Forum on Youth Homelessness had recommended an independent authority to deal with youth homelessness. The ERHA had rejected this but the latest case emphasised the need for such an authority.

He said childcare workers were 'absolutely horrified' that the girl 'has to walk around all day' without getting the help she needs.

SATURDAY, 22 JULY 2000

What Not To Do On A First Date

Louise East

First dates are not that common in Ireland, where people tend to get together at parties or in pubs after most of their inhibitions and their friends have disappeared. But there usually comes a time when, instead of relying on bumping into each other — a dating process rather reminiscent of the natural method of contraception — you decide to meet up on your own. This, then, is the first date, and it's an experience comparable only to having your molars removed as far as terror is concerned.

I can't abide the things myself — I'd rather skip straight from first snog to the argument about whose turn it is to put out the bins than go through the whole first-date rigmarole. All the good advice you've heard about how to behave is going through your head: 'Relax. Be yourself. Ask him about his interests.' But all you can really think is: 'God, what am I doing here?' With this in mind I asked my friends for their top tips on what not to do on a first date, and put together this vital, cut-out-and-keep, Winging It Guide to What Not To Do On A First Date.

- Does it go without saying that any kind of restaurant, even one serving only goat curry and tapioca, is preferable to that intimate little Italian place? Go Italian and it's tricky to order anything other than pasta or pizza — not a good idea on a first date. Further down the line, when you find everything from your new love's nocturnal farting to their phobia of using their own credit card terribly endearing, you can giggle when Arabiata sauce drips down your chin. On a first date, you need every bit of dignity you can muster.

  I would also take garlic bread, noodle soup, corn on the cob, anything that still has its head and Tayto crisps off the menu. This said, a date at a fast-food restaurant is neither funny nor post-modern. Don't go there.

- Choose your first-date activity carefully — not everything they do in the movies works. One of my friends very wisely pointed out that while nubile young American teenagers look very cute hurling themselves round a bowling alley, for most of us going bowling is a lesson in humility. The amateur bowler has a nasty habit of remaining frozen, arse in the air, while watching the ball dribble into the gutter.

  Another friend told of the bitter experience of going swimming on a first date. She had pleasant fantasies of splashing through the waves together and instead found herself hauling herself out of the deep end of a local swimming pool, feeling less like Venus rising out of the waves and more like King Kong about to take Manhattan.

- Don't talk about your ex. A first date is not a job interview so you really don't need to tell your prospective new boss why you left your last job. Hearing too much about a man's ex-girlfriend always makes me feel as though he's outlining the qualities he's looking for in the new model. It also makes me wonder whether this man shouldn't just take out a small ad asking for a mother-figure for tea, sympathy and amateur psychotherapy. Discussing every detail of past relationships is for when you're bored of arguing about the plot of EastEnders in your ninth month together, not a first date.

• When nervous, most people have a tendency to throw drink into themselves in quantities which would have kept the Gatsbys watered for an entire summer. If you imagine that you're going to end up looking cute and tipsy, think again — first-date drinking has a few well-known and documented side-effects.

If you're female, these include you insisting that you love to dance and making repeated attempts to pull your very unwilling date onto the dance floor during 'I Will Survive'. If denied, you will sulk, which could make you look as though you're slightly cross-eyed. If there's no music, you will take the alternative route into drunkenness and start talking about how nobody loves you, not even your friends, and how sometimes you just feel so alone. Tears are inevitable at this point.

If you're a male, you will not notice when the barriers between acceptable topics of conversation and the unacceptable, disappear. So you won't think it's the slightest bit odd to start giving your date an in-depth description of hilarious mooning incidents from holidays past. Nor will you notice when your date's eyes glaze over. You will, however, be rendered absolutely speechless when your date starts telling you that nobody loves her, not even her friends. You will find yourself saying: 'You're a good girl' at inappropriate moments.

• Don't go anywhere where you know a lot of people. While it may look quite swish to arrive at a bar and have the barman know your name and your favourite drink, it's not good to spend the entire evening discussing last weekend's party with a stream of friends who all mention the fact you got sick in the neighbour's garden. It may also have the effect of making you look rather like an alcoholic.

Tina Turner at the RDS. Photograph: Cyril Byrne.

• Don't whinge. Don't boast. Don't duck. Don't dive.

The following are gender-specific dating tips, so if you're female:

• Don't talk meaningfully about how deafening your body clock is.

• Don't wear new shoes. This is an entirely practical tip, inspired by my own experience of rushing out to buy shoes which I felt would subtly allude to the fact that I was hugely desirable and sophisticated with it. I soon found out that they did nothing but shout about my inability to walk while my heels were bleeding.

- Don't order a salad and then push it around your plate. Eating like a bird should be left to those with wings.
- Don't flirt too much — most men agree there's nothing more terrifying than a woman making come-to-bed eyes over the top of her Early Bird menu.

If you're male, you should avoid the following tendencies:

- Don't wear too much aftershave — even if it is a very expensive one.
- Don't laugh too loudly or too much. For some reason this is a common male mistake on first dates, no doubt because of nerves and the desire to put a woman at her ease. Instead, it can make you seem slightly simple. 'Would you like dessert?' is not a joke.
- Don't be cooler than thou. We're actually suckers for guys who aren't afraid to show that they're interested (which doesn't mean hanging on our every word or behaving like a love-sick puppy).
- (For both sexes) Don't go on a first date at all. If you want to keep somebody really keen, the best method is to refuse to go out with them in the first place. I know it's childish, I'm sure it's likely to backfire, and I realise it'll get you nowhere but, hey, it's much easier on the nerves.

SATURDAY, 22 JULY 2000

In Headiest Heaven

Mary Dowey

Somewhere on the narrow road between Margaux and Pauillac, the old cynicism melted away. I'd had three days of driving all around Bordeaux, meeting relaxed, open people instead of the predicted shoal of suits, and tasting plenty of good wines at prices even a non-chateau-dweller could afford. Now here, on a sunny July morning, was the epicentre of it all.

The great chateaux, ranged to right and left, flash by like a slide-show — turreted Palmer, palatial Gruaud-Larose, rose-fringed Leoville-Barton, fairytale Pichon-Longueville, sterner-looking Pichon-Lalande across the road, with Latour's famous tower poking up from a glossy green sea of vines. If you're anywhere remotely near Bordeaux and any way remotely interested in wine, drive the D2 through the Medoc. You'll feel a fresh frisson of excitement every minute.

It hasn't always looked this good. 'Fifteen years ago, it was a desert,' says Sylvie Cazes-Regimbeau of Chateau Lynch-Bages. 'Nobody came here. The chateaux were in terrible condition, behind big, locked gates. The owners didn't want to let anybody see anything.' Succinctly, she zips through half a century of Bordeaux history. The 1950s saw gradual recovery from the war years; the 1960s, poor vintages and lack of money; the 1970s were good until the oil crisis of 1974, with some technological advances. In the 1980s, she says: 'Everything we needed — big improvements in technology, big improvements in the vineyards, a booming world economy and a series of great vintages. All of that helped to change the landscape.'

Are we in the middle of a new golden age? Sitting in the salon of elaborately restored Chateau Pichon-Longueville, Sylvie is wary of taking all the new grandeur for granted. 'You can only speak of a golden age when it lasts. We'll have to wait and see.'

Up the road in Saint-Estephe, her friends Laurent and Thierry Gardinier represent the new generation at Chateau Phelan-Segur, a magnificent property built by Bernard Phelan of Clonmel in the 1820s. Having sold two major champagne houses, Pommery and Lanson, their father had a bundle of francs to spend on improvements when he bought into Bordeaux 15 years ago. 'Anybody who has some passion can do what we do,' says Thierry, who abandoned the perfume business to fine-tune the cellar of a grand cru. 'It's not a special talent — just a matter of enthusiasm and dedication.'

Yeah, but money helps. In all the swanky appellations, Bordeaux has been raking it in like never before through the 1990s — so while it's rewarding to see top-level wines getting consistently better, through investment in vineyards and cellar, so they jolly well should. More striking — for everyday consumers, at least — is the way the quality message is finally trickling down, through lesser regions, to plain old mass-market Bordeaux where, heaven knows, there's room for improvement. The wines are growing smoother every year, as ways are found to ripen grapes more fully and tame tannins. Praise the Lord.

First, a couple of hot tips — appellations to comb for well-made wines that don't (yet) cost the earth. The Cotes de Castillon, adjoining Saint-Emilion, is the one the smart money is on — a pretty region of family estates on soil very similar to its famous neighbour's, but at a fifth of the price. Catherine Papon of Chateau Peyrou (not yet known in Ireland, but watch this space), tells of fiery arguments with her father, a vigneron from the generation that embraced chemical fertilisers and mechanisation with glee. 'My generation is going back to more natural methods,' she says.

Still on the right bank of the Gironde but

Mr Stephen Brewer, CEO Eircell, Ms Moya Doherty and Mr John McColgan, Executive Directors Tyrone Productions and broadcaster Mr Gay Byrne, at the launch of the Eircell sponsorship of the programme 'Who Wants to be a Millionaire', which will be produced for RTÉ by Tyrone Productions. Photograph: Eric Luke.

further north, the Cotes de Blaye is another area on the up. At Chateau Bertinerie, for instance, Eric Bantegnies is fastidious in his approach, determined to strive for quality in an appellation where, despite promising and varied soils, land is still relatively inexpensive. 'You can buy a nice old house and ten hectares here for half-a-million francs — much less than the cost of a weekend house in Deauville — so people can come here and play at living the wine dream.'

Are you tempted? When Alan Johnson-Hill swapped life as a Hong Kong businessman for ownership of dreamy Chateau Meaume, he describes planting vines, struggling with the language … But the du Seuil wines — the reds every bit as impressive as the whites — suggest the effort has been worthwhile. Look out for Leoville-Barton-like labels emblazoned with a little Welsh dragon. They're even in La Coupole.

At a more basic level, the wine firms don't usually set my heart aflame, but I couldn't help noticing how much better the wines of Calvet have become, with investment in new oak barrels, a new respect for traditional wooden vats and cement tanks, and a lighter hand with filtration. Although this vast negociant house owns no vineyards, it has stepped up its strategy of working closely with growers to secure good grapes. Besides the branded wines, there are some excellent petits chateaux under the Calvet umbrella; let's hope Ireland will see Chateau Cotes de Bellevue, Cotes de Bourg and Chateau Tayac Plaisance Margaux soon.

Closer to Christmas, the season of splurging, I'll give details of the de luxe goodies encountered — cru classe Medoc, Sauternes and more. Meanwhile, here are a few more modest bottles which stood out. A tiny, tiny sampling from a region with 57 appellations, 4,800 chateaux, 13,500 growers … Just as well Bordeaux isn't the sort of wine that grows tiresome. Years of steady drinking in the name of learning lie ahead.

MONDAY, 24 JULY 2000

Derry Exit Stage But Leave Unbowed By The Front Door

Ian O'Riordan

Offaly: 2–23
Johnny Dooley 0-12 (two frees, two 65s), J Pilkington 0-5, B Murphy 2-1, C Gath 0-3, Joe Dooley 0-2.

Derry: 2-17
G McGonigle 2-3 (two frees), G Biggs 0-4 (all frees), M Collins 0-4 (one free), J O'Dwyer 0-2, O Collins 0-2 (one penalty, one sideline cut), R McCloskey 0-2.

Rarely do such heavyweight mis-matches bring such entertainment. Derry's first trip out of Ulster in 92 years was supposed to yield no more than a possible commendation and then an unintended massacre. Instead, they sent Offaly running out of Croke Park flying a flag of relief after a completely addictive and unpredictable climax.

True, Offaly won by six points in the end, but it was Derry who stole the hearts with their desire to win and did so with a quality of hurling that must have surpassed even their own expectations.

Midway through the second half, they trailed Offaly by just a point after a dramatic exchange of points, which actually confused the manual score-keeper in front of the old Hogan Stand. A few minutes later they were level and, suddenly, Derry began to believe in the impossible. Offaly had to dig a lot deeper into the reserves than anybody could have expected.

It wasn't just that Derry had Offaly on the run, it was the way they did it. Geoffrey McGonigle returned from suspension with a thud and picked off the two goals that set the game thoroughly

'... but it was Derry who stole the hearts with their desire to win and did so with a quality of hurling that must have surpassed even their own expectations.' Photograph: Eric Luke.

alight. Oliver Collins and Ronan McCloskey linked up majestically at midfield and where Kieran McKeever is finding his energy from these days only God knows.

The full-forward line of Gary Biggs, Michael Collins and John O'Dwyer picked off 0-10 between them. Compare that to Offaly's sole full-forward contribution of 0-3 from Conor Gath. More remarkable, John Troy and Gary Hanniffy were both held scoreless despite holding key scoring positions and, well before the end, both Joe Dooley and Joe Errity were called back in an effort to keep them afloat.

And it is hard to imagine a game where Johnny Dooley will be more productive or more crucial. His 12-point contribution was, to a large extent, the difference between winning and losing,

because when Offaly were forced to match Derry's scoring rate, the options were glaringly limited.

Johnny Pilkington did have a reasonably productive afternoon when he managed to break loose from the Derry defence, which, like Antrim learned a few weeks back, can be as stubborn as they come. Michael Conway had moved back from midfield to the right wing and proved himself a fistful for the opposing half forwards. In the full back line, Conce was immediately apparent. Still, Johnny Dooley was the only man to raise his game by any visible mark. After another clinical free, he searched out men with greater intent. Murphy picked off one of his passes on the hour and then smashed the net with his first shot. That restored their lead to five, but Derry weren't lying down just yet.

Michael Collins maintained their response, although McGonigle sent the first of two successive 65s wide and that seemed to allow Offaly to settle. The Dooley brothers added two more between them and, by the time McGonigle missed another chance from a free, the clock had run down.

Six points in the end, but it felt a lot closer. Derry had come down with talk about making a statement for Ulster hurling and no one argued that they hadn't succeeded. Croke Park has rarely heard such genuine applause at a full-time whistle. And rarely has it been more deserved.

SUBSTITUTES: Offaly — Joe Dooley for Gath (55 mins), J Errity for Troy (57 mins), J Ryan for Duignan (61 mins), B Whelahan for Oakley (65 mins). Derry — Greogory Biggs for McCloy (42 mins), D

McGrellis for Oliver Collins (58 mins), P McElooney for McCloskey (62 mins). REFEREE: M Wadding (Waterford). BOOKED: Offaly — Claffey (50 mins). Derry — None; SENT-OFF: None.

SATURDAY, 29 JULY 2000

EU Threatens Morris Minor Obsession

Sarah Cottle

High in Sligo's Ox Mountains, David Carroll surveys the unusual 'stock' that has subsidised his family farm for more than three decades.

Diversification has proved necessary on many small farms throughout the rural north-west. For

Car collector David Carroll at home in Lissonagh near Tubbercurry with a 1956 replica Morris Minor Million behind him, one of only 349. Photograph: Bryan O'Brien.

Mr Carroll, that meant turning his love of Morris Minors into a paying proposition.

Wild brambles and saplings grow through the rusty bodywork of dozens of Morris Minors which nestle amid land set aside for vintage cars on the 32-acre farm near Tubbercurry village. Other cars, in happier condition, include the 1948 Ford Prefect driven by Cyril Cusack in the film 'Ballroom of Romance' and featured in 'Amongst Women'. Film producers, set designers for theatre groups and vintage enthusiasts searching for rare parts are among the customers who regularly beat a path to the Carrolls' remote farm.

'My obsession began with a scrap Minor I bought for £15, patched up and drove all over Sligo on our honeymoon in 1970,' said Mr Carroll. As his interest in vintage cars developed during the 1970s, so did customers.

'People brought their cars here from miles around for David to fix. We reared a family of four on the proceeds when times were hard,' said Frances Carroll, David's wife. David, however, says that the introduction of tighter EU environmental legislation in the autumn may threaten the business he has built up over decades. An ongoing survey in the western counties commissioned by Mr Éamon Ó Cúiv, Minister of State for Arts, Heritage, Gaeltacht and the Islands, suggests that Phase 2 of the Rural Environmental Protection Scheme (REPS) will require tighter measures to gain approval from Brussels.

The REPS scheme aims to support sustainable agriculture while protecting the environment.

Eligibility for payment requires farmers to set aside land, tend hedgerows, plant broadleaf trees, build drystone walls in keeping with local tradition, attend to general maintenance and clear all obsolete vehicles and machinery.

Mr Carroll says that his 'obsolete' Morris Minors may pose an obstacle to his eligibility for REPS. 'If you want the headage, you have to do what the EU says, so maybe the cars will need to go, but it would be terrible. This land could be cleared and grazed by cattle in a few months.

'But it would be a real loss. There's no harm in the beautiful old motors,' he said.

Famous Drawn to Hill by his Charm and Personality

Brian Fallon

Derek Hill's death was not unexpected. He had been in poor health for some months and it was obvious that his sheer appetite for life and people was at last beginning to fail.

So Tory Island — his favourite retreat — will never see him again. The studio-home in Donegal is now tenantless and the house in Hampstead where he sat and painted among paintings, stacked one against another, will no longer hear his step or his unmistakable voice.

Hill was not merely an excellent (and still rather underrated) painter; he was an outsize personality who had a genius for friendship. He had so many parts they almost seem self-contradictory.

Who else could have been a successful portraitist, an outstanding landscapist, a recognised scholar of Islamic art and architecture, a world traveller, a devoted art collector, a public benefactor (particularly of Ireland, his adopted country), a patron of young artists, an able writer, a gifted stage designer, a very knowledgeable gardener, a famous host and raconteur and an organiser of exhibitions all in one?

His friendships included so many fellow artists, writers, social celebrities, musicians, stage people, politicians, explorers, academics and intellectuals that together their names would read like an artistic and social register of two or three continents.

Hill the portrait painter is represented in many collections, including the National Portrait Gallery in London which owns his paintings of the writer L.P. Hartley and the actor Alec Guinness. Hundreds more hang in private houses in Britain, Ireland and the US.

All his life Hill was a celebrity collector. Yet they gravitated towards him of their own accord, drawn as much by the charm and force of his personality as by his professional skills.

His early friendship with Bernard Berenson, for instance, grew naturally and for a time he lived in a small house in the grounds of Berenson's house in Italy, painting and profiting by the great scholar's talk and tuition.

He painted Berenson during his last months, lying back in bed while being read to by his mistress-muse, Nicky Mariano. To my knowledge he did not paint Matisse, to whom he was sent by Dorothy Bussy (sister of Lytton Strachey) and her husband, the gifted French pastelist Simon Bussy.

Otherwise, it is hard to think of many well-known personalities whom Hill did not paint. His sitters included Seamus Heaney, Arthur Rubinstein the pianist, the historian Steven Runciman, John Betjeman, Isaiah Berlin, Wilfred Thesiger, Erskine Childers, Garret FitzGerald, Tony O'Reilly, Anne Crookshank, Archbishop McQuaid of Dublin, the Duchess of Abercorn, the Tory Island painter James Dixon, et *alii multi*.

Those who liked to poke fun gently at Hill for his cherished intimacy with the British royal family might remember that he was just as likely to paint some Tory Island boatman or a small farmer in the area of Church Hill, the district in Donegal where he lived for much of the year. He was too big a man to be a social snob and his friendships embraced all sorts of people.

He sometimes became a little sensitive that many people preferred his landscapes and excellent small genre pieces to the portraits, since this implied that the latter were painted for pleasure and the former to make a living. Hill was, of course, a professional portrait-painter but he generally chose his sitters and was inimical to painting people who did not interest him.

Overall, the portraits are uneven in quality but the best of them are outstanding and show not only his excellent technique but his insight into character. In an epoch in which portraiture was either neglected or left to poorly talented academicians, he kept a great tradition alive.

The small landscapes — his 'postcard master-pieces' — are unfailingly good. Yet some of the larger ones are also masterpieces, including the big view of Tory Island in the Ulster Museum, Belfast and 'Donegal, Late Harvest', which shows a scene near his beloved Church Hill.

These two pictures would be sufficient to place Hill among the great landscape painters. And his small, deceptively 'spontaneous' pictures of musicians in action, or Greek Orthodox monks at Mount Athos or the clothesline in his garden are excellent.

His reputation as an artist seems secure and will grow with time and greater public familiarity. As for the man himself, he was so rich and kaleido-scopic a personality that only the combined reminiscences of his uncounted friends and extend-ed family could describe him in the round. He seemed to know or have known just about every-body and could relate facts or anecdotes about them.

Visitors to the house in Church Hill were asked to sign a visitors' book and once when my wife and I arrived there for a few days we noted the name Greta Garbo, dated some days previously.

'What was she like as a guest, Derek?' I asked.

'Oh,' he answered, 'she didn't do very much except eat apples and go for walks on her own.'

Hill was not afraid of dying. 'Probably it will be just like going on a trip to Tory Island.'

He also mentioned that he had finally finished, with a little help, writing his memoirs, and I can only hope they preserve some of the essence of a unique personality.

David Will, Tipperary, with Judge John Rees in the Junior Whip Competition at the Tullamore Show. Photograph: Joe St Leger.

Taking Watery Route to Fabled Fermanagh

Tim O'Brien

The Shannon, a jug of wine and thou …

We started in Killaloe, Co. Clare, which is the southern end of the Shannon navigation, at least for hire boats. This was the trip. All the way to Co. Fermanagh to see the mouth of the Ulster Canal.

We promised each other long summer evenings watching the sun descend across Lough Derg, slow journeys meandering through the flat midlands countryside and the sight of the mist as it rises off Lough Bofin on a summer's morning.

We spoke of eating outdoors, on the deck of the boat or in the waterside restaurants and pubs, of the banter with neighbouring boaters and of the slow, slow pace of it all.

And that is exactly the way it happened.

Two hours into the journey the evening was so nice we decided to spend the night at Garrykennedy on Lough Derg in Co. Tipperary. Garrykennedy consists of little other than two pubs and a harbour and many pleasant evenings have been spent in both pubs. It's popular with families, because the pubs serve food and children's meals, and you can almost hear the collective sigh when the last one goes to sleep on the boats and the deck chairs come out.

Next morning, after a choppy journey, we arrived at the swing bridge in Portumna, with enough time to cook lunch or visit Portumna Castle before the bridge opened. Left alone for a few hours, I made a classic blunder. I went back

Cruising on the River Shannon. Photograph: Brian Lynch.

out on the lake in the boat with no other craft in sight. It had become very rough and suddenly the anchor was flipped overboard and became stuck in the lake bed. Bobbing there, I blessed mobile phones and explained my predicament to the Emerald Star base in Portumna. They despatched one of their boats and between us we drove our boat across the anchor and hauled it in.

Chastened and in the calmer river section north of Lough Derg, we got through Victoria Lock without any problems, and in Banagher we prepared a meal and ate on deck. The weather was blustery, but we got chatting to other boaters; it was pleasant to sit in the fresh air and relax with a cool draught. We vowed to take Lough Ree with extreme care.

The following days slipped by slowly as the river meandered wide and slow-flowing, the boat going at no more than a fast walking pace. We passed the entrance to the Grand Canal, which leads to Dublin, and the Ballinasloe Canal, which was closed in 1961. We wandered about the monastic ruins at Clonmacnoise and then went on to Athlone, where we spent the night at the marina.

The next day we crossed Lough Ree in a convoy of boats to Lanesborough. An ESB power station is here and many miles of narrow-gauge railway bring small trains feeding the plant with peat. We passed the entrance to Richmond Harbour, where the Royal Canal enters the Shannon, and continued on under the raised bridges at Tarmonbarry and Rooskey.

We ate well in the local pub that night, but were under way early the next morning and crossed loughs Bofin and Boderg as a gentle haze rose off the water, holding the promise of really fine weather.

Here we were in the upper Shannon, my favourite part of the navigation. The sun sparkled on the water and we were tempted up the Boyle River, where the trees overhang the water. There was time for lunch at Clarandon Lock before entering Lough Key. By now, we had lost all sense

of time, and it did not seem to matter that we had turned off the route to the Shannon-Erne link. At some stage we went back, because I remember the daunting series of locks leading up to Lough Scur on the Shannon-Erne link. They are all automated and the smart cards which open them also operate showers, lavatory and laundry facilities along the way.

After Ballyconnell, we were on the Woodford River, with Fermanagh on the left and Cavan on the right. There was a turn for Belturbet on the Erne River, but we headed for the calm Quivvey Waters and the mouth of the Rinn River. At Wattle Bridge we came upon the holy grail: this is where the Ulster Canal began. With the second feasibility study under way, most boaters believe it will reopen.

Some day, when that happens, and we have a month to spare, we will be back.

WEDNESDAY, 9 AUGUST 2000

Dogs Outwit Sheepish Cunning

Eileen Battersby

Forget everything you've ever heard about sheep being stupid. They're not. At least, not in Co. Donegal. Even those who never have a good word to say about the woollies would have to concede sheep can have their moments. And at the 33rd annual Clonmany Agricultural Show at Ballyliffin, Co. Donegal, at the northern point of the Inishowen peninsula, yesterday, several sheep displayed instances of rare cunning. Some even looked slightly amused.

But such is the appeal of the sheepdog — hardworking, faithful, lively and good-natured — that there was no mistaking that as far as the crowd was concerned the sheep were the enemy and the dogs all heroes.

Despite overcast conditions and suggestions of rain throughout the day, the expected tempest never arrived. Instead, the showground area, contained within the natural bowl created by mountains, remained busy and constantly offered diversions. These ranged from mysterious Rose, the soothsayer, who sat in a trailer to the Wellington-boot-throwing competition, to the hoof-paring demonstration, to the children's pet competition — won by a pair of ferrets as tame as turtle-doves.

The Clonmany show dates from 1954. With some gaps caused by organisational difficulties in the early years, it has continued ever since, attracting visitors from all over the county and, judging by the variety of accents, people from all over Ireland and elsewhere. Even with the up-to-date equipment on show and topical themes such as Pokemon, the Simpsons and 101 Dalmatians, the show still retains a relaxing old-world feel. It could be Ireland from the 1950s.

The bouncing castles were busy and the children involved in running races, but the general attention remained firmly fixed on the sheep-judging and the various classes ranging from black-faced mountain ewe lamb and rams to cross-bred ewe border Leicester to Suffolk sheep — be they ewe, ram or lamb — to the horses and, above all, the dazzling sheepdogs.

The experienced shepherds were initially wary. Sheep become easier as the day goes on. Judging by the friskiness of some of the sheep quartets coming into the field, the dogs were being challenged. Followers of the TV programme 'One Man and His Dog' knew what to expect. The shepherd, crook in hand, whistling or shouting his commands, invariably looks concerned while the dog works, beginning his approach with a wide run, ever-narrowing its circle around the sheep.

The objective is to pen them. A couple of tourists, however, made their lack of rudimentary knowledge obvious. 'But there's only four sheep,' exclaimed a woman with expensive binoculars and new green wellies. 'I thought there'd be a flock or, well more than a few.' But most of the onlookers

were knowledgeable; and many of them not only knew the shepherds, they knew the names of the individual collies.

Dog after dog came onto the field, each displaying an eagerness and an interest. There were more border than rough collies at work yesterday. Even when the sheep proved most troublesome — such as one adventurous pair which jumped into the announcer's van — most of the dogs retained a sense of perspective.

The shepherds revealed more temperament. One man who had impressed as being poker-faced in the extreme, eventually became a vivid study in exasperation. His dog looked sympathetic.

A quartet of sheep entered with all the self-possession of a corps de ballet. The four could have been preparing to dance Swan Lake, but the deceptively young shepherd facing them had such presence that the sheep heaved a collective sigh which seemed to express their understanding that they had no option but to co-operate with the youth's happy scrap of a dog.

Also competing in the open class was Michelle McGoldrick, the winner of the young handlers' class in last year's 'One Man and His Dog' competition held in Wales. She has been herding for three years and her dog, Jess, had no doubts as to her worth. Watching the proceedings with an expression of intense interest was a fine old dog who sat for much of the afternoon with his paw on my foot. Clever, obedient, full of curiosity and intent, these working dogs in general shared the slick movements of a skilled pickpocket. But one of the most impressive had to be Nap, a collie with the stride of a 400-metre hurdler and the poise of a ballerina.

His owner, William, was about as laid back as a skilled and efficient shepherd could be. Watching the pair was to see two artists at work.

There is no doubting that Co. Donegal's sheep are a game crew and certainly know how to give good dogs a run for their money, while the dogs themselves are true entertainers. Elsewhere, the

Monkstown Combaltas Ceoltoirí dancers Fionnuala Doberty and John Considine step out for the Enniscorthy Combaltas musicians including from left: Fionntín MacNaeidhe, David Harper, Kevin McDermott, Jimmy Kavanagh, Mick Murphy and James Kelly at a reception in the Guinness Reception Centre, Dublin to announce details of the Guinness sponsored Fleadh Cheoil Na hÉireann taking place in Enniscorthy, Co. Wexford. Photograph: Matt Kavanagh.

home industries tent proved the scene of many triumphs. Patchwork quilts and dolls were among the prize winners, while the bakery section confirmed again and again that there really is nothing like a good home-baked cake.

FRIDAY, II AUGUST 2000

True to Life

Kevin Courtney

Boys often fantasise about being a movie hero like James Bond or George Clooney, but none of us really believes we will ever see ourselves on the big screen. Well, I went to see a film the other day, and there I was, 20 feet high, in glorious technicolour — but I was anything but thrilled to see my magnified mirror image.

Oh, I loved the movie. But my Doppelganger on the screen was no action hero or romantic swashbuckler, but a rather unglamorous record shop owner, music obsessive and list-o-maniac named Rob, whose emotional development had been arrested during the anti-Vietnam riots. My character was portrayed by the actor John Cusack; although he doesn't much resemble me in looks, he nailed my personality to the wall, next to the Led Zeppelin poster.

Flashback to a couple of weeks ago: I'm at a music industry gig, chatting to a fellow journalist, music obsessive and pop trivia buff, whom we shall name J. 'Have you seen "High Fidelity"?' J asks me. I reply that I haven't yet seen Stephen Frears's movie of Nick Hornby's best-selling novel. J grips my arm with a get-out-of-the-building-now-before-it-explodes urgency, leans closer to me, and says, 'Oh, my God, Kevin, we're all in it!' It felt like the moment when Richard Nixon was told that the whole Watergate cover-up was blown.

And so I scooted down to my local cineplex, and watched with a mixture of amusement and horror as John Cusack re-enacted my rather imperfect life right before my eyes. I had originally planned to bring a date to 'High Fidelity', but something told me I should make this one a solo trip, even though I might look like billy-nomates sitting alone in the cinema. Call it alpha male self-preservation instinct — I don't want to be found out just yet. Top five reasons for not bringing your girlfriend to see 'High Fidelity':

1. She will realise with a sinking feeling that the sad, hopeless bloke on screen is the same sad, hopeless bloke she's been living with for the past two years. Except not as good-looking as John Cusack.

2. You will spend the entire movie fidgeting in your seat, head averted to avoid eye contact with her. At certain points in the film, you will have to fight the urge to slide on to the floor and crawl out of the cinema.

3. Each time Rob confesses to another selfish, insensitive act of betrayal, she will stare suspiciously at you and say, 'I hope you've never done that!'

4. Every time you laugh during the film (and it is a funny film), it will be the hollow laugh of a cornered rat. Every time she laughs, it will

Ian McCormack from Crumlin, Dublin, competing in the Irish Bog Snorkelling Championships on Lisryan Bog, Co. Longford. The event marked the opening of Granard Festival with the overall winner qualifying for the World Championship in Wales. Photograph: Matt Kavanagh.

be with a wry and slightly vexed chuckle of recognition.

5. She will break up with you right after the film's credits roll — if she has any sense.

The blurb on Hornby's book reads: 'You should read it and make your partner read it, so they will no longer hate you but pity you instead.' The story concerns a record-shop owner named Rob, who, refusing to grow up and get a life, hides behind his vast array of musical knowledge and builds impregnable emotional barriers using hundreds of 12-inch-square slabs of vinyl (alphabetically sorted, of course).

Rob is the archetypal approaching-middle-age man: immature, under-achieving, obsessive and anally retentive; he knows more about music than anyone really needs to know, and knows less about relationships than is decent and acceptable in proper society. He can recall the minutest details of rock events past, but can't remember the conversation he had with his girlfriend last weekend. He can commit 100 per cent to rock bands he has never met, remaining loyal to them even through their jazz-African-concept phase, but he can't commit to the woman lying in the bed next to him.

He is often referred to as a 'Sad Bastard', but the saddest thing of all is that Rob is a painfully accurate composite of me and most of my middle-aged, trivia-driven friends. Rob spends his entire working day skulking around in a second-hand record store. I too have often spent my entire working day in a second-hand record store, seeking out Primal Scream's 'Loaded' on 12-inch vinyl when really I should have been filing my Primal Scream review for a 5 p.m. deadline.

Rob's record collection is alphabetically arranged on big wooden shelves. Once, I was entertaining a young lady at home, and she idly browsed through my CDs while I fixed us a drink. 'I don't believe it!' she exclaimed. 'Your CDs are in alphabetical order! How sad.' Blushing profusely, I tried to explain that, as a music journalist, I needed to be able to locate a record quickly, but I could already see her mentally taking note of the nearest exit. I even claimed mitigating circumstances, i.e. that only two of my shelves were so arranged, the rest being in glorious disarray, but it was no use. She was already looking at me with a mixture of contempt and fear, as though I might suddenly lock her in my basement, tie her up and show her my butterfly collection.

But 'High Fidelity' is not just about me. It's also about my male friends, colleagues and social compadres. As my trivia-loving chum said, we're all in it.

My two closest friends are in it. When the three of us meet up in our local pub, the conversational parameters are set down even before the first pint has settled. Top five things we will talk about:

1. This year's Mercury Music Prize nominations.
2. Rory Gallagher's greatest guitar solos.
3. The tracklising of Led Zeppelin's 'Houses of the Holy'.
4. Getting on the guest list for Lou Reed.
5. The Bends versus OK Computer — discuss (at length, ad nauseam).

Top five things we won't talk about:

1. Our feelings.
2. Our partner's feelings.
3. Our fears, hopes and dreams, and how to be better people.
4. Spirituality (we will, however, happily discuss Spiritualized).
5. Westlife. We will never, ever, mention those, whom we consider evil spawns of Satan.

When love breaks down, Hornby Man takes solace in his top five sad songs. 'I have my own relationship break-up songs, just like Rob,' admitted a colleague, N. 'I can track the whole trajectory of my relationships through music — happy songs to start with, sad songs to finish, and bitter songs to help get over it.'

Experts say that middle-aged men start collecting records because they're trying to recapture their youth and — by association — their fading virility. Women are becoming more empowered in the workplace and in their personal lives; men, already reeling from hair loss, falling sperm counts and soaring stress levels, are in fear of losing their place at Number One and dropping out of the human hit parade. Finding a pristine vinyl copy of The Beatles' White Album, complete with poster, seems a perfectly logical way of fighting the onslaught of change.

Now that we have been outed, however, I feel a sense of relief. No longer do I have to skulk in secondhand record shops, hiding from the real world, and nor do I have to change the subject to my Top Five punk anthems every time my girlfriend wants to discuss relationship issues. I'm finally ready to seek professional help to cure these symptoms of mid-life crisis — just as soon as I've finished cataloguing my record collection.

MONDAY, 14 AUGUST 2000

Immigrant Baby Boom Puts Pressure On Coombe

Nuala Haughey

Baby Mary is lying sleeping in her cot in the Coombe Women's Hospital in Dublin, a Bible by her tiny head, opened at Psalm 23, 'The Lord is My Shepherd'. Her mother, Olayinka Ujimakinwa, a Nigerian asylum-seeker who arrived in the State last April, is recovering well. She praises her medical treatment and, tutting and shaking her head, says that she definitely does not want to return to Nigeria.

Olayinka is one of five women in the 36-bed Our Lady's Ward today who are non-Irish nationals. They also include Angel Kabongo from Zaire who has been granted refugee status, entitling her to live in Ireland permanently, and who is expecting her third Irish-born child. The number of non-Irish nationals attending the maternity hospital has increased in line with the generally upward trend in asylum applications in the past year, and now

accounts for 10 per cent of its 7,000 patients annually. This picture is reflected in the capital's two other main maternity hospitals, the National Maternity Hospital at Holles Street and the Rotunda Hospital on Parnell Square, close to the area known as Little Africa due to the proliferation of African-owned shops.

Dr Peter McKenna, the master of the Rotunda, estimates the hospital will deliver babies for about 700 non-Irish nationals this year, out of some 6,000 births. Neither the Coombe nor the Rotunda categorises mothers on the basis of their status as asylum-seekers or refugees.

However, Holles Street hospital does, and a spokeswoman said that about 10 per cent of its 6,500 annual births are to non-Irish nationals, with half of these to asylum-seekers or refugees. In his office two floors below Our Lady's Ward, the Coombe's Master, Dr Sean Daly, says he's not interested in what brings asylum-seekers and other immigrants to Ireland, or whether they should or should not be here. What interests him is the medical care of such women, who often arrive at the hospital very late in pregnancy, having had little or no previous medical attention. 'The issue is that this hospital provides care for everybody,' he says. 'We are now seeing a range of medical disorders in pregnancy that are being presented to us so late that we are trying to catch up. And on the one hand it's challenging, but on the other it's time consuming and needs additional resources.'

The medical disorders include hepatitis, HIV and sickle cell disease — a blood disorder prevalent among Africans and associated with severe bone pain and pre-term delivery. Dr Daly recently saw a woman with sickle cell disease have a psychotic episode on the labour ward. He also recently treated his first two cases of expectant mothers with malaria.

'When I worked in the US, I had dealt with sickle cell disease, but I had never seen malaria,' he says. 'Now we investigate for malaria, but before we wouldn't have considered it in the differential diagnosis. The complexity of the pregnancies is much greater than we've been used to dealing with.' In the case of HIV infection, early treatment can reduce the blood's 'viral load' to almost zero, which means the risk of infection of the baby through vaginal delivery is minimal. However, if the viral load is not virtually zero, then consideration for Caesarean section is appropriate as this drastically cuts the risk of transmission of the AIDS virus.

If an HIV-positive patient arrives in the State already heavily pregnant, she will invariably have to have a Caesarean section, says Dr Daly. This means a slower recovery time for the patient and increased staff workload. Prompted by concerns for the welfare of heavily pregnant patients with medical complications, the hospital has set up a fast-track referral system for asylum-seekers. Dr Daly stresses that such patients are managed well and there is no risk to other patients. 'The staff are becoming more familiar with the diseases, but we could certainly do with more expertise in dealing with the complexity of cases,' he says.

This complexity goes well beyond just the women's medical needs. There are obvious issues such as language barriers, gender sensitivities, cultural nuances and dietary needs. And then there are less obvious matters, such as taking into account the trauma or distress the women may have recently fled.

Angel Kabongo and children, Divine, aged one (left) and Grace, aged two years, at the Coombe Hospital. Photograph: Matt Kavanagh.

'You might ask someone, "Is your husband going to come?" and they say: "Well he doesn't know where I am and I have no way of contacting him",' says Rosemary Grant, the hospital's head medical social worker.

Grant says her staff have learned when dealing with immigrants to suspend the normal assumptions they make when dealing with Irish nationals.

'What does it mean to have a Down's syndrome baby if you are from another country?' she asks. 'You can't take for granted that the ways we think here are going to fit. You have to learn about what would be the norm in the woman's country.'

Staff are constantly learning about the sensitivities involved in dealing with such patients, she adds. For example, staff formerly used family members or friends to interpret for women who did not speak English, 'but then we realised that the women might not want to talk about intimate issues in front of people they know, so we changed that'.

For the women too, Irish practices may take some getting used to. For example, in some African states, women might bring their children to stay in the hospital with them when they are having their new baby. 'So the idea of having to organise someone to look after them is difficult for the women and the husband who is used to sending them all off to hospital together,' says Grant.

The system of direct provision for asylum-seekers — where they are placed in full-board accommodation and paid £15 per week comfort money per adult and £7.50 per child — places additional stresses on new mothers, says Grant. While grants for clothing, cots and prams are available to asylum-seekers on the same basis as Irish nationals, asylum-seekers usually have fewer family members or friends to rely on to supplement State benefits. 'Irish people would have someone they could borrow a carry cot from, or hand-me-down clothes, whereas most of the asylum-seekers wouldn't, and they could go home from hospital without anything to put the baby in and no one to ask "Could you lend me that for the week?",' Grant explains.

Dr Daly has written to the Minister for Justice, John O'Donoghue, telling him it is difficult for staff to maintain the current level of service in the face of such challenges. He says he is not publicising these issues 'as a stick to beat the Government with. People are concerned in this hospital that the numbers coming through are going to increase and our ability to deliver quality care could be compromised ultimately.'

In his letter, Dr Daly advises the Minister that asylum-seekers with complicated pregnancies should remain in Dublin rather than being sent to towns and villages around the State under the mandatory dispersal programme.

'We deliver more than 7,000 babies per year, we have a lot of consultations and therefore it's easier for us to deal with complicated pregnancies than a two or three-doctor unit down the country which is not used to dealing with them. I think we should look after those women but I think we should get extra funding to do it,' he says.

Dr Daly returns to the guiding philosophy behind the hospital, set up by a philanthrophist, Margaret Boyle, in 1826. 'Margaret Boyle set up the hospital 175 years ago next year because two pregnant women died in the snow trying to get to the Rotunda,' he says. 'This hospital has always offered care to women who wanted it or needed it and what brings them to the door is not something of concern to us. We should care for people if they need it. Other issues are superfluous to us.'

TUESDAY, 15 AUGUST 2000

As Good As It Got

John Connolly

In the summer of 1991, on the night before I travelled to the US for the first time, my father expressed his regret that we hadn't managed to have a drink together. By that time the pubs were closed so it was too late to go, but it was a major concession on my father's part.

Colin Byrne, representing Wicklow, taking a Poc on the slopes of Annaverna mountain during the All-Ireland Poc Fada Final 2000 in the Cooley Mountains. Photograph: Alan Betson.

You see, we drank in very different bars, my father and I. He had abandoned his favourite drinking spot, the County Bar in Rialto, after it was desecrated by the addition of carpets. My father, being a socialist, a trade unionist and a fan of horse racing, had an ingrained suspicion of public houses with carpet on the floor. I, on the other hand, had no difficulty with carpets, or comfortable stools, or toilet floors that didn't soak my suede boots or the ends of my jeans with overflow. Our paths, therefore, tended not to cross in bars.

That was in June, and we never did get to have that drink together. I went away to the US and when I came back in September my father was dying. The illness that was taking his life had altered his appearance so dramatically that I had to check the names on the ends of the beds in the ward before I could find him.

I had brought him back a cardigan, which he never got to wear, and a book, which he never got

to read. (It was *The Wit and Wisdom of Spiro T. Agnew* and had no writing in it, but I thought he might appreciate the joke.)

I used to wheel him down to the toilets so he could smoke a crafty cigarette after it was explained to him that lighting up beside his oxygen tank was not something with which the hospital authorities, or his fellow patients, were entirely comfortable. I think I had about three weeks with him before he died, during which he was lucid for no more than a few days.

But all of that came later. That evening, it didn't bother me so much that my father and I had missed an opportunity for a drink together, because I was 23, I could drink as much as I wanted in an American bar, and I was leaving for Delaware the next morning.

I didn't stay in Delaware for very long. (Anybody who has ever been to Delaware, proud home of the du Pont chemical corporation, will probably understand why.) I departed my place of employment after my boss, a 70-year-old woman, stabbed me in the arm with a fruit knife. I think she'd just forgotten that she was holding the knife, as some 70-year-olds will do, but I still decided that it was time to leave before I became a statistic, my grave an object of gruesome pilgrimage for fans of homicide.

I fled north to a luxury hotel called the Black Point Inn at Prouts Neck, an area formerly home to the painter Winslow Homer and part of the coastal region of Scarborough, Maine. Eight years after my first visit, I would publish the first of a series of books inspired, at least in part, by Scarborough.

I grew to love its salt marshes, its coastline and, within cycling distance to the north, the small city of Portland. I even grew to love — in a strictly non-sexual way, of course — the policemen who lurked by the roadside in an effort to apprehend speeding motorists and unwelcome poor people, poor people having no place in Prouts Neck unless they were being paid by the hour. (I still return to Maine each year, but I have never yet stayed in the Black Point Inn. I can't afford it. If I ever have children, I don't want to have to tell them that daddy blew their inheritance on a couple of nights in a hotel.)

That summer in Prouts Neck I learned, among other things, that the rich really are different. In August, the governor of the state announced the evacuation of the coast because of an impending hurricane. Buses were laid on to take away the evacuees, but the guests at the Black Point Inn were made of sterner stuff. The majority insisted on staying and the only real concession made to the elements was the application of black adhesive tape to the windows, so that we would not be shredded by flying glass when they eventually caved in.

In addition the waiting staff were permitted, for one night only, to dispense with their usual bow ties. How this might assist us in the event of the building being torn apart by the hurricane was unclear, unless the management was concerned that our bow ties might catch on a piece of hotel

property as the high winds swept us away, thereby causing us to choke and leaving the hotel open to potentially ruinous lawsuits by our next-of-kin.

That night, I sat on the edge of the cliffs at Prouts Neck and watched the waves pummel Crescent Beach and Old Orchard. I wasn't afraid of being swept away. I was immortal, as all young men are.

Meanwhile, my father was having difficulty sleeping because of pains in his back. He was being treated for a trapped nerve, despite the fact that he was dying of cancer. This might explain why he didn't seem to get any better.

Actually, I suspect my father already knew that he had cancer; I don't believe that the body allows rogue cells to colonise its lungs, its spine and its brain without sending a message to the mind that something is terribly wrong. Still, my father elected not to tell anybody, partly because he didn't want people worrying but also, I think, because if he chose not to admit it then it might not be true. Unfortunately, this ranked alongside soluble painkillers, my father's other preferred treatment option, as an effective way of combating the disease.

I was in New York, walking with a friend in Central Park, on the day I finally learned that he was dying. I made the call home from a bank of pay phones close by the statue of Alice in Wonderland. Afterwards, instead of raging and tearing my hair out, I went to a performance by the magicians Penn and Teller, who specialised in undermining other magicians by explaining to the audience how their illusions were performed. In essence, they took the mystery out of magic: there was no enigma, just sleight of hand, trickery, and people's desire to believe that, somehow, miracles beyond nature might be possible. It seemed kind of apt. That night I lost my jacket, but I found it again. As far as miracles went, that was as good as it got for the next few weeks. I went home the next day.

A few nights before he died, my father spent an hour drawing a map of the hospital on the back of a cigarette packet, so he'd know where he was going when they eventually let him out of the ward. The irony of attempting to plot his escape on materials salvaged from the very things that were killing him escaped him, but you had to admire him for trying.

My father passed away on 8 October 1991, at the age of 62. I have only visited his grave once since then, because I don't get any sense of him there. He is somewhere else, probably complaining about the new carpets and trying to find out the winner of the 3.30 at Kempton.

I think my father would be surprised that I am making a living from writing fiction; not unhappy, and certainly proud, but just a little taken aback. He was a clever, educated man, an idealistic realist (or realistic idealist) who worked for Dublin Corporation all his life, but for him writing fiction would have been on a par with pavement art and busking as a reliable way of earning a crust. He always hated being proved wrong, so maybe it was for that reason that I dedicated a book to him.

I did it partly because I loved him.

But, mostly, I did it to annoy him.

SATURDAY, 26 AUGUST 2000

How to Read a Novel?

John Banville

How to Read and Why, by Harold Bloom. Fourth Estate. 283pp, Stg£15.99

Harold Bloom is an old trooper in the culture wars. He has skirmished with literary theorists of all hues — structuralists (remember them?), deconstructionists, feminists, the political correctors — and in the heat of battle has delivered many a sword-cut, and taken a few slashes himself. He is an unreconstructed humanist, firmly in the line of his heroes Johnson and Hazlitt; as such, he is one of the last, if not, indeed, the last, of his kind. *How to Read and Why* is his Big Red Book, a primer for all those potential readers who in his judgment have been betrayed by contemporary arbiters of culture, including the universities. It is also a barricade thrown up against the seemingly unstoppable advance of the new academic Levellers who firmly reject the Western Canon and whose aim appears to be, in the formulation of his namesake, Allan Bloom, the closing of the American mind — and the minds of the rest of us, too.

Bloom — Harold, that is — in his preface quotes approvingly Virginia Woolf's remark about Hazlitt, that 'He is one of those rare critics who have thought so much that they can dispense with reading.' The same may not be said of Bloom, not because he has not thought a very great deal, over the nearly 50 years of his career as critic and teacher, but because he would never dream of dispensing with reading. He is stoutly and intentionally unfashionable in the answers he adduces to the question with which the book opens, 'Why Read?' Readers must read, he declares, 'for and in their own interest'. Books will not make us better in our dealings with the world, or not directly, anyway — as Auden said, poetry makes nothing happen — but they will help to refine and expand the self.

'I turn to reading as a solitary praxis,' Bloom writes, 'rather than as an educational enterprise.' This is a more radical statement than it may seem at first sight, especially from the pen of a man who surely must be one of the great educators of our time. He is Professor of Humanities at Yale, and Professor of English at New York University. Although he declares, contra Auden, perhaps, that 'poetry is the only "self-help" that works, because ... [it] strengthens my own spirit,' his expectations from reading are sensibly limited. Of Chekhov's work he observes that 'while he doesn't make me simple, more truthful, more myself, I do wish I could be better (though I can't be). My wish seems to me an aesthetic rather than a moral phenomenon...'

The key word there, surely, is 'aesthetic'. There is a pseudo-liberal notion abroad in these

Actors Eric Lacey (left) as Mercury and Mikel Murfi as Jupiter, members of the cast of the Barabbas production of 'God's Gift', one of the shows in this year's Eircom Dublin Theatre Festival arriving at Eircom Headquarters in St Stephen's Green to publicise the programme for the event. 'God's Gift' is a new version by Irish author John Banville of Heinrich von Kleist's 'Amphitryon'. Photograph: Bryan O'Brien.

times that art, the doing and the receiving of it, is good for you, because it both 'takes you out of yourself' and out of a violent and stressful world ('prevents wrinkles', as the Lyric FM advertisement has it), and at the same time allows you to express yourself, and aids you in achieving the highest aspirations of your soul. Sadly, this is nonsense, as any serious artist, if he is honest, will tell you. It is also pernicious, in that it is a clandestine, or perhaps just unconscious, assault on real art, which does not aim to help or assuage or vindicate, is not directed at the public good, will not cure your Angst or mend your broken heart, but nevertheless is a moral force, an inert moral force, if only because it represents the closest to perfection that the artist, a frail, flawed human being like the rest of us, could manage to get. Whatever it is we expect from art, 'we must not,' as Bloom warns, 'impose upon fiction [or art in general] the burden of improving society'.

Bloom recognises, and acknowledges, that there is far less of quotidian reality in literature, even in fiction, than we like to think. 'Only literature can be made into literature,' he points out, 'though life must get into the mix, almost always as provender rather than as form.' Although Bloom is, to say it again, a great humanist, unshakeable in his insistence that the organic life of a great work of art will resist and survive any theoretical onslaught, whether from extreme deconstructionists, 'cultural studies' gauleiters, or the proponents of 'art for everyone' — which really means 'art for no one' — he will not allow us for a moment to lose sight of the fact that literature is made out of words and thoughts, not flesh and blood, which is as true of the novel as it is of poetry, no matter how high a level of verisimilitude the novelist may achieve. Anthony Burgess, a wise commentator as well as a good novelist, whose wisdom and work alike seem for the moment forgotten, put it simply and truly when he bade us to keep in mind that 'art is a game, life is not'. Wallace Stevens, one of Bloom's heroes, expresses something of the same, but more gnomically, when in his great poem 'The Man with the Blue Guitar' he writes that 'Things as they are/Are changed upon the blue guitar'.

In its organisation, *How to Read and Why* is as awkward as its title. It begins with a splendidly two-fisted preface — 'The poems of our climate [Stevens again] have been replaced by the body stockings of our culture' — which, after an initial promise that there will be 'no polemics here', plunges straight into attacks upon 'our new Materialists' who 'assert that they work in the name of the Reality Principle. The life of the mind must yield to the death of the body, yet that hardly requires the cheerleading of an academic sect.' Next comes a long section devoted, lovingly, to the short story, then one on poems, then 'Novels Part I', followed by 'Plays', 'Novels Part II', and a faintly transcendental Epilogue. Poets, novels, novelists, plays and playwrights, are considered in short, two- or three-page sections that have the flourish and urgency of mini-tutorials. Bloom's choice of authors and works is eclectic: Housman sits beside Blake, Henry James rubs shoulders with Thomas Pynchon, Shakespeare's sonnets come hard on the heels of 'Sir Patrick Spence'.

Favourites are apparent: Shakespeare, of course — Bloom's most recent book claimed the Bard to be 'The Inventor of the Human' — Blake, Emily Dickinson, Proust, Melville; but he is also accommodating to writers whose presence here may surprise: for instance, Toni Morrison — wisely, he chooses an early work, *Song of Solomon* — Nathanael West, Cormac McCarthy (*Blood Meridian*) and the versatile Anon., whose 'Tom O'Bedlam' he ranks with the best of Shakespeare's songs.

One might argue with Bloom's sometimes overly commonsensical, Johnsonian stone-kicking. Not all Theory is deplorable: fierce reality-instructors such as Paul de Man and Jean Baudrillard do

manage to expose much of the pietistic cant that lesser critics than Harold Bloom indulge in. What is deplorable, however, is the Tyranny of Theory, driven by mediocrities and academic time-servers and what Bloom witheringly refers to as 'our current campus Puritans', in other words, by those with a case to prove or an axe to grind or an inadequacy to compensate for at our expense. Also, Bloom chooses not to engage the question of the possible implication of High Culture in the political catastrophes of the last century; for instance, surely there is a connection, however tenuous, between the fascist tendencies of many of the great Modernists — with the glorious exception of James Joyce — and the political and cultural collapse of the 1930s. But this is to yearn for the book that Bloom did not write, instead of celebrating the wonderful one that he did.

Bloom, who is touching 70, appeals to the reader in us — perhaps, in many of us, the lost reader — with the desperate urgency of a man who towards the close of his professional life has been forced to contemplate the coming of a cultural darkness into which many of the beautiful, lofty things that make life worth living may disappear. He is pessimistic on the future of the novel, in our image-obsessed age; although he does not say so, he is probably fearful that the finest poetry, too, may be drowned in the rising tide of popular culture, most of which is not culture in any sense, but a means for a few shrewd individuals and multinational corporations to make a very great deal of money by deceiving the young. Bloom writes with passion of those writers whom he loves, and whose work for him affirms life, but throughout his book there persists an apprehensive, sorrowing note.

'Despite Proust's healing power, I cannot read a novel in quite the way I did half a century ago, when I lost myself in what I read. I fell in love (if I remember accurately) not with an actual girl but with Mary South in Thomas Hardy's *The Woodlanders*, and I grieved dreadfully when she cut off her beautiful hair in order to sell it. Few other experiences quite touch the reality of falling in love with a heroine, and with her book. One measures oncoming old age by its deepening of Proust, and its deepening by Proust. How to read a novel? Lovingly, if it shows itself capable of accommodating one's love; and jealously, because it can become the image of one's limitation in time and space, and yet give the Proustian blessing of more life.'

SATURDAY, 2 SEPTEMBER 2000

Tragedies Stemming from Middle-class Malaise

Breda O'Brien

An act of violence outside a nightclub in Dublin ended another life tragically and senselessly this week. How many more young people like Brian Murphy will have to die before we are disturbed, not just briefly and in passing, but at a level which prompts deeper questions about the kind of society we have become?

I did not know Brian, but I know his parents and sisters, and it is almost beyond comprehension that this loving and closeknit family should have been devastated in this way. Details are still sketchy, but it appears that some sort of rivalry escalated until it became lethal. I was struck, however, by one phrase used in news reports on the day after his death. Garda referred to it as an 'isolated incident'.

By what reckoning is it an isolated incident? The telephones on RTÉ Radio 1's 'Liveline' programme hummed all summer with a litany of similar events: unprovoked assaults, scuffles which suddenly turned viciously aggressive, muggings, beatings. Far from being an isolated incident, it is part of a disturbing trend.

By coincidence, a few days before Brian's death I was at a gathering of adults who work with young people. One of them was a man who has been involved for many years with summer courses. This

Passers by look at the flowers left on the railing of the Burlington Hotel, Dublin, near where Brian Murphy died. Photograph: Bryan O'Brien.

man has dealt with teenagers for two decades, but admitted that this summer he was deeply troubled by the level of wanton destructiveness which he witnessed among some of the students.

He was stunned by these young people's blank incomprehension of the antisocial nature of their activities and by how oblivious they seemed to the effects of their behaviour on other people. Worse still, many, though not all, of the parents seemed more concerned with blaming others for their child's wrongdoing. Far from accepting responsibility or attempting to challenge and change their child's behaviour, they attempted to obfuscate and deny the seriousness of their child's actions.

In our snobbery, we associate this with areas of poverty, but these were not deprived children, but some of the most privileged teenagers in the country, who attend select and sought-after schools in south-side Dublin. Yet these teenagers vandalised and dismantled both public and private property, causing thousands of pounds worth of damage. When confronted with their actions, effectively they shrugged and implied that money would fix the damage, so what was the problem?

The expression, knowing the price of everything and the value of nothing, might have been coined for them.

More serious than property damage was the systematic, orchestrated bullying which led to one youngster being seriously beaten. A small core group was behind almost every incident, and resisted every attempt to make them realise the seriousness of what they were doing.

Bullying and destructiveness is not new. What is new is how widespread it is, and the obvious feelings of impunity which those who perpetrate such acts have. New, too, is the degree of parental indifference.

It would seem absolutely basic that parents should be easy to contact while their children are away from home — but no. Those who run summer courses have reported occasions when a child became ill or was in trouble of some kind, but no parent was to be found, for the simple reason that they were out of the country on holiday.

These parents left no contact number, nor did they nominate any other adult who would be capable of taking responsibility while they were gone. It defies belief that any parent should be so casual, but apparently it happens.

There is a malaise among the middle-classes, a deadly mix of affluence and indifference which means that children are indulged in every way possible materially, but a solid grounding in basic values is absent. How else do you explain teenagers who seem incapable of understanding the nature of right and wrong and who sneer in derision at those who try to explain it to them?

It is important not to exaggerate the degree of the problem. Most parents still care for their children and struggle to do their best for them. However, the degree of damage which is done by those who do not care in this way for their children extends far beyond the family circle.

The man of whom I spoke earlier who runs summer courses had another perceptive comment to make. The majority of teenagers present were sane and sensible and would not dream of indulging in the kind of vicious behaviour which came so easily to some, but none was willing to alert the adults to what was going on, or to shout stop.

That morality is a matter of personal choice has become an increasingly pervasive philosophy. The greatest crime is to impose your morality on another, or to judge someone whose beliefs or actions do not accord with yours. In that atmosphere, common standards of behaviour cannot be taken for granted or maintained.

To challenge others' behaviour contradicts the idea that morality is purely private, so few are willing to do that. That reflects a change in the wider society. We can wring our hands and moan about what has happened to young people, but a better question might be, what has happened to us?

This generation of parents is the first to be unsure of its role. Character formation seems to

Ian Mahon of Colmcille National School in Ballybrack, at the Children's Playground, St Stephen's Green. Photograph: Pat Langan.

have been dropped from the job description. An authoritarian way of being a parent disappeared almost overnight, and I for one am not sorry to see it go, but what has replaced it? Many parents seem fearful of setting any boundaries or incapable of enforcing them if they do set them.

Parenting is a labour-intensive job. Quality time is a myth. Quality time happens within huge swathes of quantity time, and not to a schedule. Yet our whole society seems hell-bent on making it as difficult as possible for parents to do a good job, by demanding both parents work outside the home, and often long hours as well.

Excellent parents sometimes still have troubled children, but for the most part, we reap what we sow in parenting. A crucial part of that process is

spending enough time with our children to spot their signs of distress early on, but that needs support from the wider society, too.

It is completely naive to believe that young people will somehow have the ability to resist temptation, to be sensible about alcohol and other drugs and to postpone sexual activity in a society which sends them ambivalent messages about all those things.

Adults are particularly ambivalent about alcohol, probably because most of us have been plastered out of our skulls on occasion. Perhaps that is why we are so willing to accept the ludicrous fact that alcohol abuse is a routine element of many young people's social lives. We have one of the youngest ages of experimentation with drugs and alcohol in Europe, yet we adults seem paralysed and helpless in the face of such realities.

Recent tragic events have shown us the frightening price paid by some families for our paralysis.

THURSDAY, 14 SEPTEMBER 2000

Review Bob Dylan, Vicar Street

Tony Clayton-Lea

Where to start? Simply, Dylan's history dictates he has little right to be as good as he was last night at Vicar Street.

There are people topping the charts these days at a quarter his age who have no more talent than a budgerigar's whistle. Flanked by emphatic, intuitive musicians clearly the match of both The Band and those rock'n'roll rascals in the Rolling Thunder Review — with the added bonus of the sterling, duelling guitarist in Charlie Sexton — Bob Dylan jauntily strolled through his back pages with no secrets to conceal and plenty of surprises in store.

Chinese whispers said he would be playing an acoustic gig, but the reality of a rock set became apparent when the good, the great and the fans walked into the venue and saw a full band system.

Displaying a remarkable sense of time and place, Dylan's iconic status, so dismissed by both himself and his most staunch critics in the past, was reinforced by a set that encompassed the completely unfamiliar (one song at least foxed the Dylanologists) with the universally known: *Blowin' In The Wind*, *Tangled Up In Blue*, *Highway 61*, *Ramona*, *Girl From The North Country*, *Like A Rolling Stone*, *Just Like A Woman* and *Desolation Row*.

For those in attendance whose knowledge of Dylan was such that they barely recognised one song from another, this gig was a beginner's guide in learning what the fuss was all about. For Dylan fans, it was a confirmation of the man's considerable stature and a reason to die happy.

O'Reilly Departs Heinz As Boom Times Fade

Elaine Lafferty

There was a time, not so long ago, when it was pretty easy to elicit criticism of Dr Tony O'Reilly, who inarguably was and is an easy target. A multimillionaire who flaunts his wealth, a flamboyant personality who sometimes crosses the border of good taste, a businessman who has made decisions to close factories and put people out of work ... as they say in New York, what's not to hate?

Even in the US, where getting filthy rich by whatever means necessary is perhaps not frowned upon as much as in Ireland, Dr O'Reilly has faced harsh criticism over the years. On 2 December 1997, when H.J. Heinz, the Pittsburgh Pennsylvania-based $9 billion (€10 billion) food company, announced that Dr O'Reilly would be stepping down as chief executive, 'Businessweek' magazine online declared, 'Tony O'Reilly steps down at Heinz — and investors cheer'. Indeed, on that news alone, investors drove Heinz's stock price to a 52-week high.

This week, Dr O'Reilly leaves Heinz altogether, as he relinquishes the chairmanship of the company, a position which he retained even after stepping down as chief executive.

By many Wall Street analyst estimates, Heinz is in a shambles. Sales rose fourfold in the two decades Dr O'Reilly was in charge. But demand has slowed, especially for its tuna and pet foods.

In the 52 weeks to 13 August, Heinz recorded sales declines in its tuna, ketchup and canned and dry pet food businesses, according to supermarket data collected by Information Resources.

The company's shares fell 30 per cent in the fiscal year to 3 May, their worst performance ever. They've fallen another 3 per cent since. 'Heinz is a merge, purge or scourge story,' US Trust analyst

Mr Herb Achey told *Bloomberg News*. The stock's drop of almost 40 per cent over the past 22 months may spur the board and Dr O'Reilly's successor, Mr William Johnson, to consider moves such as selling products, merging with rivals or setting lower profit targets.

Mr Achey said Heinz's options include merging with a rival such as Campbell Soup, buying the rest of Hain Celestial or selling off lesser performing businesses such as the pet-food unit.

In the absence of some action, Heinz's shares will continue to be reviled on sales concerns, he said. Critics say that Dr O'Reilly began turning his attention elsewhere several years ago, spending more time on his other business interests. As he leaves Heinz, he is chairman of Waterford Wedgwood and executive chairman of Independent News & Media. He holds considerable stakes in numerous other businesses, including oil exploration and financial services.

And yet some of the people most critical of Dr O'Reilly years ago are now more muted in their analysis of his tenure.

It may be mere nostalgia for the heyday of a great businessman, a recognition that no one individual could have turned the tide for a company suffering inevitable problems plaguing the entire food industry, or a simple reluctance to target a media mogul who promises to be around for a long time still. (Mark Twain had a point when he noted it unwise to criticise 'a man who buys his ink by the barrel'.)

'Tony's tenure at Heinz is a study in extremes,' said Mr John McMillian, an analyst with Prudential Securities, who in the past levelled harsh critiques at Dr O'Reilly. 'He did extraordinarily well in the 1980s. And then there was the other side.

'It's true he is leaving Heinz with the stock flat on its back. But as low as Heinz is now, that's how high it was in the 1980s. But I think his accomplishments in the 1980s outweigh the difficulties. His tenure is one of accomplishment despite difficulties.'

The 1980s were without doubt the heyday for Dr O'Reilly and Heinz. During his 18-year reign as chief executive, Dr O'Reilly presided over major growth. Sales leapt from $2.15 billion to $9.3 billion. Average annual return to shareholders was 21 per cent. During the 1980s, it was closer to 31 per cent.

Dr O'Reilly became a star chief executive. He graced magazine covers and was the subject of many flattering profiles. He wined and dined Wall Street analysts at his 18th century castle in Co. Kildare.

'If there is one image that would say it all about Tony,' said Mr McMillian, who was one of those analysts invited to Castlemartin, 'it would be the picture of the pool at the back of his castle in Ireland. There is a telephone next to the pool. Now a lot of people have phones near the pool. But this is different. It looks like an office. Even when Tony is relaxing he is working. Business is his life.'

That life and that business was by all accounts quite a party, especially in the 1980s. Dr O'Reilly threw lavish parties at his 18-room Tudor home in Fox Chapel in Pittsburgh. Three-day bashes were held in Dublin, where friends and other business leaders were flown in from around the world.

Dr O'Reilly became one of the highest paid chief executives in the world. During one six-year period, his total compensation from Heinz was $182.9 million, according to 'Businessweek' magazine. Then came the 1990s, and the party ended with a thunk. With most US companies having restructured and laid off employees, there was little room to squeeze more profits and analysts say the prospects for growth into new markets is limited.

As a consequence, most food companies are showing flat profits, including Campbell Soup and Bestfoods. Moreover, the rules of the business game have changed. The stars of American business are now largely in high technology and entertainment companies. Dr O'Reilly, while never a

Pass the ketchup… Tony O'Reilly (left) who handed over the reins of H.J. Heinz to William Johnson.

household name in the US, was eclipsed even in his own industry by Mr David Johnson, chairman of arch rival Campbell Soup. Says Mr McMillian: 'Mr Johnson took the applause from him. Mr Johnson began to get most of the acclaim in the 1990s.'

In a scathing 1997 story that some believe may have contributed to the end of Dr O'Reilly's tenure as chief executive, 'Businessweek' magazine compared Dr O'Reilly unfavourably to Mr Johnson, and also continued its criticism of the way Heinz was being run.

It accused Dr O'Reilly of stacking his board with cronies and insiders, and charged that the lack of independent thinking from the board was hurting the company's performance. Dr O'Reilly vehemently denied the charge. Analyst Mr McMillian feels that, during the second half of his tenure at Heinz, Dr O'Reilly simply had 'too many balls in the air. In the 1980s he was hailed. In

the 1990s the industry environment became more difficult. They undernourished brands. They cut advertising'.

Mr McMillian says Heinz also stumbled because of Dr O'Reilly's policy of having individual managers for each country where the products were sold. 'There were no brands that were pan-European. They needed more centralisation,' he said.

Back in Pittsburgh, where the family-owned Heinz had been a major presence since its founding, Dr O'Reilly continued a tradition of generous contributions to charity.

'I got to know Tony very well,' said Mr Dan Rooney, a co-founder of The Ireland Fund and the owner of the Pittsburgh Steelers, a major football team.

Mr Rooney explains that Pittsburgh was once a major industrial centre in the US, home to major manufacturing companies such as Alcoa Steel, US

Steel and Gulf Oil. But as the economy changed and Pittsburgh lost its industrial base, the H.J. Heinz company became even more important to the city, remaining a major employer and cultural presence.

'I was the chairman of United Way (a major US national charity) and Heinz was key to us,' said Mr Rooney. 'I went to Tony and asked him for a million dollars. Personally. And he gave us $1 million over four years. Tony says I'm the most expensive friend he has.'

But Mr Rooney says that a complete picture of Dr O'Reilly should not be limited either to his status as a businessman or a force in official charity.

'I've seen Tony give away money to people you don't even know about. The kind of thing that doesn't make the paper. He has been very generous to people in trouble.'

A less flattering perspective is offered by others.

'As a person he is famously gregarious and a great talker,' said Ms Michelle Pilecki, executive editor of 'Pittsburgh' magazine. 'But if you ask people in Pittsburgh what is Tony O'Reilly most known for?, I'd have to say it's the huge rock he gave his wife.

'Of course, there's nothing wrong with giving a ring to your wife. (Dr O'Reilly purchased the ring that Aristotle Onassis at one time gave to Jacqueline Kennedy.) But I guess I'm saying he didn't get that involved in local arts groups or charities. He and his wife didn't sit on a lot of boards. Some people feel he did not give as much money as he should have.'

However, Dr O'Reilly's lavish recreational spending did not go unappreciated, said Ms Pilecki. 'Listen, conspicuous consumption is not the hallmark of the Pittsburgh millionaire. Most Pittsburgh millionaires don't flash the cash. Dr O'Reilly did. And it never hurts a city to have a handsome, charming millionaire around.'

There was also much speculation as to Dr O'Reilly's political leanings and ambitions, given his social friendships with well known Republicans such as President George Bush and Mr Henry Kissinger.

'His political impact? Not a ripple. His politics are business,' said Ms Pilecki.

As Dr O'Reilly returns to Ireland, and turns his full-time attention to both his media empire and his involvement in the luxury goods market, he may re-emerge on the world business stage in a new incarnation, one more suited both to the 21st century and his native inclinations.

Dr O'Reilly always seemed more suited to a business environment more glamorous and influential than beans and ketchup.

In fact, the stars of the business world today are the entertainment and information barons — Mr Gerald Levin and Mr Steve Case of Time Warner/AOL, Mr Rupert Murdoch and Mr Michael Eisner of Disney. With his personality and a drive that seems undiminished, Dr O'Reilly appears poised for the second act of a stunning career, one that could potentially eclipse his profile of the 1980s.

Like anything he has ever done, this act will be well worth watching.

MONDAY, 18 SEPTEMBER 2000

Great Lengths Taken to Restore Pool's Purity

Tom Humphries

He strolls out onto the pool deck and because he's wearing the little knapsack on his back you can fleetingly see the 17-year-old boy living within the man. Yet 17,500 people are roaring at him and he gives them a smile and a wave. Just a smile and a wave. No diffidence and no hubris. Then he goes to work.

It might be no exaggeration to say that Ian Thorpe has saved swimming. Saturday night and we hard-nosed hacks congregated in a big media tent not unlike the one we used in Atlanta four years ago. On that particular Saturday night in Georgia the air was sour with mistrust. The tone-deaf Irish were celebrating. The rest of the world was asking hard questions.

Our own Michelle Smith had changed the nature of swimming. People who loved the sport and knew the sport were close to tears, close to anger. The Chinese and the East Germans they had been able to view as victims of their statehood. Smith, they suspected, was the first big-time, privatised, calculating, brass-necked cheat to infest their sport. The mood was horrible. Swimming wasn't a blue skies event anymore.

On Saturday night in Sydney, embarrassingly, journalists were pestering Ian Thorpe for his autograph. Journalists were calling him Thorpey. Every other swimmer who came through the tent answered more questions about Thorpe than anything else.

Here was a champion you could believe in, a phenomenon since he was a kid, a guy who ends the doping arguments by offering to have his blood frozen and made available for any tests which may become available. You looked at the wonder that was Ian Thorpe this Saturday night and you believed in him. The heart jumped a beat. Sport has become so murky and so weak with cynicism that the Olympic Games needed a tonic beginning like this just to survive the fortnight. We all did.

What a night. Four finals. Five world records. The Homebush sky lit by flares of patriotism. Ian Thorpe won his first two gold medals in the space of an hour. 400 freestyle metres swum he confessed with a little tiredness, but yielding a gold and a world record. Then the wonder of wonders, a relay race for the ages.

Dawn Fraser called the 4 x 100m men's freestyle race the greatest relay she had ever seen. There was no reason to doubt her. The context was perfect: a long-held rivalry between the USA and Australia which heated up to boiling point last week. The venue was right: A madhouse of swim fans. The execution was perfect from Michael Klim's opening-leg demolition of Popov's six-

Ian Thorpe of Australia leaves the pool after the Mens 200m Freestyle Heats at the Sydney Aquatic Centre during day two of the Sydney Olympic Games in Sydney, Australia. Photograph: Al Bello/Allsport.

The start of the Toyota Liffey Swim from Victoria Quay — the 80th year of the race, which was won by Brian Mongey (Millennium Swimming Club). Photograph: Cyril Byrne.

year-old 100m freestyle record to the unforgettable last leg.

The Americans, unbeaten forever in the Olympics and world championships, used to have this event as an exhibition. Until 1988 they broke a world record every time they won gold. On Saturday night, they broke their own world record by 1.5 seconds. Not enough. Gary Hall Jnr touched the wall just after Ian Thorpe did.

Thorpe absorbed it all. His only suggestion of excitement was oblique. 'This,' he had told himself walking out, 'is what the Colosseum was like for the gladiatars.' An oddly boyish thought which

reminded us that this is just a kid with his career and his life in front of him.

We thought of the old story of Dawn Fraser, the swimming icon of 1956, then a 17-year-old herself. The night before her first race she slept fitfully, woken again and again by a nightmare. So we wanted to know how flustered this 17-year-old was, now carrying a nation on his shoulders as he swam along. Between the cracks of his words it became clear that we were talking a different language. He told the story of his exchange with Michael Klim, when Klim climbed out of the pool after swimming the first leg.

'It was funny,' said Thorpe. 'I'm not really a 100m swimmer so I wasn't 100 per cent sure of the 100 free world record, but I was pretty sure it was 48.21, but I didn't want to tell Michael he'd broken the record, just in case. So I said, "Michael, you've just done 48.18 seconds."'

'And Michael looked at me, he wasn't realising he'd done it. So I said, "Michael" (and he raises his voice as if speaking to a slow child), "YOU SWAM 48.18 sec".'

That's a weak little story until you colour in the background. Ten minutes earlier Thorpe had been on the Olympic podium with his first gold medal around his neck and listening to Advance Australia Fair.

He'd come off. Posed for the snappers, blown kisses to his mother, spoken to Channel Seven, heard his name called for the relays, rushed away, needed four people to get him into his body suit again, dashed out as the relay teams were being introduced.

Suddenly, the race was on, Klim finished his leg. Thorpe who should have been nervous, who should have been flighty, who might have been tired, Thorpe who was swimming perhaps the most pressured swim of his life in 90 seconds does the following:

He registers Klim's precise time on the scoreboard. Recalls the world record time. Decides he's not sure. Decides to tell Klim, but frame the statement in a neutral way so as not to cause embarrassment or unwonted excitement. Tells Klim. Detects that Klim is too excited and can't register the numbers. Tells him again like he's a six-year-old.

Then he steps up and swims the anchor leg of the greatest relay in history.

This is the nature of cool.

By yesterday morning, Australia was beginning to absorb the immensity of it. Already the perfection of the opening ceremony had been topped. We looked across at those FINA blazers, presiding over it all, at Gunnar Werner and the boys who have struggled for decades to restore the purity of their sport. East Germans. Chinese. Michelle. It's been a long war and they've lost many many battles, been afraid to even fight others.

It will be longer again, but yesterday, beneath untroubled faces, their hands were clapping furiously and, above, the skies were briefly blue. It was worth it for this.

WEDNESDAY, 20 SEPTEMBER 2000

Olympic LockerRoom: Why I've Become an Aussie

Tom Humphries

I swore I'd never begin a column like this, but here goes: G'day mates. Gidday. Gidday. Gidday. How ya goin'?

Things are different. As of yesterday I am officially an Australian. I have renounced Irishry and all it stands for. I now come from a land down under. Let me explain. You'll remember Jimmy The Greek Snyder, of course. Jimmy The Greek was the man whose impromptu exploration of sporting Darwinism had him removed from the airwaves in America before you could say 'Jackie Robinson'. Jimmy The Greek felt that black athletes might owe their greatness to their ancestors' years of slavery. Displaying profound ignorance on a range of issues Jimmy mused that slavery had bred black Americans to be good at the sort of things which athletes are now good at.

Jimmy The Greek was wrong and what's more he was a moron, but I feel his analysis should be brought to bear on the current crisis in Irish sport. Surely it's time for even the most diehard olé olé olé merchant to wake up and smell the whatever is rotting where the coffee should be.

We are not a great sporting nation. We never have been. We just like the idea of being one. If being a great sporting nation is going to cost us more than a couple of shillings count us out.

I write this as a proud Australian and as one who has been slightly involved in compiling the list of war dead that is the daily report of Irish involvement in the Olympics. I feel the OCI should have two forms of standard letter to send to families of the failed.

Dear Mr and Mrs ———-,

It is my solemn duty to inform you … it may be of some solace … he/she was eliminated doing his/her personal best…

Yours etc,

Or Dear Mr and Mrs ———-,

It is my solemn duty to inform you … I am obliged to add that he/she was eliminated without coming near their personal best.

Yours etc,

In this Olympics we Australians are expected to win medals of one hue or another in 21 different sports (that is counting track and field as one sport). In Atlanta we medalled in 14 sports.

Ireland has a chance of winning a medal on the track, to go with the last one — for the marathon — which arrived 16 years ago. Between times there's been three swimming golds which, as Susie O'Neill would say, were pretty suss. And two boxing medals, one for Wayne McCullough, who had the benefit of the pommie system, and one for Michael Carruth, who was trained by his Da. You might ask how five million of you Irish can fairly be compared with 19 million of us Aussies but, look mates, when we are beating the Americans at swimming we don't make a fuss about there being 272 million Americans.

Including swimming — include it if you must — Ireland has won Olympic medals in four sports in 27 Olympiads. Counting Michelle de Bruin Ireland has 19 medals in over a century of Olympic competition. Nineteen!

Here I would like to call Jimmy the Greek as an expert witness. See. I blame the Irish middle classes. I do. Big fat self-protecting bunch of soft-ass sheilas. I ask you to bring the Jimmy the Greek analysis to a brief comparison of the Irish and Australian experience of sport.

From the Flight of the Earls to the Famine to the recession the brightest and the best have always scarpered. Add me to that list now.

The rest, the dumbest and the worst and the least co-ordinated, have always stayed behind working for their daddies and running for office in the junior chamber. So. Irish sport is riddled with the Irish class system. The more middle class the sport the worse Ireland are at it. Rugby. Golf. Yachting. Cricket. If Tallaght ever gets independence the soccer is sunk too.

We Australians on the other hand have the opposite experience. We had to endure five months of scurvy just to get here. The weakest died on boats coming over and if they didn't they died soon after. The tough, adventurous ones served their time or moved through the bush till they found enough viable land to make a farm.

Once settled, they set about making a society which, superficially at any rate, is classless.

Take a few stories. Bob's me mate and he drove me in a taxi down the Gold Coast last week. I said to him about our Australian nation's ability to be good, bloody good at a range of sports simultaneously. He gave me a 20-minute talk about his life.

As kids he and his friends would organise bike races across the sands on the little spits and islands along the Gold Coast. His Dad, a truck driver, was captain of the golf club, so all Bob's family played and Bob, who is nearly 70, still plays. Bob swam all his life and was captain of the swim team at school. Until recently everyone played in a regional tennis tournament which lasted through the summer and guaranteed a couple of games a week.

'But,' said Bob reflectively. 'I was never really what you'd call sporty.'

Sonia O'Sullivan (left) winning an Olympic silver medal while striving to catch Gabriela Szabo of Romania who took gold in the Women's 5,000 metres final in Sydney. Photograph: Eric Luke.

Then there's Chen. Chen's me mate too. He arrived here 15 years ago having squeezed out of Vietnam with his family and having spent two years in a hellish camp in Indonesia.

He plays rugby but prefers running and has joined a triathlon club. His younger brother is a good golfer and the two of them have taken up surfing. His cousin, a swimmer, is hoping to get into the Australian Institute of Sport.

The AIS is what this country created after the Montreal Olympics, which went badly. The purpose is coaching and training and education. The philosophy is the propagation of sport, the development through a whole raft of policies of both an élite class of sports persons and a massive well-catered-for underclass of people just healthily playing whatever they enjoy.

The grants are good, the science and facilities are world class, the results are on display every day here at the Games.

Any wonder we're putting on the happiest Olympics ever. Any wonder I've evolved into an Aussie.

'Best land in the world,' Chen tells me. 'Who ya tellin' mate,' I say to him.

MONDAY, 26 SEPTEMBER 2000

Sonia's Sweetest Medal of Them All

Tom Humphries

Did you leap out of the chair and roar or did you slip into the kitchen and cry? Were you whispering silent prayers or was your fist clenched and pumping as she came down the straight?

This was the sweetest medal in our sporting history, a triumph, a redemption song, a perfect aria delivered by our greatest ever athlete, the one we've been through the most with and known the longest. Sonia O'Sullivan, happy and brilliant again. Could you have been Irish and been unmoved?

She said afterwards it wasn't the hardest race she has ever run. Maybe so but it was the bravest.

Yesterday Sonia O'Sullivan claimed the Olympic moment she deserved in a race which compressed the agonies of the last few crazy years into 12 and a half laps.

She came off the track and her face was shining and happy. She'd found a part of herself again.

This Olympic 5,000 metre final was one of the great races, an epic struggle to the finish line between two great rivals who won't like each other any better this morning but who respect each other a whole lot more. Gabriela Szabo of Romania did what we thought she couldn't do. She held off Sonia in a sprint.

This is what sport is about. This is what you came for. Afterwards you saw her stand in a little knot of love with her partner Nick and her daughter Ciara and the distance from Atlanta seemed incalculable. 'That was nightmare,' she said, 'this was a dream.'

Gete Wami, the third placed finisher, explained afterwards that the Ethiopians had planned to run as a team and 'then just before the race we decided it was wrong, not the fair thing to do.' For her grace, Wami was rewarded with bronze.

And for Sonia, silver. Fate owed her this at least. She'd wanted it all so badly that it almost destroyed her back in 1996. She crumbled in front of us all.

'On the fourth lap, I felt like I was dropping off. It wasn't the pace, I don't know what it was. I was nearly gone. It was that voice in your head "do you want to go with this?"'

She did. She did. She survived by hanging on to Jo Pavey from Britain for a while and then getting between two Kenyans.

'Then I discovered I was so close to winning. I came off the bend. I was so shocked I almost stopped. I'm glad I didn't.'

And so she lived to fight her way down the straight, an epic slugging match right to the line. She glanced up, wasted but happy and saw the race times on the scoreboard. Two thoughts: So close. How did we run so fast?

She left finally to jog off into the cool Sydney night to warm down loyal muscles, to put order on a wild day, to think about running the 10,000 metres later in the week. She had a silver medal in her pocket, the Australian sky was inky blue and the torch was still burning. Does it get any better?

An Olympic win at last… Sonia O'Sullivan with her silver medal for coming second in the Women's 5,000 metres final in Sydney. Photograph: Eric Luke.

Corrections and Clarifications

A report in yesterday's edition on criticism voiced by a senior Army officer on Thursday at an official function attended by the Minister for Defence, Mr Smith, in Collins Barracks, Cork, quoted the officer in question as referring to an 'empty old mess and armoury'. In fact, Col. Brownen referred to an 'NCOs' mess and armoury'. The error occurred in transmission.

SATURDAY, 8 APRIL 2000

In last Saturday's On The Town column, the title of Gerald Dawe's new collection of essays was given incorrectly as Strong Dogs And Dark Days. *It should have been* Stray Dogs And Dark Horses.

TUESDAY, 6 JUNE 2000

Several errors occurred in the report headed 'Health problems of builders revealed' in Thursday's edition. The figure of 977 potential years lost through premature retirement on health grounds was an average annual figure, not the total for the years 1972 to 1996 as stated.

The figures given as days a year in lost production for cardiovascular disease (22,406), bronchitis, emphysema and asthma (15,481) and infectious diseases (67,194) were not days a year, but total days lost over the period 1981 to 1996. The high of 14 per cent in 1986 (referring to rate of early retirement) should have been 14 per 1,000.

Finally, the name of the author of the report, 'Pattern of ill-health in Irish Construction Workers', is Dr Harold Brenner, not Bremmer as stated.

SATURDAY, 20 JUNE 2000

Where errors occur it is the policy of *The Irish Times* to correct or clarify as soon as practicable. Readers may contact the Readers' Representative's Office at email readersrep@irish-times.ie or by telephoning 01-679-2022 from 11 a.m. to 4 p.m, Monday to Friday. Outside these times they may contact the Duty Editor.

Index